The Courage to Be a Single Mother

Becoming Whole Again After Divorce

SHEILA ELLISON

HarperSanFrancisco
A Division of HarperCollinsPublishers

HarperCollins books may be purchased for educational, business, or sales promotional use. For information please write: Special Markets Department, HarperCollins Publishers Inc., 10 East 53rd Street, New York, NY 10022.

HarperCollins Web site: http://www.harpercollins.com

HarperCollins®, ☗®, and HarperSanFrancisco™ are trademarks of Harper-Collins Publishers Inc.

FIRST HARPERCOLLINS PAPERBACK EDITION PUBLISHED IN 2001

Designed by Jessica Shatan

Library of Congress Cataloging-in-Publication Data
Ellison, Sheila.
   The courage to be a single mother : becoming whole again after divorce / Sheila Ellison. — 1st ed.
      p. cm.
   ISBN 0–06–251651–5 (cloth)
   ISBN 0–06–251652–3 (pbk.)
   1. Single mothers—United States—Psychology. 2. Divorced mothers—United States—Psychology. 3. Single-parent families—United States. 4. Self-esteem in women—United States. I. Title.

HQ759.45.E52 2000
306.85'6'0973—dc21

                                                              00–035017

01 02 03 04 05 ❖/RRD (H) 10 9 8 7 6 5 4 3 2 1

To my children,

Wesley, Brooke, Rhett, and Troy,

for bringing light into the darkness

Contents

Introduction ix

1 • Knowing It's Over 1

2 • Stripping Away the Old 16

3 • Telling the World 39

4 • Too Many Decisions 55

5 • Finding Support 70

6 • The Divorce Process 86

7 • What Is Best for the Children? 106

8 • Grieving the End 130

9 • Who Am I Now? 145

10 • On Your Own 161

11 • Feeling Good 176

12 • New Romance 192

13 • From Survival to Living Again 211

14 • Time to Dream 226

15 • Passion Discovered 236

Epilogue 247

Acknowledgments 251

Introduction

I'm picking up the towel from the floor in the boys' bathroom, putting it over the shower door and holding on to the edges of the towel as tears run down my face. Harvey, our black lab, rubs my legs. He hears all my cries. Nobody is here, the kids have all left for school, but all the lights are on, stereos are still playing, breakfast dishes line the sink, and a huge pile of laundry sits on the couch and reminds me of all the things that need to be done. I'm sick. I should probably be in bed resting, trying to get well, but there is no one but me to make the lunches, to give a hug and say, "Have a great day!" and I have a writing assignment due today that isn't finished. I'm still holding on to that towel, wondering how many more mornings like this I will have, how much longer I can carry the weight of it all. I make myself let go of the towel, tell myself in my most authoritative voice, "Pull yourself together. It isn't so bad."

I remember just a few days ago when I was in a different space. Why is it that I can fall apart in a single instant for what seems like no reason? I somehow make it out to my office with a thermos of tea in hand, and here I sit writing. I don't feel well, I don't feel inspired, I'm still crying, but I'm sitting here and willing my fingers to type. I know I have to. My kids don't have anyone else they can count on.

There are many reasons marriages don't work. I can't begin to define or even understand all the reasons mine didn't. I got divorced because I could no longer survive without love. It was the hardest decision I've ever made. Ron* and I had grown up together; we married in 1982, a year before I graduated from college. I had just turned twenty-two. Two years later we had our first child. By the time I was thirty I had four children under the age of six. My husband Ron worked for ten years as a professional athlete, and I wrote part-time and took care of the kids. When his career was over, we decided to take a year off to have some time together as a family. The marriage wasn't going so well, and we both agreed that our relationship needed attention. In September 1993 we decided to rent out our house in California and take the kids to New Zealand, where we rented a house for one year. Ron was born in New Zealand, so it was a natural choice.

The marriage was falling apart. It wasn't helped when Ron's agent fraudulently signed our names on a bad business deal, losing most of our savings, so in June 1994 we were forced to sell our house in California. Ron hadn't decided what his next career move would be, and I still was trying to make the marriage work, so in July 1994 we bought a house in Christchurch, New Zealand, with the hope that we could start over with a new and simpler lifestyle.

Six months later, in December 1994, my youngest son, Troy, who had just turned four, was diagnosed with autism. After months of researching treatment facilities in New Zealand, I discovered that our only option was to go back to California. Ron and I had grown further and further apart. When I told him I had to take the kids back to the United States so Troy could get help, he told me that he would only allow me to take Troy. But I wasn't about to leave three children behind with a man who rarely attended to their needs. In April 1995, when Ron was in the United States on business, I packed up our house in New Zealand and took my children home. It wasn't as sudden as it

* For privacy reasons, all the names in this book have been changed.

sounds—we'd been talking about divorce and I'd been living in the guest room for six months.

Ron was furious and in June 1995 charged me with abducting the kids. That suit stopped me from being able to get divorced, have child support, or provide for the family. (The suit was eventually dropped. Even Ron knew it wasn't true.)

When the California courts decided not to take our case, Ron was free to take all of our money and move it to New Zealand, which meant that I had no access to our joint assets for the next two years. I ran out of money in June 1996, so the children and I moved into a rented studio apartment. Desperate for guidance and companionship, I joined a single mother support group. For fifteen months we lived in that studio while I waited for a trial date in New Zealand. Finally, in June 1997 I appeared in a New Zealand court and was awarded half of our assets. I immediately sold the house in Christchurch and in November 1997 bought a one-bedroom cottage down the street from the studio we had been living in. Since then we have added an addition to the cottage and begun to rebuild our lives.

If someone had outlined for me what I would have to face over that two-year period, I would have thought myself incapable of surviving it. I didn't mean to be courageous. I had to make some hard decisions because my marriage didn't work. Over the last years of my marriage I wrestled with my obligation as a wife, my responsibility as a mother, my own feelings as a woman—what did each mean? Was I selfish, or was I saving my life and in doing so being a better mother for my children? Now I stand in the middle of a life that will never be black and white, with four kids whose homework won't get done, a house that refuses to stay clean, and mornings spent crying into a towel.

I've learned that it takes courage to make a decision to do the best you can in both worlds, as a woman and as a mother. I want to tell you that if you are a single mother picking up this book, you have courage. This is what I've learned about courage—you have to move forward, do the difficult things, and make those difficult decisions. Part of courage is experiencing your fears, facing something even when you are afraid. Courage is taking reasonable risks for a good cause, standing up for what you believe, standing up for the rights of others, and being who you are regardless of others' opinions. Courage does not have to be a grand or heroic feat. It can be as simple as saying no. Taking on the process of divorce, getting up each day and living life in whatever state of mind you find yourself, takes courage. Life can become a scary place very fast when all that you've hoped for has changed. Every woman reading this book got out of bed this morning and has chosen to live her life today—that is courage.

The set designer on a kids' show I was filming recently complimented me on the ring I was wearing as she lined up the paint, markers, and posterboard on the table in front of me. I told her it was my wedding ring melted down and redesigned—just like my life. She laughed as the cameramen looked on, wondering if I was serious. Later she confided in me that the only time she felt lonely was when her husband of ten years was sharing an evening at home with her and their son. She said she'd been thinking about getting a divorce for a year. I wanted to scream, "Don't do it! Raising children as a single mother is the toughest thing in the world, and not just because of conflicting soccer games, financial instability, and late-night trips to the emergency room alone. The problem is that you can't raise your kids if you aren't whole yourself. There is no time to focus on becoming whole, so there you are stuck on a daily treadmill of survival. It's like fixing the car when it's not just running but moving!"

The goal of this book is to teach you how to fix the car while it is moving. You see, there is a timeline to all of this. Remember when you had your first baby and you wondered how a mother could pick up her three-year-old when you were having problems carrying an infant? You probably swore that you'd never be able to lift a heavy child every day. You will grow the muscles to manage your new role as a single mother just as you grew muscles to lift your child. You can learn to create a new life full of passion and dreams of a new future. When I joined a single mothers group, I remember someone telling me that it would be two years before I felt a shift toward wholeness. That woman was right, and now I tell everyone—hold on for the first two years.

Psychologists call divorce a "process." We start by grieving the relationship, we work our way toward a different life—changing, growing, and stretching along the way—and then we arrive someplace. "Arriving" for me has been a place where I stopped feeling like I was surviving each day and started feeling a little bit like I was living each moment secure in myself, my direction, my worth, my purpose, and my abilities. I've realized many things through this process, the most important of which was that it wasn't just the mental and physical aspects of myself that needed to grow. I needed faith to live in a world that wasn't black and white. When I didn't know what the next day would bring, I hoped that there was something out there bigger than I was. I now have a job and am earning money, and the future doesn't scare me so much anymore. I put time into creating a support system and have close friends and a growing love relationship. All of this took time. The goal is not to look backward pointing fingers but instead to point our hands and hearts forward to new possibilities.

There are some stories in here that my kids aren't crazy about, and some stories that they feel make them look too good. But I felt that, to be of any help, I had to be honest, so I'm going to tell you the way it is, not the way the psychologists and psychiatrists tell you it should be. This is what happens in the life of single mothers, mess and all. I will tell you my stories and other women's stories. You'll find that running through all of them is the idea that a sense of balance happens as a result of having courage.

This book won't give you instructions on how to get credit in your own name, how to get a job after years at home, or how to get the child support you need. It will, however, let you *feel*— laugh, cry, rejoice, and doubt—with the voices of many single mothers around the country who were willing to share how they grieved the loss of their marriage, how they struggled to survive, and how they made the changes necessary to courageously create new lives. Society has given us beliefs about ourselves as women, our mothers have given us their views—now it's time to tell the truth and to teach each other. One promise—you will not feel alone after reading these pages.

The Courage
to Be a
Single Mother

··

ONE

Knowing It's Over

We were sitting on a porch swing, slowly swaying back and forth, facing our beautifully shaped, one-hundred-year-old oak tree, glancing over the top of the blooming rose bushes at our children playing on the lawn that we had planted together. It was the usual scenario. I was crying, telling him that I needed changes in the relationship, that I was unhappy and felt unimportant to him. Ron, my husband, said that I didn't understand him, that he was grieving the loss of his career and needed time to himself.

Our anniversary was two days later. I couldn't stay in the house, so I wrote a long letter that said nothing new and flew to Los Angeles to help my best friend deliver her first child. Her labor was long, so I sat day after day watching the way her husband looked at her, touched her face, and responded to her calls. Their words were soft, comforting, and intimate. I would leave the room when I couldn't stand it anymore and sob, physically shaking as I tried to calm myself in the locked bathroom stall. I couldn't remember ever feeling such tenderness. I sat wallowing, allowing painful scenes to flash through my mind, silly things . . . being eight months pregnant and asking for help carrying groceries but getting the response "It's good exercise, you can do it!" . . . the times he would ask me to walk backward toward our bed so that he could pretend I wasn't pregnant . . . his question for the doctor just seconds after my second daughter was born: "When can she get pregnant again?" I felt I had nothing.

I wanted a divorce, but I was an unemployed, stay-at-home mom with four children under eight years old. I wasn't ready for a fight; my baby was only two. Instead, I returned home from my friend's birth experience with renewed fervor for making the marriage work. My new plan: rent out our house and take the whole family to New Zealand for a year. Ron was born in New Zealand. We'd planned on spending a year there at some point so the kids could get to know their relatives and experience life outside the United States. I was sure that a change of location could save the marriage. We would be together in a new place with time on our hands to reconnect and heal.

Finding a renter for our house was easy, and receiving information from private schools in Christchurch was fun. The job of planning the adventure replaced my pain. At the time I was seeing a therapist who had the insight to point out a pattern she saw in my life. Instead of admitting to the world, to myself, and to my husband how bad the marriage felt, and doing something about it, I would take on a new and exciting project that kept my attention and creative energy focused forward. She told me that my pregnancies had been such projects. I knew she was right, but I wasn't ready to deal with the reality behind my feelings, so it was onward to New Zealand.

Each child packed one huge duffel bag full of a few bedroom treasures, clothing, a pillow, a blanket, and books. I packed all of our household goods into boxes and put them up in the attic, leaving the furniture in place for the renters. Through all the preparations I painted a picture for friends, family, and the kids of an incredible adventure: our family going away together to explore a new country. Then I worked to make this story a reality. Nobody knew that the whole production was really my last-ditch effort to save my marriage.

I would hear a version of this denial over and over again as I talked to women who had become single mothers. Even when they knew absolutely in their hearts that the love was gone, or that there was no way to rebuild the relationship, somehow, just as I had done, they kept hoping and hanging on, afraid to face or utter the truth. Suzanne, a thirty-four-year-old marketing executive with two children ages eight and twelve, says she hung on for five years even though she knew that her husband was having affairs. "It wasn't because I loved him and couldn't stand living without him. I had been the one who earned the income in our family since we were married the year after I graduated from college. My husband wanted to be an actor, so he would be in productions and other dramatic projects and work odd jobs on the side. One day I opened a letter addressed to him from a town where I knew he had been filming recently. The letter was from a woman who was professing her love and devotion. She begged him to come back to her. She talked about their intense lovemaking and how she knew he couldn't love his wife if he could love her so completely. I went to the bathroom and threw up.

"I confronted him that night, and he apologized profusely and promised not to respond to the woman and never to hurt me again. He was going to be faithful, and he used his 'actor's ability' to convince me that the affair meant nothing, that he had been away from me for three weeks, and that we hadn't been making love much, so he made this big mistake.

"Some of his argument did make sense. I did work late hours (but that was only because he wasn't making any money at all). I did have the freedom to make all my own decisions, while he had to discuss his plans with me, because most of his plans included spending money that we didn't have. He was the one who was home with our boys in the afternoon until I returned from work, and he did make dinner most nights. So I decided that he had a few good points—we did need to make sex a more important part of the relationship.

"I set the goal to make love at least once a week, and the relationship got better. But I have to admit I didn't let myself go in our lovemaking, I was sort of just there, going through the motions, while all the time I resented that he chose to share this intimacy with someone else 'so completely.' I also knew this wasn't his first affair, but I didn't bring it up because I was afraid to know the truth. Each night I would ask myself if his infidelity was a good enough reason to break up the family."

So many women seem to have an internal voice that tells them to hold the family together at all costs, even if the price is losing themselves, their energy, their inspiration, and their self-worth. When I arrived in Christchurch with my three oldest children (Ron was to bring the baby and join us a few days later), I was excited about finding a place to live, helping the kids make friends, and settling into a new relationship with the man who I wanted to love. The kids were to start school the day after we arrived, so there was no time to waste. We had to buy school uniforms and get settled into a hotel. I managed to get them all enrolled in school, miraculously to find a huge house to rent, and to have us all moved in within ten days.

Once we settled into a regular household routine, I noticed that even though neither Ron nor I was working, we seemed to spend our days doing our own thing. In no time Ron had joined a rugby club and a cricket club and found all the best fishing spots in the area. Once all the creative work of making sure my kids were settled and happy was finished, it became painfully obvious to me how far from home I really was.

I believed that it was possible for women to move "home" with them wherever they went, and that mothers were "home" to their children forever, so this sense of isolation even among welcoming new friends confused me. My goal had been to get to a place where my husband and I would have to depend on each other, but the plan seemed to be backfiring. I realized that all those people who participated in my life back in the United States had filled an emotional void in my marriage. Now I felt completely alone. Moving had exposed—not filled in—the holes. The move had made the marriage worse, but I still wasn't able to admit defeat.

We had lived in the rented house in Christchurch for six months when I decided that maybe if we bought a house in Christchurch and moved our furniture from the United States things would feel better, more like home. I wanted so badly to stay married. I threw myself into the search for a new home and before long we purchased one of the oldest homesteads in Christchurch. Another perfect project for me. I worked side by side with carpenters, painters, and plumbers for three months with a sense of devotion and purpose that I meant to be putting into my marriage. The kids were thrilled to decorate their new rooms and await the arrival of their personal treasures. Life was easier for me to bear with something to look forward to.

"I think it's amazing the amount of pain mothers will go through to make the family look intact," says Jenny, a twenty-seven-year-old artist and mother of a five-year-old daughter. "When I met my husband, we both had this idea that life should be fun and free. We were both living abroad, we were young, and we didn't think things through. I became pregnant and of course had to stop partying—but he didn't want to. It didn't feel like we were in this marriage together, although we were in love and were both excited to be parents.

"My dedication to painting and my creative energy were great while I was pregnant. All my ideas seemed to dance on the canvas. An art studio picked up my work, and life seemed to be an upward spiral. I thought that he'd be happy, but he really changed, drinking more, staying out with friends, and I didn't feel as close to him as I once did. Our daughter was born; we both adored her and focused our energy away from each other and the problems we had.

"When our daughter was two years old, my mom decided to visit us in London. A few days before her arrival my husband came home from a night out with friends and beat me. When I picked my mom up at the airport with a swollen face and stitches across one eyebrow, I looked her straight in the eye and told her I had been mugged. I made up this elaborate story that a robber ran into me while I was walking home from the gallery, that I had been beaten and my purse stolen. Three years later, when we divorced and I returned to the United States with my daughter, I told my mom the truth. At the time I didn't want to end the marriage, and I was afraid that if I told my mom the truth I'd look like an idiot for staying."

There is another kind of hiding the truth for those women whose husbands choose to leave them. "I still loved my husband with my whole heart the day I found that e-mail from his lover, giving him the flight information for their scheduled trip to Hawaii," says Janet, a forty-year-old mother of four. "Because everyone around me reacted with such outrage at his betrayal, I felt that I had to hate him too. I couldn't admit to any of my friends or family that I still loved him and wanted him back. I was numb, devastated, and in a state of shock, so I think it was the energy of the people around me that determined my decisions.

"I called him in Hawaii (where he had claimed to be on a business trip) about the time I knew he liked to take a shower at night. The woman answered the phone, and I said with a confidence I wasn't feeling, 'This is (I gave the name of his business) calling. May I speak to Mr. _____?' He came immediately to the phone, and I said, 'I want a divorce, all of your belongings are in the garage, I've changed the locks.' And then I hung up.

"I don't think I ate or slept for days. Friends said I was acting as if someone had died. What they didn't understand was that someone had died—me. He didn't come rushing home as I had hoped to beg for my forgiveness and ask me to take him back. Instead, he returned righteous and with an attitude of relief.

"The next week I was out to lunch with two of the kids and we saw him walk by our window with a woman who was about twenty-two years old. Our oldest daughter, who was seventeen years old, went outside and called to him, but he kept walking, acting like he didn't hear her. Maybe he couldn't, but my heart broke. Even then I would have taken him back, but I never told anyone how much I still loved him."

The Moment You Know

Recently my daughter Brooke asked me, "What was the happiest day of your life?" After thinking for a few minutes I had to say, my wedding. All my friends were there, my family surrounded me with their love and support, and Ron and I professed our dedication and were full of hope for our future. We promised to love, honor, and cherish . . . all the days of our lives. Then one day I woke up and wondered how I had moved in such a short time from feeling like Cinderella, in my wedding gown dancing the night away in the arms of my lover, to a bitter woman.

What had created the huge space in my marriage? I was lonely, sad, and disillusioned. The realization that divorce was a definite possibility came to me (after four years of therapy) in five minutes when the therapist I had been seeing asked me to bring one of my journals from five years before to our next appointment. She then asked me to read three to four pages from this old journal out loud. After I did this, she asked me to read three pages from my current journal. They were the same. I stared at those pages, willing them to be different, sure that we had made some progress. Then she asked me, almost too soft to hear, when I thought my husband would begin the change I was so sure he could achieve. In that moment I knew the truth. Where could I go from that moment?

There seems to be a defining moment when divorce is the decided outcome. Women can spend years being battered, knowing about an affair, waking up depressed, contemplating suicide, having an affair of their own, knowing that their relationship isn't what they'd hoped for—and still they stay. Then at some point they decide (or it's decided for them), and they or their husband has the clarity and courage to say, "No more."

For me there were several moments that solidified my belief that marriage vows were living promises, not simply a prison cell that held two hearts. I spent hours wrestling with the guilt that mine would be the first divorce in my entire extended family, that I had made a promise until death did us part to love, honor, and cherish, for better and for worse. I wavered back and forth, trying to define how unhappy I should really be before considering the actual act of leaving. Once I even wrote the wedding vows down and went through each one, deciding whether I had held to my part of the bargain.

My problem was that I loved him the way I thought I was supposed to love him—more than he loved me. When I had created enough evidence in my mind that I wasn't loved, honored, or cherished in return, I was able to let the word *divorce* cross my lips. Years before someone asked me, "Have you ever considered divorce?" My response was, "Absolutely not, never!" Just letting the idea in and believing that I deserved to feel loved was the first step.

"The moment I knew," says Mary, a computer programmer with a three-year-old son, "was when we attended a friend's wedding. I had bought a dress that I loved and was all ready to go when he made some small comment about not liking the length of the skirt. I let the criticism go. When we got to the reception, I had many men compliment my dress and tell me how great I looked in it. I was so relieved to get away from my husband's criticism and spend some time with people who seemed to appreciate and like me.

"I know it seems like such a petty thing, but as I thought about it that comment was just the tip of the iceberg. He didn't like the way I cooked, the way I mothered, how much time I spent at work, or my choice in friends, and we argued about these things constantly. He spent so much of our 'alone time' telling me how I should be that I didn't feel appreciated for who I actually was. I used to think that our relationship could stand any amount of 'meanness,' but I now realize that love is a very fragile thing that has to be nurtured. We both understood this in counseling, but by then it was too late. We didn't like each other by that time."

Sometimes a relationship can move, in a matter of hours, to a place where there is no turning back to heal the marriage. "We had been working outside the day our lives fell apart," says Martha, the mother of two teenagers. "There had been tension for a few weeks because my husband had forbidden us to socialize with a family that we all really liked. He thought the father was getting too close to our children. He was jealous, and it was important to him that he could control all of us.

"Well, he went camping one weekend with our son, Chad, who was thirteen at the time, so my daughter Karen and I decided to visit this family. I later decided to tell Chuck about our visit because I felt uncomfortable that Karen had to lie. We were out to lunch one day, and I told him. He blew up, I'd never seen him that angry with me. He kept yelling, 'How could you do something that I forbid?'

"The next day, after we had all worked in the yard under Chuck's direction, the kids and I sat down to watch a movie.

When the movie was over, I asked the kids to get up and help me start dinner. The kids didn't get up right away, so I asked again in a more forceful way. Chuck then interjected and started yelling. The kids were kind of staring at him because he looked so out of control. He then told them to run up and down the stairs fifteen times for being disrespectful. They grumbled, so he said run the stairs thirty times. By the end of his yelling spree the kids were supposed to run the stairs seventy-five times.

"Karen stood up for herself and said that he couldn't make her do that. That is when he went after her. He took her head and started shaking it violently. Mama lion woke up in me, and that was it. I tried to step in, and he said that he'd had enough from me. He started to go upstairs toward Karen's room, and I was going up after him. Chad begged me not to go, but I said I couldn't leave Karen alone with him. Chad said he was going to call the police. I got to the top of the stairs and physically put my body between him and the door so that he couldn't shut it. He then started strangling me. All the while Chad was on the phone with the police. I blacked out. The kids heard sirens, and the next thing I remember was looking out the window to see Chuck assuring the police that everything was fine. The police came into the house to question us and decided to arrest Chuck.

"This was the first time he had physically attacked any of us, although there had always been a force behind his control so we were all terrified to misbehave. I decided that instant that I had allowed his abusive behavior to go on too long because I was a coward. But after he threatened my children, I knew that my next move would be to get a restraining order and file for divorce."

One of those "living promises" I thought would be inherent in the marriage commitment was support for each other. I took my job to support my husband, a professional athlete, very seriously. I nursed him through five surgeries, listened nightly to his work woes, attended all of his in-town games, and met him at the door most nights with dinner prepared and kids ready for bed. I was his psychologist, friend, business partner, and lover. In the beginning it didn't bother me that he wasn't that interested in supporting me in my life. To him, financial support was his most important contribution, so I took refuge in my female friends, my sisters, and my mother, looking to them to validate my accomplishments. It worked for a while, until we had kids and I started to resent the way our lives all revolved around him.

One night when we were out with friends Ron started talking about the books I'd written. I thought it odd, since he had shown no interest in my books in the past. To make my point (and embarrass him), I asked him what the title of one of my books was, and he couldn't remember. Then I asked him what the books were about, and all he could say was, "Things to do with your kids." I regularly complained, in a way that he labeled "manipulative," about his lack of interest in my life, but I did nothing about it.

One of my moments of knowing the marriage was over came five months before I actually left. We had just moved into the house we bought and remodeled in Christchurch. My son Troy, who was four years old at the time, had been undergoing many developmental tests. Ron thought I was being neurotic, creating a problem where there was none. Finally, the doctor said, "Troy's tests point to childhood autism. Do you know what that is?" Of course I knew what it was—I had lived it for the last four years. I knew it from the second day of Troy's life. When Troy didn't look at me, or want to nurse, or cry, or make any sound, I knew there was something wrong. I watched him alone in his own world and wished there were a way to get in. I felt a sense of relief to finally have a name for his problem. When I arrived home to share the news with my husband, he said, "It's your fault; you must have done something to him." In that moment it was as if all the lack of support in the past came into fine focus—there was no turning back. My heart switched off.

Many women stay in the marriage, sometimes for years, after their moment of knowing. Sandra, a Realtor and mother of a nine-year-old daughter, says that it took her three years to leave. "The moment I knew it was over was one day in October. My husband took his sister and our three-year-old daughter to the beach. When they returned, I could tell he'd been drinking, and for some reason I can't remember now he just blew up. I'm sure people could hear him for ten miles. His sister grabbed my daughter and hid. I think they thought he was going to kill me.

"I took that energy, that hateful destructive energy, and used it to fuel my resolve to escape. We had a house that we had borrowed money from my family to buy. We were in the construction business, which fell on hard times in the early 1990s, so I felt a responsibility to my family and my daughter to have some financial stability before I left. I needed time to create a plan to sell the house so I could give that money back. I decided to focus all my attention on finding a vehicle that could carry me from the marriage. I knew that vehicle was a job of some sort. I needed to have training, and I needed to be sure that I could make adequate money to support my daughter and myself. I wanted a plan before I picked up and left.

"I know it sounds manipulative," says Sandra, "and I guess it was, but I did what I had to do. I went to real estate school. After I graduated, I convinced my husband that we should sell the house to help the business (with a capital investment) and to pay back our debts. I listed the house with my new real estate license, sold it within a week, closed the deal within three weeks, and we moved into a hotel. My husband took our daughter to Sacramento on business for a few days, and while he was gone I received a call from a friend letting me know that she had just listed a rental unit that sounded perfect for us. I went with my mother to storage, and with her continued repetition of the words 'You're doing the right thing, honey!' I got the furniture I needed and (even though I was scared) moved into the rental.

"When he returned, I asked him to meet me for lunch in a very public place and told him it was over. Since that time I always meet with him in public. I feel safer that way. That was the opportunity I had been working toward and waiting for. But I had to be ready; I was focused on the goal of leaving, I had a job, I had paid back my debts, and I had thought through my new life as a single mother. It was three years from the moment I knew I was going to divorce until I was able to leave."

Pam, a forty-two-year-old stay-at-home mother of three, says that her divorce came as a complete surprise. "I spent all my energy taking care of the kids. We didn't have a great relationship, but I had no idea that he was thinking about divorce. My husband made a lot of money, so I never worried about paying bills, nor did I concern myself with understanding all of our investments.

"I first learned about my husband's affair when I was out looking for a new car. I had found the car I wanted and began to give my name and number to the salesman so that he could get back to me on a color choice I had made, when he said, 'I hate to ruin the surprise, but your husband just bought you a car. It was delivered yesterday.' I drove home excited, thinking that there would be a new car in the driveway. There was no car. When I asked him about it that evening, he said that the salesman must have made a mistake. I had this feeling that something was wrong, so I went to that car dealership and found out the address where the car was delivered. I'm a very passive person, but I decided to drive by the address and check it out. There was no car in the driveway, so I sat and read a book for an hour. Later a woman pulled into the driveway with a new car. She got out, and I could see she was around thirty, tall and pretty. My heart sank—I knew that my husband was having an affair and that he had bought her that car.

"It took weeks for me to put the pieces of the puzzle together, but in the end I found out he had also bought her a house five years before. For five years he was living with us pretending he was a dedicated family man while all along he had this woman on the side. I didn't know where to begin. I really knew nothing of our financial state. As soon as I told him I knew the truth, he immediately packed and took all the records from our house. If I could give women one general piece of advice it would be to get some working knowledge of the family's financial affairs. Make sure your name is on all property purchased once married, ask to see bank and stock statements, and take an active and equal role in financial planning. I didn't, and it's pretty much cost me any assets I might have gotten from the divorce."

Time to Feel

Taking that first step of admitting to myself that the marriage had failed and deciding what to do about it was emotionally the hardest part of the divorce process for me. Maybe it's because I was grieving slowly, letting go of the relationship bit by bit over a period of years, yet not letting it go, working hard to rebuild and not wanting the end to be what it was. Fear for my kids' future compelled me to stay, and choosing to stay was as hard as choosing to leave.

Living with the lack of intimacy, not feeling close to the person you share a life, a family, and home with, is something to which all the women I interviewed related strongly. The action we take regarding the marriage (how we know, how we decide to leave, what we do) can be seen by the outside world, and it's possible that the image we create can be orchestrated to look a certain way to some extent. Nobody sees the desperation in a woman as she drives the carpool to school, helps with homework, or reads bedtime stories. Most women outwardly seem to hold it together.

There is a place that is impossible to see, a place that is hard to put into words, that inner space where a woman sits alone with her thoughts and feelings. That is the place where the doubt, the guilt, and the fear jump out at any moment when the mind is allowed to be at rest. Even though we've reasoned out the decision, have the support of family and friends, and know that the choice is made, from this place the tears come unexpectedly, and in moments of complete distress we scream inside, "This can't be real."

I wrote in my journal: "God help me now. Can I let myself feel the tragedy of this life I've painted, of the years that I allowed myself to be lost? I want to let go of my thoughts, to be able to smile again and feel it. Will I ever feel inwardly the happiness I've made it look like I feel on the outside?"

Suzanne, the woman whose actor-husband had affairs, says, "That inner questioning would go on all day in my head, asking myself if his infidelity was a good enough reason to leave him. Going back and forth between rage (wanting to kill him for the betrayal), guilt (my part in the relationship not working), and despair (I love this man, we are a family, what will happen to the kids, etc.) made me feel like I was going mad. I was so preoccupied I almost lost my job."

Jenny, the artist whose husband beat her, says, "I had a spiritual friend who kept telling me that nature tries to teach us that it takes death to bring new life, that I needed to leave—to let the marriage die and then I'd be able to grow. When she was talking to me, I'd get really inspired and resolve to go home and end it. Then I'd be walking up the steps to our apartment, hear my daughter and husband playing inside, and my thoughts would take over, convincing me that death hurts, change is hard, and that my decision would cause suffering for all of us."

Janet, the woman who discovered her husband vacationing in Hawaii with his girlfriend, says, "I don't even want to admit how many times I thought about killing myself. I would wake up so depressed, and I'd go to bed so depressed. I kept thinking that not waking up again, if I could do it without feeling pain, would be such a relief. Sometimes I would even figure out in my head who would take the kids and what their life would be like. Ultimately it was the responsibility I felt toward the kids that pulled me out of this space."

Mary, the woman whose husband was critical about everything, says she also contemplated suicide. "I really couldn't deal with this deep feeling of failure. My self-esteem was pretty low, and I hadn't realized it. I had this vision of my life as a grown woman—of being a mother, of being loved by this incredible man, of being successful. I allowed negative messages to dance across my mind all day: that there was something wrong with me if I couldn't make my marriage work, that my daughter would be screwed up, that I'd never find anyone who would want someone with a child. There were moments when I couldn't find anything in life I could hold on to."

Janis was a thirty-eight-year-old homemaker and mother of two who left and rented her own apartment. "I can't explain the paralyzed feelings of fear I had about making it on my own. I hadn't worked in years, so I had no idea how I would support myself. Images would cross my mind of having to work bagging groceries, as a cleaning lady, or a waitress. Then I'd imagine my husband walking into the place I was working, pointing and laughing. In the beginning I could feel only fear, but as the months passed I began to think more clearly and to examine options like going back to school."

• • •

It is very important to recognize the feelings and thoughts a woman has in this beginning stage because it is from this pain, from the seemingly endless despair, doubt, and fear, that the transformation begins that allows a woman to face herself, to survive this change in direction.

My own first thoughts were about ruining my kids' lives. I was terrified of being unable to make it alone, not knowing where I would go or how I would support my kids. There was a desperate feeling of wasted time, the years spent building a life. I felt I'd declined as a human being. I'd entered marriage a whole person, and now I was going to leave in little pieces. I had birthed four babies, nursed them, and loved them, yet my energy had been so devoted to repairing my marriage that sometimes I felt too drained to mother them.

I often thought about the question my mother asked me the day before our wedding: "If you knew he would not change from today, would you still marry him?" I laughed and said, "No . . . but he's changed so much already." The end was my fault—I believed I could change him into the husband I wanted, and he remained exactly who he was.

There were moments of feeling crazy, of wanting to die instead of facing my life. Sometimes I'd think that I had talked myself into the situation—things weren't as bad as I thought. It took years, but I was finally able to let go of my dream of the perfect family, my lifelong hope to have the perfect marriage, and the fifteen-year connection and memories I shared with my husband. I knew it was time to have the courage to move forward toward healing, toward the reality of the failed relationship, and into acknowledging that my feelings had purpose.

Stripping Away the Old

When I was married, I had strong opinions about divorce. I judged friends who chose divorce as lazy individuals—too selfish to put their kids first and work on their relationship. When a woman would come to me with relationship issues, I often suggested that she look for ways to change herself, since I was sure she could not change her husband. I had built a compact and sturdy brick wall around myself. Each brick contained my rules for life, what I believed about myself, and a list of right and wrong decisions. This brick enclosure made me feel like I was stronger, better than other human beings who seemed to make decisions based on how they felt. When friends told me their troubles, I could listen, offer advice, and feel empathy, but inside I labeled them as weak. I had trained myself to brush aside my own feelings and to focus on the goal, whatever it was at the time. When I felt alone, I'd call a girlfriend and go out to lunch. Instead of recognizing the emptiness I felt inside the marriage and doing something about it, I added more activities so there could be no time to feel the emptiness. When I craved intimacy, I focused on my role as a mother.

My brick wall kept me safe until the day our regular babysitter (who had worked for me for five years and was more like a daughter) asked me if I had ever been happy in my marriage. I couldn't believe she had so clearly seen what I was hiding even from myself. I think I answered, "Marriage is a commitment, and like all relationships, it has its ups and downs. If you're unhappy, it is your own choice." Still ensconced behind the brick wall of my rules, I went to my room and cried, feeling the truth yet unable to speak it. This conversation happened four years before I left my husband.

It takes a lifetime of experiences to shape a human being. Born naked and completely dependent on others, we grow and learn things about the world, the people around us, and ourselves. For thirty-three years I gathered information. I was shaped by my family's belief structure. I had decided who I was and what my life would be like well before I was married at twenty-one. When I started thinking about what I'd lost, I had to go back to the very beginning of my marriage relationship.

I entered marriage without the life experiences I needed to determine who I wanted to be. I was still a young girl, bringing to marriage my understanding of what it meant to be a wife and mother according to the Catholic Church, the movies I'd seen, the examples from my own family, and our community's guidelines. During the first ten years of the marriage it didn't even cross my mind to ask what I thought about the many ideas that had been planted in my head. I just skipped along living and accepting my many roles, feeling happiness at times and feeling very alone at others. As time went on I found myself reading books on relationship, motherhood, or family and integrating all of these ideas into my life. I wanted it to feel just right. I wanted to be the perfect wife and mother.

Most of my days were spent learning what is still the most difficult challenge of my life—how to be a mother. I still remember the months it took me to decide something as simple as whether I would use a playpen. During those early years I was so unsure of my choices that it was hard to stick to my decisions when my mother made comments (in an advisory sort of way) that questioned my direction. "Don't you think Brooke would be more comfortable in a playpen? You would know where she was, her toys would stay clean, and all babies spend a few hours a day in one." She would then go on to tell me stories from her own "motherhood file." Like the day my sister Karen, who had to be tied with a harness to the inside of the playpen because she had the habit of escaping, pulled the playpen out of the front yard and down the street. I saw the image in my mind of a child with a harness on, pulling a playpen down the street, and replied, "Don't you think Karen was a little big for a playpen if she could crawl out of it and take it for a walk?" We both laughed.

She listened patiently to my theory that children who were put in playpens would go wild when they reached the "terrible twos." I explained it like this: "You see, Mom, if children are never restrained, they will learn early what they should and shouldn't touch. They will have seen enough pots, pans, boxes, stereo knobs, and television buttons that they will be sick of playing with them." She respected my efforts to learn my new profession and followed my wishes even though it meant she had to chase Brooke around the house to keep her safe every minute of the day. She said nothing more about playpens until Brooke was an adolescent throwing a temper tantrum. That day my mother looked at me and said, "Maybe we should have put her in a playpen!"

I could have earned a Ph.D. with all the reading, research, and fieldwork I did on mothering! And I'm sure I grew some unhealthy body cells from the stress I felt, wondering if I was doing it right.

I had put so much of myself into my family and my marriage that talking to anyone about my unfulfilled expectations would have shattered the perfect world I'd worked to create. When my marriage failed, that perfect world blew up. The ideas that had been planted in my head as a child were mutating into concepts I couldn't quite get a hold of. The words I had used to define who I was in the world had been replaced with new terms, and the terms came with new roles that I would have to learn how to play. I was reading from a script that seemed to belong to someone else's life. I was still a mother, but not under any circumstance I recognized. I was no longer a wife. Instead of being someone who fit into my community, I became a woman who stuck out. I felt like I was standing naked, exposed to some harsh environment, and I hadn't even noticed the layers of my clothing (or roles) being stripped away.

The Relationship We Wanted

When I met Ron, we were college freshmen and a perfect example of the "opposites attract" theory. I was an eighteen-year-old idealist who was sure she could save the world. Anyone who needed help, any social injustice, any child in need, had to be helped. I had planned on becoming a missionary, a thought that took hold of me while attending a summer Bible school when I was seven years old. Perhaps it was Father Thomas, the priest I adored, or the movie *The Singing Nun,* or perhaps it was all the Sundays my family spent feeding the poor in community soup kitchens. I was sold on the idea that I would make a difference in the world by helping others. So when I met Ron, I couldn't believe my luck—he was a gold mine of possible changes. I felt the challenge immediately—if only he were given the right advice, guidance, and personal attention, he would emerge a wonderful human being. I had no idea what I expected, wanted, or needed from a relationship. I was simply searching for the feeling of purpose and connection.

I believed our vast differences would open my mind and expand my awareness of others. I was intrigued by his ability to lie on the grass and look up at the stars, enjoying nature when he should have been studying for a test or writing a paper. He was a free spirit, and I admired him for being unaffected by his grades, by his teachers, by rules, or frankly by anything else. My attitude was so different. I wouldn't even talk on the phone when I had a test or paper due. He was the first atheist I had ever met. I spent most Sunday mornings of my childhood lined up with my five siblings, sitting on the hard pew in a Catholic church. Before dinner each night my family prayed a litany of prayers ending with one last "Hail Mary" for world peace. He liked violent movies, and I disliked violence of any kind. Sometimes we went to the same theater and watched different movies, and I convinced myself that this was evidence of our ability to think independently. He went to boarding school from the time he was eight years old and didn't spend much of his childhood with his family. My parents rented a houseboat or a cabin on a lake each summer, so we couldn't go anywhere alone or do anything but bond with each other. My family contained my most important relationships.

Ron was a star athlete. Sports ruled his life, and he thought that any talented person should be dedicated to the pursuit of greatness in just one area. I had nothing of any great merit to put on my résumé but was good at many things and didn't care to be devoted to any particular one. I fell in love with all the differences. All I could see was potential. Reality was the furthest thing from my mind.

As our relationship grew in years, so did my list of disappointments. We had completely different needs. When I asked for my needs to be met, he felt controlled. When he didn't respond, I felt unloved. It was like we were both on a spiral path heading away from each other. Even in life's most precious moments, like the birth of our first son, we were on different frequencies. I desperately wanted a home birth, but Ron insisted on a birthing center or hospital. I don't remember coming to any conclusion over this disagreement. I simply decided I would have it my way. I didn't care what he thought.

When the night arrived, even though I knew I was in labor, I waited until after he had fallen asleep to wake him up and tell him the news. I figured that a sleeping man was less likely to want to get dressed, pack up, and drive someplace else to birth a baby. My plan worked. He lifted his head for a brief ten seconds and said, "Sure," and fell immediately back to sleep. I felt triumphant. I was going to have the home birth I had planned and nothing stood in my way. (I had given up on the "partnership" idea after failing too many times to count.)

I put on a heavy sweater and went outside. My thought was to walk around until I couldn't walk anymore. The moon was full and the stars were so bright that I could see the road as if it were day. I looked at the big oak tree in the backyard as it cast a shadow onto the grass. Past it I could see the eight cherry trees that lined the creek. I walked the path in front of our home, stopping with each contraction to breathe in the cool night air.

While I was out walking, my midwife, Kay, had arrived with her nurse. I found them in the kitchen making a pot of tea. We drank it together, laughed, and talked about the three hundred babies Kay had delivered. Kay was beside me whenever I needed her. She massaged my back, encouraged me to walk around, helped me in and out of the bathtub, and laughed with me as Ron slept on our king-size bed. Every once in a while he would bolt upright, open his eyes, and yell something completely incoherent like, "Green, over past ten, yes down!"

This went on until 3:00 A.M. It was only when I said, "Go wake up the girls," that he sat wide awake, realizing that the baby would be arriving in ten minutes. He had missed the entire labor. I felt only a dull pain over this because I had long since given up begging for his attention. I wanted him to choose to love me. I had worked for years to convince him of my value and believed, even at that point in the marriage, that choosing to be alone was much better than asking to be loved when I already knew that my request would only be ignored.

These feelings are not unique to me. Vicka, an immigrant to the United States, was the only member of her family in this country. When she first arrived, she was living with a family she had met when they were visiting Russia. "Everything was so different in the United States," she tells me. "My English was not great, so it took a long time to establish friendships. I met a Russian man at our church, and we started dating. I was twenty-three years old. We fell in love immediately and were married six months later. Now we have three little boys.

"For the last three years I've known in my heart that we need to get a divorce. He drinks and is irresponsible with the money we both earn. It's funny, I had this ideal dream for our lives. When we met, my heart surrounded him as a lost part of my past. We had the same history, the same language, and the same homeland. I think I missed Russia so much that I imagined him to be much better for me than he actually is. I'm very lonely with him. As much as we have in common, sometimes I feel like he doesn't know me at all. I never really feel like he wants to be with me. Sure, he will play with the boys, but he isn't very interested in talking to me or supporting my ideas or thoughts."

Sometimes we want the relationship to work so badly that we're willing to put our feelings aside, as Jodi did during the birth of her first baby. "Even though my husband walked out on me when I was pregnant, I still allowed him to be with me when our daughter was born," says Jodi. "I thought that sharing this intimate experience would be a reminder to him of the relationship that we once had and the connection we still shared. Instead, I felt so compromised and vulnerable. When it came down to it, I realized that I couldn't trust him to be supportive, reliable, or nonjudgmental. I regret that I didn't ask someone else to be a birth partner for me. Instead of enjoying the birth experience, I spent much of my energy focusing on the fantasy relationship I wanted to have rather than the relationship we actually had. Now when I teach childbirth classes, I spend a lot of time telling women that just because a man is the father of their child doesn't mean he has a right to share in the experience if the woman feels compromised in any way."

Like these women, I expected many behaviors from Ron that I could never seem to get out of him. Weren't husbands supposed to carry groceries, play with children, listen attentively, encourage and adore their wives, and so on? My long list is laughable to me now, but the behaviors seemed within reach while I was married. Divorce stripped away my ideas and forced me to examine who I was in that relationship. What did I expect, and how did I react when my expectations weren't met? The layers of questioning began to erode all that I had once believed. The seeds that had been planted in my head about what a relationship was supposed to be had died, choked off by the weeds of reality, to be replaced with something else, something at that time unknown, when the space was fertile again.

No Longer a Wife

I was twenty years old when Ron asked me to marry him on New Year's Eve. When I said yes, I had a feeling of belonging to someone, of being wanted and loved. I couldn't wait to return to college and surprise everyone with the news. When someone became engaged in our sorority house, we celebrated with a lovely tradition I'd participated in only once before. Nevertheless, I had already picked out the poems I would have three of my friends read. The room would be dark as a circle of girls passed around a lit candle, each waiting anxiously to find out who was lucky enough to have secured a husband! My three friends would each read something as everyone else tried to figure out which girl had chosen these friends. My closest sorority sister, Julia, read my favorite passage from *The Prophet* by Gibran:

> Love one another, but make not a bond of love:
> Let it rather be a moving sea between the shores of your
>   souls.
> Fill each other's cup but drink not from one cup.
> Give one another of your bread but eat not from the same
>   loaf.
> Sing and dance together and be joyous, but let each one of
>   you be alone,
> Even as the strings of a lute are alone though they quiver
>   with the same music.

I had chosen this poem because I knew that our strongest trait as a couple was our individuality, our ability to be alone and still feel fulfilled. As the candle touched my fingers and I softly blew it out, Ron appeared from the front hallway with all of his fraternity brothers to sing songs to me.

We were married six months later, returning to a one-bedroom apartment in Los Angeles so Ron could finish his senior year in college. He had decided to play one last year of sports even though he had had four major knee surgeries. I thought he was the most focused person I had ever met when I saw him wrapped in tape and metal knee braces, determined to have the best year of his career. All through college I had nursed his injuries, carrying his backpack to classes and bringing food to his fraternity room. We were rarely apart except during summers, when I would go home to Minnesota and he to Arizona. His energy was like a magnet for me, endless, determined, and original. I knew that I was not the most important thing in his life, but I was willing to accept that fact believing that perhaps over time his passion would be directed toward me. I was very proud to be Ron's wife. He had accomplished so much in his life, excelled at whatever he did, and was admired by many people. Nevertheless, we were shocked when Ron was drafted to a professional sports team—knee problems and all.

In some ways my self-worth was dependent on him. I felt important being married to someone whose talent was recognized by others. With the birth of four children within six years, I had little time to focus on myself and was content to live my life vicariously through his accomplishments. I felt a sense of belonging to him—I wore a ring on my finger, and his children surrounded me. But I never felt like we were a team, like he would do for me what I had always been willing to do for him—setting myself aside to support emotionally the person he was becoming.

My mother was visiting once when she noticed during dinner that Ron asked me to get a glass of water and I got it for him. After Ron had left the dinner table to go to his office she quietly told me that I should make him get his own water. I told her it was nothing, but she said that she had never seen him do anything like that for me, and that in general, why would anyone do anything for himself if someone was always willing to do it for him? I think that over time, in order to feel equal with his accomplishments, I lost myself as I tried to become the person he wanted—a wife first and a person second. I wanted his love so badly. Part of the difficulty in making the decision to divorce was admitting to myself that I had failed to capture that love. I believed that it was my fault; I wasn't interesting, exciting, athletic, or sexy enough.

Like me, Dawna felt she lived in her husband's shadow. "When I married my husband, I was thirty and had a son from a previous relationship," says Dawna. "My husband was a professional baseball player, well recognized in the community and sought after by women wherever he went. I admit to feeling a sense of gratefulness that he chose me. We were both from the South, and I had never had much materially in my life before we married. I had a college degree; in fact, by the time we married I had an M.B.A. He was so self-centered, the world revolved around him and his perceived talent. I can't believe I went on to have three children with him. I'm not the same person I was when we were married. At that time being his wife made me believe I was somebody. Now I know a lot more about myself, and I value my accomplishments.

I actually ended up marrying the father of my first child four years after the divorce was final. This time around I may be someone's wife, but that is only one of the important roles in my life."

Thirty years ago divorce was not as common as it is today, and many women valued themselves based on their role as wife and mother. "My husband left me thirty years ago when my three daughters were six, nine, and eleven," says Nancy. "I look back on it now, and I can laugh at the story I'm about to tell, but at the time I thought my world had ended. My best friend lived right next door, and she had two daughters. Both of our husbands wrote us letters telling us they were going to leave us. They gave them to us on the same evening, then left together. They were friends too, and I guess they were ready for newer models.

"He made quite a bit of money, so I didn't have to work, but divorce was not as common then as it is today, and I felt like a total failure. I had been raised to believe that my greatest value was as a wife and mother. All of a sudden I felt useless, unwanted, and confused. The only saving grace was that my best friend was going through the same thing.

"We decided that we weren't going to let those men, with their twenty-year-old girlfriends, defeat us. Our dream was to make so much money that we wouldn't need to depend on a man's affection again. We started an investment club. First it was just the two of us, but it didn't take long until other friends asked to join. You know that we both became extremely rich. I know that is hard to believe, but we took all our energy and devoted it to reading and learning about the stock market, real estate, whatever we could get our hands on. We even bought old houses for a while, remodeled them, and sold them at quite a profit. To this day my friend and I go on a vacation the same time each year. We leave for vacation on the anniversary of our husbands' leaving."

After my divorce I had to figure out who I was, standing alone without the relationship that had filled so much of my life. Becoming his wife had transformed me into someone different, someone who believed that in marriage you were supposed to become one, to sacrifice for each other and for the relationship. I fell from my role of wife back into myself. From that place I looked at my own accomplishments and felt that I had done nothing important with my life except marry someone important. I realized that I hadn't even taken the time or energy to acknowledge the importance of my role as mother, because it hadn't been valued or nurtured within our marriage. It had simply been expected.

From Mother to Single Mother

I actually became a single mother long before the divorce. I had just returned home after attending my brother's wedding. Ron greeted me at the airport. Actually, he didn't even say hi. He just picked up one of my bags and walked ahead of Troy and me. Later that afternoon we were talking briefly in the kitchen, and out of the blue he brought up the concept of only agreeing to pay child support if I became a "full-time" mother. I was furious at what I took to be an accusation that I was something short of a full-time mother. He then went on to say that he deserved to have the kids six months a year. It made my blood boil. One of my biggest complaints over the life of the marriage was that I was parenting the kids completely alone. He didn't wake in the middle of the night to feed babies, he didn't give baths, change diapers, attend school meetings, do homework, cook, clean, or do anything relating to the children. When he was caring for the children, he called it babysitting and acted like he was doing me a great favor. Yet there he stood demanding proof of my service in exchange for his financial support.

He watched cricket that afternoon, ate dinner, and went running. When he returned from running, all of the kids were in bed but still awake. For the past few months I had not been sleeping in our bedroom, but in a small room we had remodeled off the garage. I walked downstairs to tell Ron that I wanted to sleep in our bedroom, since I was tired from the long flight. We had agreed, since Ron spent so much time away on business, that when he was home he would have our bedroom. I asked nicely if he could sleep somewhere else that night. He then told me the kitchen needed to be cleaned. (I had cleaned it spotless after dinner, but one of the kids had left a few homework papers on the counter.) Exploding, I responded with, "You are an adult too. Why are you telling me it's a mess?" He then went upstairs and asked Wesley if he could sleep on her pullout bed, explaining that I had kicked him out of his bed. Then he stood in the middle of the hallway shouting to Brooke and Rhett, "Mom has problems with me!" and on and on, describing our problems in a very juvenile way. I followed him downstairs and told him that if he talked to the kids like that again I would make his life miserable. He put his face one inch from mine and said, "I'm not afraid of you. Go on, threaten me," making grunting sounds to make fun of the huffy mood I was in as he pushed me against the wall so he could walk out his office door. I slapped him twice, as hard as I could, but he didn't respond at all. I went into the living room a while later, and all he could say to me was that the laundry needed to be done. I dumped the basket on top of him and screamed as if I had lost my mind. I wasn't screaming any words; it was more of a scream that I hoped could reach the center of the earth. That's as close as I've come to a breakdown, and unfortunately the kids heard every word.

Until that night there had been some sort of boundary between the adults and the children in our family. The kids hadn't been involved in our problems. I had made every effort to have the kids believe that nothing was wrong with our marriage. Divorce had been on my mind for at least four years, but I had been willing to stay married for the kids' sake, believing that keeping the family together was much more important than my personal happiness. But after that night we made no attempt to hide the contempt we felt for each other. This was my baptism into single motherhood! As this process of emotional separation began, I felt myself drawing closer and closer to the children, telling them things I would not have told them in the past, just because I felt a need to explain the behavior they were seeing. Instead of the husband-wife relationship being the center of our family, I felt we had formed two separate groups—me and the kids, and Ron and the kids.

Months later, when I physically left the marriage, I technically became a single mother. The kids and I had been living on our own a few months when Wesley and I had our first real argument. She punched me in the stomach—not hard enough to knock me over, just hard enough to hurt. The argument was about respect. I felt that things had changed between us, that she and the other kids had an air of superiority, like we were equal or like they were more important than I was. She said that her dad told her she didn't have to respect me, but she clearly understood that her father judged me to be the lowest creature on the earth.

Somehow the concept of "mother" had changed for them. Until that point, they hadn't heard anyone say mean things about me. To them I was the one who had always loved them—a spirit who appeared at their bedside on dark nights, at sick times, and at school to teach art classes. Now I was suspect. The other person upon whom they had depended thought I was worthless, and their thoughts were caught somewhere in between.

When I look back on those first few months as a single mother, I can remember only confusion. I wasn't sure how much to tell the kids. When they accused me of something that mirrored Ron's words, I didn't know whether I should give them the whole story or simply dismiss it. I did both, and now I wish I had dismissed every word with the same response: "Your father is very angry at me. He is saying mean and untrue things." My kids lost their innocence and their view of the world as a safe and loving place. I was left with the wreckage—both the children's sadness and my guilt at having caused their lives to fall apart.

Sometimes the role a mother has within the family changes against her will when she makes the difficult choice to move out of the family home. "I was the one who moved out of the house," says Joanne, a pediatrician with two sons. "My husband had a string of affairs over a period of years. I chose to ignore them or to believe his promises to stop. When my youngest son was twelve, I had had enough. My husband was furious because I was the main breadwinner in the family. He had gone to law school in his thirties and had just secured a low-paying job with a prestigious firm. My income was still twice his, and he wanted to make sure I would be paying him to maintain his life. I wanted to tell the boys exactly why I was leaving, but I didn't see the point in giving them all the details. They were both very close to their dad, and I was afraid the sixteen-year-old would want to get involved by trying to convince his dad to stop the womanizing.

"About a week after I moved out I called the boys on the phone, and they refused to talk to me. I called every day for a while, and we talked just a few of those times. I would invite the boys to come and visit my apartment, which was only a few blocks away, but they weren't interested. The relationship I had with the boys was excellent before I left. Even though I had worked full-time to support the family, I had also been very involved with their schools and with sports teams they played on. It broke my heart how I went from being their mother to being an outcast of sorts. My husband was so angry that he spent his energy brainwashing my boys into believing that I had chosen to leave, that it was all my fault. The boys were told that if they ignored me completely I would miss them so much that I would have to come back to the marriage.

"This behavior went on for eight months. I think I saw the boys only twice at my apartment in that time and talked to them on the phone maybe once a week. I did get a schedule for their school and athletic events and made sure to attend as often as possible, but they would often ignore me if their father was around. I felt so out of control. I couldn't get near them because they had been brainwashed into believing that they didn't want me in their lives."

While I was married, I had a very clear vision of the kind of mother I wanted to be. I would make play dough, finger-paint, bake cookies, dance in the moonlight, and have established bedtime rituals that would send my babies off to dreamland secure and happy. I would never put the housework or other unimportant, everyday jobs above my children. I would teach them responsibility through folding laundry, doing dishes, and cleaning their own rooms. As they grew, I would teach them to communicate, to have values, to use manners, and to believe that they could achieve anything they wanted in their lives. I would surround them with people who loved and supported them. Unlike other parents, I would not go through rough periods, such as adolescence, because I would know what I was doing. I truly saw the value in my "full-time" job as their mother. Throughout the marriage I had certainly succeeded in becoming the kind of mother I wanted to be. We had money to hire help with household maintenance so I could devote my life to the kids. I was able to find time for myself, to take drawing and dance classes to restore my energy whenever I needed to.

After the divorce I was an emotional wreck. Nothing was the same. I was so busy trying to put my own legal case together in order to save on attorney fees, running the household, doing chores, and managing the kids that I seemed to become another person. There was a knot in my stomach every day as I navigated this new role as mother. We all felt my shift from "mother" to "manager" in different ways. Comments like, "You never read us stories before bedtime anymore," "Can we buy some clay and make stuff like we used to?" and "This house is always so messy," were heard every day. I didn't have the energy to fix things, to care for everyone, or to enjoy each day as I had in the past. Often I would fall onto my bed at the end of the day in an exhausted heap, sure that it was impossible to heal from my own process and raise my kids at the same time. I felt I was failing so completely that my children would never recover from the shock.

Whole Family to Broken Family

One of the core beliefs I brought to the marriage was that it was a woman's job to hold the family together. It just seemed to make sense. During our marriage I had many experiences that confirmed my expectations on this point. When I left for a day or two, I'd return to find that everything was out of order. The kids had survived on cereal, there was at least one major injury, they had "accidentally" watched the evening news, resulting in numerous nightmares, and Dad had let them crawl on the roof to remove leaves from the gutters. No complaints from the kids, of course—their days were packed with fun! But I knew that it was my responsibility to put everything back together and to get everyone back in a routine.

In some families maybe the father plays this role, but for our family my presence provided stability. One of the reasons I waited so long to get a divorce was because I couldn't imagine Ron with that responsibility. I couldn't imagine dropping them off at his house and picking them up three days later. I was afraid to hand over my influence and control in their lives. I didn't want them to have two rooms with two sets of clothes, two sets of rules, and two telephone numbers so friends wouldn't know where to reach them.

I'd read dreadful statistics that outlined all the disadvantages experienced by children from divorced homes, and I hated myself for choosing to add my children to that number. This information bothered me enough that I sought the advice of a psychologist about how my children's lives might be affected by a divorce. She said, "Your children are learning what relationship is by watching the two of you. If you stay in the marriage, the chances are very good that your children will find themselves in similar relationships as they grow up." Her response helped me to redefine what we were actually giving our children as a family. Until that point I had been focusing on the ideal family instead of the reality of our situation.

Children have the difficult job of trying to understand the divorce as they split time between their parents and miss their old lives. "We have this class in school called 'Choices,'" says Carla, an eighth-grader. "In one class the teacher asked each person to say what made them the happiest and what made them the saddest. Over half of the kids in the class said one of two things made them the saddest: not seeing their dad, or the divorce. I guess it helps a little that so many kids are going through the same thing. But even though it is more acceptable to come from a divorced family, it doesn't mean it's easy to live with just one parent.

"Kids lose a lot when their parents divorce, and parents don't seem to care. They are so selfish thinking that if they are unhappy they can just leave a marriage. What does that teach us about commitment? In the beginning I worried that if my mom could so easily leave my dad, what would stop her from leaving me? I was only eight then and didn't understand relationships as I do now. My life really fell apart, but I didn't act like it. Mom probably wouldn't have noticed even if I did. She was falling apart herself, so I felt like the best thing I could do was make it seem like I didn't mind, that I understood, that we would still be a family. It's been a few years, so now life with just one parent at a time feels normal. Even so, there are times like birthdays when I feel very sad that we can't all be together."

Issues created by a divorce can carry on into adulthood, as Brea, a thirty-five-year-old advertising executive, found out when she was planning her wedding. "My parents were divorced when I was ten. That is twenty-five years ago, and still my dad refused to pay for the wedding if my mom had anything to do with the planning," she says. "How juvenile is that? You would think that they could grow up over time.

"The hardest thing as a child of divorced parents is to balance everything. You have to make sure you don't say anything that will make the other parent question you, or think that you like them better, or are on someone's side. I also remember having to think really hard before answering any question because I didn't want to be the cause of a fight over something like my curfew, or whether or not someone paid for a dance class. I'm an adult, and I still feel torn when I'm invited to two houses for Christmas and I have to choose. Sometimes I'm scared that my marriage might end the same way. Maybe that's why I analyzed each relationship over the years until it fell apart under all the scrutiny.

"There are positive things I've learned from the divorce as well. I'm very independent, I have been able to support myself since college, and I have confidence in my decisions and life. I didn't have two parents doting on my every move because they were too busy working and living their own lives. I liked that. It gave me a chance to decide what I wanted my own life to be."

Personal issues between feuding parents can alienate children, pushing them to choose sides in order to gain a parent's love. "Our family is literally broken into two groups: me and Karen, and Chuck and Chad," says Martha. "When I think of how my son became alienated from me, there are two thoughts that come to mind. First, he was thirteen at the time, a stage when it would have been natural for him to separate from his mother. He also knew without a doubt, and probably still knows, that I would love him no matter what. Chuck forced Chad to choose between us or lose his father's love. Chad saw Chuck discard friends for practically no reason. So Chad knew that his dad would go on with his life without him and think nothing of it. Chad, on the other hand, needed his father.

"I have to say, even though our family is broken, Karen and I are very happy in our new life. We have redefined what family means to us and become more whole. We are now seeing my sisters and brothers, whom Chuck had forbidden me to see when we were married, so Karen has cousins and all sorts of new adults who love her. I do hope that Karen and Chad will reunite at some point. I'm proud that she has grown so much stronger in her ability to stand up for her own rights. The last few times the kids were together it seemed that Chad was becoming very much like his dad in his narrow-mindedness. He was verbally abusive with Karen, not respecting her thoughts or wishes, and that hurt her, so presently she doesn't want to see Chad either. I've resigned myself to the possibility that Chad will not come back into my life until he moves away from his father and can have a clearer picture of what actually happened."

The changes within our family structure as we moved from a whole family to a broken family were dramatic. My moving from caretaker to worker left the kids to organize their own lives at times. I was not available to make lunches, clean clothes with only a day's notice, or drive them to the mall to buy an outfit for that night's dance. The kids were angry, believing I'd driven their dad away, that it was my fault when he didn't call or see them for months on end.

Every decision I was faced with had a piece that related to the kids and how they would feel. My thoughts were filled with indecision, guilt, and hopelessness as I tried to determine what might work for the family, what I could handle myself, and how the kids might respond. Sometimes I found solutions that worked for everyone, but often the choices I made greatly disappointed my kids. Looking daily into my children's faces, knowing that I had to make decisions that would cause them pain, was the hardest part of the divorce.

Kids seem to identify the change in family structure as the worst part of the divorce. Things don't look the way they used to look. Instead of sitting together at school events, Mom and Dad sit across the gym from each other and do the best they can to avoid contact. People ask questions that are difficult for a child to answer. One of the parents stays away from the house for extended periods of time or takes a job out of the area.

My kids were sad about the divorce, and they missed their father, but their biggest fear was what might happen next. Would we have to move again? Would they have to miss a friend's birthday party because it was their dad's weekend? Would they be able to go to summer camp with their friends? Would their father have other children and forget about them? What would their friends think? I would often remind myself that I had had years to contemplate the divorce, to go over in my head what it would feel like to be living on my own, to come to terms with a new family structure. My kids were blindsided by the divorce. They expected me to put order back into their lives, to make the problems go away, to give them the security they had lost.

From Homemaker to Career Woman

I'm not sure what kinds of freedom women were searching for years ago when they demanded their right to work! Every mother has a full-time job whether she gets paid or not. So what have we really gained but the right to work endlessly at home *and* at the office? Of course, most single mothers have no choice but to go back to work—the courts order it, there isn't enough money to pay the bills otherwise, and let's face it, the sooner independence can be won the sooner the bombs stop dropping.

I admit to feeling a sense of fulfillment in my part-time writing during the marriage, but there is a huge difference between working for fun and working because your house is about to be foreclosed. I can still remember a friend of my husband's saying angrily, "Well, he worked to support all of you to this point. Now it's your turn." I replied, "Wouldn't that be a great deal now that the kids don't wear diapers, do their own homework, feed themselves, and almost drive!" Not that I'm lazy—it simply feels unbalanced.

There is one thing I do notice about myself and many single

mothers I know: the mother makes the doctor appointments, she stays home when a child is sick, she arranges for emergency day care, she finds the extracurricular activities, and so on. "I never really went from homemaker to career person," says Amy, a marketing director with a nine-year-old daughter. "I was already working when I was pregnant, and because of the divorce I went back to work when Rebecca was six weeks old. I feel like the responsibility for Rebecca is mine. Brett will do things if I ask and give him a specific list, but he would not voluntarily come up with the idea. There have been countless situations when I have had to drop everything at work and just leave in order to take care of an emergency. I cancel meetings that he would never cancel. I found a way to volunteer in the classroom by trading with another mother who works. He doesn't volunteer. It has been hard with my job. I manage many people, and I had to work with my manager to arrange schedules. Sometimes it works, and sometimes it doesn't work. The difference between the two of us is that I'm willing to adjust my career to fit my duties at home, and he doesn't have to adjust because he knows that I won't let Rebecca down."

Some mothers are forced into making a career choice with little work experience after spending years at home as the primary caregiver for their children. "I will never forget that day in court when the judge ordered me to make $2,500 per month starting immediately," says Karen, a sixty-four-year-old professional. "I was fifty, had just ushered my second oldest off to college, and thought that I would have some time to enjoy my life after raising five children. My youngest was still a freshman in high school when my husband asked for a divorce. I hadn't worked in twenty-five years. I thought that the judge would adjust alimony and child support to cover our living expenses, but he didn't. Actually, I had no relevant work experience and hadn't even finished college before we married and I started having children.

"My attorney was a great help. She suggested that I ask the judge to have my husband pay for career counseling. She also suggested that I go back to school and get a degree. I spent a few months searching my heart for areas of interest—something I could do for the next twenty years that might be fulfilling. The frustrating thing about it was that I had to decide on a career based on the money I could make. I knew that in five years I wouldn't be receiving child support, so I would have to be able to support myself by then. I thought real estate might be a nice career but found out that I would have to be able to guarantee a monthly income.

"The next time we went to court I had a plan to propose to the judge. I would go to school for four years and get a degree in education. After that I would student-teach for a year and be ready to work full-time in five years. The judge was pleased that I had a direction to follow. My husband tried to protest, saying that I could make much more money in a different field, but the judge said that he would have to pay alimony until my retirement at sixty-five. We had been married close to thirty years. I finished the plan and went into teaching. I love what I do, but I still resent the way I was forced into doing it by someone else's choice to divorce."

Soul Loss

I was a religion and psychology major in college, I've studied Eastern philosophy, meditation, shamanism, and yoga, and I have a living knowledge of Western Christianity through the Catholic Church. During college I spent four months in Poland sleeping on the ground in support of my Christian beliefs, attempting to bring Jesus to (at that time) an oppressed people. I taught Bible studies throughout college and was a youth minister at a Catholic church in downtown Los Angeles, where I saw gang fights that should have terrified me but didn't because I felt protected by God. I believed God's promise that "whatever is asked in God's name will be granted."

So I prayed for years, starting in the beginning of the marriage, for God to work through me to make the marriage work. I remember going to confession with one of my favorite priests, watching the sadness in his eyes when he said that I was the spiritual leader in the relationship and that God's answer might not yet be clear. When my marriage started falling apart, I left the church, feeling that God had abandoned me when I needed Him most. After years of praying and trusting, my reverent pleading

turned to screaming in the face of whatever divinity existed—
"Where are you, God? Why haven't you answered my prayers?"
In my darkest times, instead of depending on my faith and
knowledge, I turned away, believing that God could not save me,
God could not hear me, and God surely was not as competent as
I was or He would have done something already!

For many women, leaving a relationship that no longer
works requires breaking old patterns, and that's not easy to do.
"Many people experience soul loss as children through trauma,
abuse, neglect, or illness and then continue those patterns into
their adult life, choosing relationships with people who continue doing the same thing," says Victoria Marina, director of
Flight of the Hawk Center for Contemporary Shamanism. "In
terms of direct soul loss, it happens any time you give away part
of yourself in exchange for something, like love and approval.
For instance, when you put your own needs aside or you allow
yourself to be physically or emotionally abused in order to be in
the relationship or even for financial security, these are all ways
that we give away part of ourselves. There are also circumstances when energy is taken from us or stolen through acts like
incest or rape.

"When a woman experiences soul loss, it is possible to reclaim
the lost parts through therapeutic work, support groups, or taking care of herself. It's like a woman who is all wrapped up,
bound up so her arms can't move and her feet can't move. When
she breaks free of the old patterns, she's like a butterfly coming
out of a cocoon. When we are in relationships that aren't working, we often say, 'I know there is something more for me in my
life.' But we don't know how to make that happen when we're
all wrapped up. One has to be willing to be in a state of not
knowing. Like the butterfly, you're changing from one form to
another, and that's really uncomfortable. It takes hard work.
Simply put, to reclaim parts of yourself that have been lost you
have to do the work. It's essential to find whatever resources you
can, wherever they are.

"If a woman feels trapped, like there is no way out, she needs
to look for inspiration outside of herself and realize that if she
could take one step at a time, it would lead her to a new life."

Divorce strips away the facade of a happy family and lets the world in on a painful personal secret. Women who've been living the married life—parenting is done together, there is one house with one set of rules, two people are carrying the burden of running the household—now face the responsibility of life alone. When divorce happens, it can be like starting over with your life as it was before marriage, with one exception: you now have children for whom you are responsible. As children are born, many women either stop working or veer off their career path, so they reenter the workforce with less earning capacity and little work experience. Often some sort of spiritual shift occurs. Some of the important role expectations that defined a woman in the past are gone.

Yet there is an amazing freedom in revealing and finally living the truth, in having everyone see the imperfection, in surviving this huge life change with your sense of self intact. Many women I interviewed said the same thing: "Materially, I may have nothing, but I am closer to myself, closer to my kids, and stronger than I ever was within the marriage." Sometimes divorce doesn't involve having material goods stripped away, but it still feels like a sort of cleansing. Each woman I interviewed felt that she got to a place where she reevaluated everything: what she valued, the way she parented, her financial responsibilities, her relationships with family and friends, life priorities, career objectives, and relationship patterns within the former marriage. Being able to strip away the old may be necessary to create space in your life for the rebuilding to come.

THREE

Telling the World

A few weeks ago I was walking with a good friend, chatting about the usual things like how the kids were doing in school, personal struggles, and everyday experiences, when she burst out in tears and said her marriage was over. My brain jumped into action and started asking her all sorts of questions, giving her advice as to what she had to do, how she needed to organize finances, be prepared, and so on. She looked at me still crying and said, "I'm not ready for what you're saying. My mind is still spinning from the realization that this is actually happening to me. You are the first person I've told."

I had forgotten what the beginning of the end felt like—how hard it was for me to admit my decision, how foreign it had all felt, how long it took, and how fragile I was. There were many steps between admitting to myself that I thought divorce was inevitable and actually arranging to leave. I had expected this friend to be ready to move on too fast, to get on with her life, when she hadn't decided what that meant. For some women the telling is easy—they've been hurt, they've been betrayed, or they've been abused. For most, telling is admitting to the biggest failure of their lives. It's incredibly difficult, and it takes time, sometimes months or years, to move toward the end.

"I was too in shock to use the word *divorce*," says Bonnie, a mother with four children ages nine to fourteen months. "We had two children and had tried for years to have a third, so I was on fertility medicine. The day he walked out I was six weeks pregnant with twins. He left with another woman, whom he met at work; she was the manager's wife, so the same night he walked out on me they were both fired.

"I thought that the pregnancy might make him come back, but when I told him he became vicious. He and his girlfriend called me constantly, threatening to kill me if I didn't get an abortion. Once he chased me into the house, spit in my face, and screamed that I was just having the babies to get money. I was on the phone talking to a friend, who called the police—my two girls witnessed this. I got a restraining order, but it didn't stop the harassment. I even had to go to court because his girlfriend claimed I swerved my car to try and hit her in the street, that I went to her work and called her a slut, and that I called and cussed her daughter out. The charges were dropped when I went to court and proved that I was at work at the time and on the days when the accusations were made. She still calls me and promises that she will find a way to refer my kids to social services, which makes me so paranoid about even the tiniest scratch on one of the kids' bodies.

"I made it through the pregnancy but lost twenty-five pounds because I was so depressed. My attorney advised me not to file for divorce while I was pregnant, so we filed the day they were born. Until that time I just told the girls that Daddy had found someone else he wanted to live with. I didn't want to call it divorce until I knew there was no way to work it out. I realize how stupid this sounds, but I still loved him and wanted to believe that this was just some phase he was going through."

As I began to use the word *divorce*, the concept of being a quitter haunted me. I had spent years weighing the obligation to be true to myself against my obligation as a wife and my responsibility as a mother. My heart was being torn between my personal needs and the kind of life I wanted for my children. I was quitting my marriage. In the past quitting something had brought a sense of relief. When I left a job, it was because I had something more interesting or exciting to go to. When I quit a committee, I left knowing that I had contributed substantial ideas and work to the cause. But I felt only loss when I quit my marriage. I had been taught throughout my life that quitters were failures, people who were afraid to take on a challenge. Yet I found that making the decision to divorce took more courage than anything I had faced to that point in my life.

Telling the Children

Once a woman has made the decision to divorce, often the next and hardest step is telling her children. For months I couldn't bring myself to tell the kids anything about the problems in the marriage even though I knew they heard the random arguments. I was afraid that once they heard me say "divorce," their innocence would be gone—it wouldn't be possible to go back to "not knowing." So I waited until the last minute, when I knew the decision was absolute.

I wished we had been able to tell them together, but Ron had already told me in the therapist's office that he would not leave the house unless the police came and took him away in handcuffs. He believed it was my decision, and he wanted the kids to know that it was my choice. I waited until Ron was out of town so the kids could digest the news at their own pace. I was sitting under a big tree in front of the YMCA talking to my eldest son, Rhett, while Wesley, my oldest daughter, was inside taking a dance class. It was rare for me to have a moment alone with just one child, so I decided to tell Rhett about the divorce.

He was only seven years old, so his response didn't surprise me. He wanted to know what a divorce meant. When would he see his father? Where would we live? Did his dad know about it? Why was I doing this? The last was the hardest question to answer, and as I looked at his sad eyes I wished I'd gone to the library to get a book that could have given me directions on how to tell a child that his life was about to change forever. I felt a sense of relief in having told him the truth, but also the greatest sense of failing him as a mother.

Sometimes there is no time to plan what you are going to say, as Vickie, a broadcast journalist with two young girls, found out. "One night Tom told me he wanted a divorce, completely out of the blue," she says. "He said he was almost forty years old and that he had spent the first half of his adult life with me. He then continued by saying that we weren't where he had wanted to be and that he only had a few good years left to find someone to spend the rest of his life with. Tom was also a broadcast journalist, was good-looking, and had apparently decided that I was not quite up to the standards he had imagined for his wife.

"I tried to remain calm and told him that I loved him and that I wanted to work it out. I suggested he was stressed out at work and told him it was hard to find someone to share a life with who is fun, someone you like and who you can have a romance with. I was his first girlfriend, so I tried to convince him of what it would be like out there in the dating world. He said he still wanted a divorce.

"The girls were in the next room, so when they heard the arguing start, they came in to see what was going on. I began to hurry around the house getting the girls ready to leave with me for a hotel when I stopped in midstream and told him that he was the one who would have to leave. I put my arms around my daughters' shoulders and said, 'Daddy wants a divorce, and that's why you are hearing us fight.' He then said, 'Your mother is a fucking idiot.' I told him to leave that moment. He left the house, and the three of us slept in one bed that night. They were so young at the time, so I don't think they even knew what it meant. They didn't start crying or seem upset in any way over the idea of divorce. They were upset to see us fighting."

Sometimes your decision to divorce makes your children so angry that they choose to live with their father. "I'd been married for fifteen years when I decided that I couldn't stay in the marriage any longer," says Hannah. "We were both musicians playing in an orchestra when we met. We fell passionately in love, moved in with each other three weeks later, and were married a year later. He was ten years older. We have a son who is now fourteen. We had been in and out of family therapy for five years when I made the decision to leave.

"It seemed that we had both gone in completely different directions. I became interested in spiritual work, and his focus continued to be on music. We weren't communicating, and there didn't seem to be any connection. I'd gained a lot of weight and thought it was my fault that he wasn't attracted to me anymore, so I decided to lose weight. I lost thirty pounds, and he didn't even notice. During this time I went on a trip to Santa Fe with some friends. One of the men on this trip had been a friend to me for a while. I discovered that I had fallen in love with him. When I called home from that trip, my son Samuel asked me if I was having a relationship with this man. I told him I was, and his response broke my heart. He said, 'Please don't leave me.' I came home, packed up my stuff, and never slept another night in our house. I asked Sam to come with me, but he refused."

Kids Respond

When you're going through the divorce process, the divorce seems to be the only thing on your mind, so you think it must be the only thing on your children's minds. In fact, you are sure that they're looking sad, feeling depressed and angry, leaving their room a mess, and skirting homework assignments all because of your news about the divorce.

Kids have varied reactions, however, to this news. They may be devastated, relieved that they don't have to hear the arguing anymore, or afraid that they won't have contact with one of their parents. A parent may say that the divorce is all for the best, but in a child's opinion it stinks! Your kids' world may feel out of control, they may be disrespectful in order to get attention, their grades may fall, they may be sick more often, or they may deny that the situation is happening at all. You may even feel guilty, as I did, thinking these moods and problems are your fault. This seems to be a mother's job, especially when you have something to do with the situation the family is in. After all, nobody gets married hoping for a divorce, and the situation is seldom explainable to a ten-year-old who adores her father.

Three months after the separation, and after many yelling sessions (her yelling at me), I decided to write my then ten-year-old daughter Wesley a letter, to take her someplace where we could be alone, and to talk heart to heart about the divorce (at least my heart to hers). More than that, I wanted to tell her how sorry I was, how much I loved her, and how I wanted to help her through this hard time. So I took her on a picnic and read her this letter I wrote.

Dear Wesley,

The strongest, most courageous people do not base their view of life on what they wished they had, or what they have lost. They walk forward each day in a direction, even if they don't know exactly where their steps might take them. I am trying to do that now. What I'm doing is letting go of what I wanted and dreamed my life would look like. I wanted to be married and to stay married, and I did everything I could to make that happen, but sometimes someone can hurt you enough that you cannot feel love for him or her anymore.

I want to help you. I know this divorce may make you sad for a long time, but I am the one person you cannot shut out because I am the one mother you have. I am the one who felt your body move in me for the first time. My arms have always been around you when you cried. When you woke afraid or sick in the middle of the night, I was there. When you had no friends at school, I came and met you for lunch. I have listened to you, and loved you. I can help you if you let me. Please let me. A mother is like a guide: she points out things you might miss, and she pulls you up steep hills and sometimes pushes you into things you may fear. But mothers always walk with their children down life's path until the child can walk alone. You are not ready to walk alone. You can turn to other people with your problems right now, but nobody will hold you as tightly as I can, and nobody can love and accept you the same way I do. I love you without question. I hope that someday you will understand this.

She listened attentively as I read the letter. Then she said, "Mom, thanks for sharing that with me, but I have been upset the last few weeks because I don't understand my Spanish. All the kids at school have had two years of Spanish, and since we were in New Zealand I haven't had any. I feel so stupid when the teacher calls on me."

I learned a great lesson here, one that I will never forget. I had been looking so deeply into my own pain that I assumed that my daughter's life revolved around my problem and me. What I learned was that she had her own life and struggles, and that her struggles were those of a ten-year-old girl—problems like having someone to eat lunch with, reading a report in front of the class, being too tall, being the best or worst swimmer, and so on. For some kids their parents' divorce is more problematic, but many kids go on with their lives, grieving faster and recovering more quickly than their mothers, who have just lost the main relationship in their lives. Kids, by contrast, often still have both their parents, and their relationship with each one hasn't really changed—their lives have just been rearranged in an uncomfortable, sad way.

Some kids end up being so hurt by one parent that they don't want to see that parent for a long time. "My parents had been arguing that night," says Rachel, a fifteen-year-old high school student. "My dad sounded like he was getting out of control, so I went upstairs to see if my mom was all right. He yelled at me to mind my own business, but I heard him hit her, which to my knowledge had never happened before. I was scared, so I called the police. When the police got there, they asked me a lot of questions, and my father was charged with assault and battery. He moved out that night, and I didn't want to see him for a few months.

"I knew that he blamed me for everything because I was the one who called the police and got the whole divorce ball rolling. I see a therapist, and she tells me that it isn't my fault. My mom tells me the same thing, and all my friends think I did the right thing, but sometimes I just wish it didn't happen, that our lives could go back to the way they were before that fight. Mom says that the divorce was inevitable, that the fight was just a sign of how bad it already was. We have to move out of the house now. The good thing is that I've always been able to talk to my mom. She is great at listening to how I feel."

Divorce is one of the scariest ideas that children can face, so their "moment of knowing" usually comes much later than it does for their parents. Most kids, even though they understand on some level that the relationship between their parents isn't working, don't believe it's over until someone actually leaves the home. Allison, a ten-year-old, says that she could hear the arguing from her bed but she wouldn't let herself think about divorce. "I would go to sleep at night, and the yelling would wake me up. I'd put a pillow over my head because I didn't want to hear it, and I kept thinking that they just disagreed about things. I had a best friend whose parents were divorced, and she never sees her dad anymore. What really made me sad was thinking that I might not see one of my parents as much. I was an only child, so my mom talked to me sometimes about how she wanted to leave, but she said she wouldn't leave my dad because of me. I wish she wouldn't have said that, because every time they would fight I'd feel guilty knowing that my mom would be happier living without my dad if it weren't for me.

"I knew it was over when my dad didn't come home from a business trip. He called me and told me how much he loved me and that he'd still see me, just not with my mom. I was really angry at my mom—I still don't understand why they can't get along."

Family and Friends

Family and friends have their own reactions to the announcement of a divorce. Among the most common are disbelief that the couple had any trouble, relief that the relationship is finally over, or confusion as to whose side to take.

Ron and I went to the same college. We were both out-of-staters, so we spent most of our weekends on campus. We had the same set of friends, and we kept those friendships long after college. Each summer we invited our closest college friends to a USC reunion at our house. It was called the USC Olympics because every activity was worth points: walking to the breakfast restaurant the fastest, jumping on the trampoline the highest, playing Trivial Pursuit the best, throwing the football the furthest, and so on. I can't remember what the winners received, but the fun we had trying to win still brings a smile to my face. Since the divorce we haven't had a USC Olympics, and I haven't seen any of those friends from college. I don't feel like they are taking sides, and I received calls or letters from most expressing sadness that we had divorced and inviting me to please call or visit if ever in their area. But I haven't called, and they haven't called. Why, I'm not sure.

Most of our friends were very surprised. We certainly managed to look happy and in love with each other—full of life, success, and hope for our future together. Once the news was out, one of my closest friends told me that she never liked the way Ron treated me, that she didn't come to our house because she felt uncomfortable. It was interesting to me how many friends told me their honest thoughts once I was divorced. Their input might have helped when I was struggling within the marriage to make everything look so good! When I asked them why they hadn't said anything, their answer was simple: "You loved him so much."

Sometimes friends can be more supportive than family. "My friends were very supportive about the divorce," says Meg, a receptionist with two boys ages seven and ten. "Some said they were surprised it had taken that long. They were able to see how much of an energy drain it was for me to be married to an alcoholic. My mom was pretty shocked, and his mom cried when I told her. I felt from my mother a combination of surprise, sadness, and anger. She didn't really express the anger directly, but she offered to loan me some money, then she called the next day and told me she would only give me half of it. She wanted to support me but couldn't understand my decision. She felt my husband was a strong, reliable, hardworking person. She thought I was overreacting about what she called 'occasional drinking.' The message I got from her was, why wasn't it enough. I guess she was willing to settle for less in her life and marriage. She didn't tell anyone in my family for months. She kept saying that we shouldn't tell anyone until it was final."

Friends may also tend to take sides, especially if they were friends with one of you before the marriage, as Amy found out, having moved to her husband's hometown. "When we separated, I felt like I'd lost all my friends," says Amy. "I was six months pregnant at the time, and I internalized everything, thinking it was my fault because I loved my job and worked such long hours.

He had been telling me for months that I worked too much and was not in the relationship. The problem was that he wasn't working, so I felt a responsibility to provide some sort of life for my baby-to-be. He could see how much I loved what I was doing, so maybe he was jealous and was looking for some excuse.

"We saw a counselor for about three months. I had moved to his hometown when we married, so most of the friends we had were couples he had known before me. They all blamed me because he was such a nice, funny, and kind person. I had a few friends at work, but I'd only been there for a year when this happened. I felt really alone and too embarrassed to let anyone at work know that I was six months pregnant and my husband had already moved out."

Actions Speak Louder—Ending It

Transitioning from a life together as a family into some unknown living situation is what makes the divorce a reality. Knowing it's going to end is one thing, but acting on that knowledge takes an incredible amount of resolve, which is usually accompanied by sadness, doubt, guilt, and fear.

My departure was dramatic. Ron and I had already had many arguments about whether I would leave New Zealand with the kids. I'd spent a lot of time checking into schools in Christchurch that might teach autistic children. Finding nothing, I decided to take a trip to Los Angeles to check out schools in the United States and found information that disturbed me: autistic children who entered therapy after the age of five had little chance of language recovery. I then found a program in the San Francisco area—close to where we had lived before going to New Zealand—that would be perfect for four-year-old Troy.

On my return to Christchurch, I was determined to take Troy home to the United States immediately to begin therapy. But Ron insisted that the other children stay in New Zealand. Since for the previous six months he had been in the United States three weeks out of each month trying to get a business venture going, I couldn't imagine who would care for the kids. His solution was to enroll the children as boarders in the private schools they were already attending. We fought long and loud about this.

I knew I was going to leave him at some point in the near future, but the urgency I felt about beginning Troy's therapy as soon as possible fueled my desire to leave immediately. I went to see an attorney the next day to ask her if I had a right as the kids' mother to take them home to the United States even if their dad disapproved, and her words stunned me: "Your children have lived in New Zealand for over six months. New Zealand is now the children's home state."

She then asked me, "If you leave the country, will your husband charge you with abducting the children?" Never having thought of this as a possibility, I responded, "Of course he won't! He knows that we are in New Zealand temporarily so he can figure out his next career move. He's read Troy's medical diagnosis and is aware that there is no adequate treatment available for him in New Zealand. We disagree about my taking the kids, but they are United States citizens."

That night Ron and I had another argument, and he told me outright that he would block the kids from leaving the country. He left the next morning for the United States on a business trip. As I dropped him off at the airport, his last comment was, "Don't do anything drastic." I told him he could count on my doing something drastic, to which he replied, "I have this feeling I won't be seeing you again in our house."

My mother flew out the next day after listening to me sob my way through a description of the situation over the phone. She took one look at my gray skin and red eyes (I'd been sick for a month with some unknown illness that had required trips in and out of the hospital) and told me to start packing. She was not going to leave New Zealand without me. We called a moving company, and within a week we had the house packed up. Trying to be fair, I left him half of the furniture and household necessities, wrote a note, and left it on the table before closing the door for the last time.

He called once during the packing time. I told the kids they weren't allowed to tell him we were leaving (a strategy I greatly regret). I was afraid that he would contact his New Zealand attorney, who would in turn flag the kids' passports in some way so that I wouldn't be able to take them to the United States with me.

Three days later I boarded a plane for the United States with two of my children. My mother boarded a different plane with the other two. As the plane left the ground in New Zealand, a feeling came over me like I had never felt. It was like running across a burning field to safety, or being in a war zone when all the bullets stop. I had made a decision that was irreversible. I cried and laughed, held my head in my shaky hands, and answered my children's stares with, "I'm all right, don't worry." My past threats to leave him, the boundaries I had set but didn't enforce, the times I had cried for attention—it was all behind me. And in turning away from the marriage I made the move that would save me—I turned toward myself. For the first time in twelve years I chose to fulfill my own needs. I made the toughest decision of my life, and now I believed I could survive anything. I definitely had left him.

Many women do not leave their marriage so abruptly. Many couples continue to live together through some of the court process, for financial reasons or simply because it hasn't been determined who should leave. Kim, a stewardess and the mother of two young daughters, says, "I had such a wacky work schedule flying three days every week that we decided to live in the same house while we went through mediation and figured out a schedule. We didn't sleep in the same room, but we did have dinners as a family and continued to attend the kids' school and extracurricular events together.

"It was like having a dual personality. We'd be civil to each other around the children and almost act as if nothing were happening. The kids were only two and four, so we felt it would be too confusing to explain the divorce before one of us was ready to leave the house. Then we'd go to mediation and bite each other's heads off, arguing and saying all sorts of things just to get our point across. We had decided that the first rule of living together during mediation was that we would never discuss anything at home. It was so weird. This went on for three months, until I told the mediator that it was unbearable, so he suggested that my husband leave the house.

"I think mediation and the whole divorce process would have

gone better if one of us had moved out immediately. We each brought so much unexpressed agitation to the mediation that agreeing on a custody arrangement or how the assets were to be divided was impossible. We ended up in court in what felt like a competition to see who could win the most. It was dreadful."

Some mothers feel that the only way to get on with their lives and to remove themselves from a bad situation is to move out. "For nine months I had asked my husband to leave the house, and I told him clearly that I wanted a separation," says Janis, "but he refused to go. I felt like I had no other option than to get an apartment myself. My kids were thirteen and fifteen at the time, so I thought they would be old enough to understand. I was sure that once we got to court the judge would order my husband to leave and I would be able to live in the house with my kids (since I had been the main caretaker up until that point).

"The day after I moved out I called to talk to the boys, and my husband wouldn't let them talk to me. By the time I did talk to them I couldn't believe the picture my husband had painted in their heads. All of a sudden I had become the villain, the one who wanted the divorce, the one who was ruining our family, the one who would ultimately cause my children to move from their home, and most importantly, the one who had moved out. By the time we got to court my husband had rearranged his work schedule so that he could be home after school with the boys. He was asking the court for full custody, requesting that I get visitation rights. He intended to stay in the house. We ended up having to sell the house, with both of us buying condos and the kids splitting time equally. But I can still hear my attorney's voice at that first meeting: 'Judges don't look kindly on mothers who leave their children. It would have been easier for you to get custody had you stayed in the house.'"

Some couples are actually able to live alternately in the same house. The kids stay in one place, and the adults move in and out. Susan, a waitress with two daughters ages seven and ten, and her husband decided that they wanted to make the divorce as easy as possible on their children. "We don't make a lot of money, and the idea of having two homes that were equally appealing to the girls seemed impossible. One of us would have to be in a small apartment that the girls would most likely not want to visit. So we decided to rent a studio apartment that we would share at alternate times.

"To make it easier on all of us, we alternated entire weeks. That way I could buy groceries for the week at the apartment and give family and friends a dependable schedule when I could be reached at home (the first and third weeks of the month) and when I'd be at the apartment. Neither my husband nor I was involved in another relationship when the marriage broke up, so I guess that also made sharing the same space easier. We agreed not to listen to each other's messages, had two phone lines installed, and cleaned the dishes, laundry, and apartment in general when we left on Sunday. This arrangement worked really well. I have to admit I'm really proud of myself and my husband for being able to work together as parents, putting the needs of the girls before our own problems with each other.

"This living arrangement worked for three years until I met a man I wanted to marry. At that time we sold the house (which had gone up in value), so we were both able to buy something near each other in a safe area where the girls could attend a good school."

Sometimes a mother is able to leave the instant she knows the marriage is over. Angela couldn't believe her daughter's words when she said her father was molesting her. "I loved my husband. We had a good relationship. There was no sign that I had ever picked up that he was sexually molesting our daughter. When my daughter, who was fourteen at the time, came to me and said this had been going on since she was ten, my gut reaction was that she had to be lying. She said that she loved her father, but that she had contemplated suicide and had planned to run away many times but could never do it.

"She had heard a speaker at school that day, a woman who had been molested herself, and she decided she had to tell me. Once I looked into her eyes and saw all the pain, the pain of still loving her father, of loving me and not wanting to hurt me, I decided we were leaving. I felt so betrayed I wasn't sure I could even look at his face. We had no family in the area, and I wasn't ready to spill the story to my close friends, so we went to a hotel. I left my husband a note and told him that I'd call him in the morning and that I knew what he had done.

"I called the school counselor in the morning and asked for help. She gave me the name of an organization where my daughter could talk to other girls and get into a support group. I got the name of a therapist and made an appointment for the next day. She suggested that my husband not be included until we had a chance to meet with her and create a plan that my daughter felt comfortable with.

"I felt my life was a waking nightmare. One day my husband and family were fine, and the next day I was thinking about divorce. Even though I still loved him, my heart had decided the moment I knew my daughter was telling the truth that I would not stay married to this man. We went back home a month later, after he moved out, and my daughter (after a year of therapy) is rebuilding her relationship with her father."

The most common outcome seems to be that the father moves out of the family home. "I was the one who had the affair," says Anna, a forty-year-old architect and mother of two girls ages nine and thirteen. "I told my husband that I was in love with someone else, but he still wanted to stay in the house and try to work things out. When I think back on it, I can't believe how cruel I was. I actually went out with the person, and he would stay home with the kids.

"We were married young, and I guess I thought my husband had the qualities I needed. At the time I met this other man I was already very unhappy in the marriage, but I hadn't had the courage to admit it. This new love gave me the strength to tell the truth about my feelings. My husband gave up trying a few months later and moved into an apartment close by, where the girls could see him often. There were perks at his apartment, things we didn't have at home which made the visit special: a pool, game room, and sports area."

Introducing Miss_____

I still remember my husband's words: "I know that I ignored you and the kids for years while I focused on my career, but I never thought you'd actually leave me." Weeks later I found a pad of paper dated fifteen months prior to that conversation in Ron's handwriting. In short, he had written: (1) She's afraid to leave because she can't support the kids. (2) Her self-image is attached to the concept of being married. (3) She's staying to see if my business is successful. In the end he decided to work on the marriage for six months, and if it didn't work to get divorced.

Reading this, I realized that, after all those years of trying and crying to make things work, taking the family to New Zealand, selling our house, and going to a marriage counselor, my husband wasn't happy in the marriage either. He'd actually checked out of the relationship years before and admitted that to me, but he didn't want the divorce to be his idea. It had to be my fault.

In the aftermath of hearing the news, everyone asks why. How could this have happened to the parents they loved, to the brother or sister they thought they knew so well, the best friend who never complained of marital problems, the son or daughter who looked happy enough whenever Mom or Dad was in town? Telling the world the truth seems to be an open invitation to begin making accusations and passing judgment. A sort of battleground is drawn. Friends and family feel they can't be supportive of both people. Kids feel like one or the other parent is more to blame, and people in general draw their own conclusions based on hearsay.

Welcome to a new reality—you are now a single mother, with a completely different social image from what you had as a married woman, and with the difficult and exciting challenge of putting the pieces of your life back together. Your marriage was a declaration of the love you had for the person you were marrying. Could it be that the divorce in some way is a declaration of the love you have for yourself? During most weddings there is a moment when the husband and wife are introduced to those in attendance as Mr. and Mrs._____ . It is customary for everyone to clap, encouraging this new commitment. A party follows. When a woman tells her children, family, and friends about her decision to divorce, it is also a sort of declaration, one that takes great courage to make. Maybe a party should follow!

....

FOUR

Too Many Decisions

Having to make many important decisions within a short period of time while continuing to juggle the daily decisionmaking and family organizational needs adds significant stress to the divorce process. Especially in the beginning, almost everything seems to need immediate attention. The school calls to report that one of the kids is acting out. Summer camp registration is due, and you don't know yet if you have a job that requires child care. Meanwhile, you need to reach a visitation agreement, sell the house, find an apartment in a new community with safe schools, divide the storage space and household furnishings, find a job—and the list goes on. Trying to juggle the roles of divorcing wife and supportive mother from a position of emotional exhaustion sends many women over the stress edge.

The First Year

It took so much of my energy to orchestrate our departure from New Zealand that by the time our plane touched down in the United States I had only figured out the first week of my new life. We landed in Los Angeles to spend a week at Disneyland. I had little cash with me since I couldn't withdraw money from our New Zealand account. I immediately called our U.S. bank to make sure my name was still on that account. I was relieved to find out that U.S. banks aren't allowed to change joint accounts into private accounts without a signature from both parties, so of course my name was still listed.

Leaving my kids in the hotel at Disneyland with my mom, I flew up to northern California to take money from our account. I took what I knew I'd need to live on for a year, plus funds for the cost of Troy's therapy. Ron was already in the United States on business, so I had planned to call him as soon as I had the money in a different account. Coincidentally, he called the bank five minutes after I left, and the woman who withdrew the money for me told him enthusiastically that she had just seen me and that she was so happy we were moving back into the area. I had no idea he would find out this way.

Later that day, after returning to Disneyland, I called his closest friend in the area to find out how I might reach him. She was the one who told me how he found out I had withdrawn the money; she said that he had already contacted an attorney and that I was to put all the money back. He wanted to know where we were. I'd checked into the hotel under a different name so that we would have a week of peace before any confrontation occurred. I was too emotionally drained to have him show up at the door.

After our one-week fantasy stay at Disneyland, we flew up north and moved into my brother and sister-in-law's two-bedroom apartment. All five of us were sleeping in their extra room. Somehow it didn't seem small to me. It felt good to be with family—to be home. During that week I made just two decisions—the kids would go back to their old schools so that they would have a familiar environment, and Troy would get the therapy he needed. A few weeks later I found the perfect house to rent in our old neighborhood, where the kids could attend their old school. I was thrilled and paid an entire year of rent up front.

Knowing our living situation was taken care of for a year helped me with all the other decisions waiting to be made. Sometimes it's like that—one big decision crystallizes many others. I'd also made the second decision before leaving New Zealand—to make a commitment to at least one year of intensive behavior modification therapy for Troy. I knew that to do that I had to talk my way into a therapy program with a two-year waiting list, start interviewing tutors, set up a place in the house for his therapy to take place, and read a pile of books on the subject. I set aside enough money to pay for this year of therapy.

One of my personal strengths is organization and clearheadedness under pressure. It became evident as our divorce battle heated up that my best decision so far had been to take that money from our U.S. bank account upon returning home. At least I had bought myself one year without any real financial worries. At that point it seemed like a year would be more than enough time to settle the rest of our divorce issues.

When I look back now on that year, the decisions about my children were the only real ones I made, but carrying them out required intense concentration. I believed I could save Troy from the most debilitating aspects of his autism if I worked hard enough, so I took all the energy I had and directed it toward him.

It was July when we began six-hour days of tutoring, starting with the simple command "Look at me." Two months passed. Still we worked six hours a day: "Give me ball," "Raise your arms," "Say Mama." Each response was followed by a reward— M&Ms and raisins were his favorite. Troy learned fast. Two months after we started his program he put three words together: "Give me ball." No one understood him except me, but everyone understood my tears. I hugged his tutors and danced around in a circle, celebrating as Troy looked on blankly.

Each week we challenged Troy with new skills. Sometimes he learned them within a few days, sometimes it took months. I would put on a cassette tape of music and dance, trying to move Troy's arms and legs to the music as he stiffly resisted. After a while he would slowly sway, and following many attempts, with me holding his hands and moving his body, he danced.

Troy lacked the ability to understand make-believe. He didn't know how to play dress-up, put on a puppet show, or make animal sounds. I stood behind him, wrapped my arms across his back, then swung my arms with his, pretending to be an elephant. He seemed to hate this, but all the books I read told me to drag Troy into my world, to not let him retreat. I dragged him into the normal world of a preschooler for six hours a day. We played until I had no energy left. His speech was monotone and difficult to understand, but he was communicating.

One afternoon the kids decided to teach Troy how to answer the front door. Until then he always ran and hid whenever the doorbell rang. We each knocked on the door pretending to be a visitor. Troy watched as the other kids greeted the person at the door with "Hi, how are you? Please come in." Those were triumphant moments when he finally mastered a skill we had all been working on for weeks.

At other times his brother and sisters would be so embarrassed by his outbursts in public that they would walk away pretending they didn't know him. I knew how they felt one day as I stood in the middle of the cereal aisle with Troy lying flat on the ground, face to the dirty, cold floor, screaming louder than the store alarm, "You're mean," in his hard-to-understand English. I spoke in a tense, quiet voice into his ear: "Get up, I mean it, stop yelling." He yelled louder. I held him, trying to lift him off the ground. He screamed, "Stop hurting me!" A middle-aged woman was trying to get around us with her cart, so I slid his body to one side of the aisle as I gave her an apologetic smile. She looked away in disgust, as if I beat Troy regularly. As I sat there knowing it would take a few minutes for Troy to calm down, I fantasized about having a T-shirt printed for him to wear that would read: "I'm autistic. Life is too stimulating for me sometimes, so I scream. It's not my mother's fault."

One day in April, when I was overwhelmed by the stress of my life and the reality of being a single mother with too much to manage, I lay crying on the couch. My son Troy, who was not supposed to understand compassion, sat next to me and patted me on the back. He had learned how to copy, and we had all showed him how to care.

Troy made incredible progress in these daily sessions. I was able to enroll him in a community preschool with a tutor at his side. It was a triumphant feeling for all of us to see Troy emerge as his own person, with a sense of humor. This therapy took all of my energy, including any thoughts about the divorce. It seems now that I let this year slide by almost in a state of denial, as if the divorce hadn't happened. The only divorce-related struggle was defending the child abduction accusation and keeping my kids in the country. But that was easy compared to Troy's daily sessions. The other kids complained very little about my intense focus on Troy. They knew that his progress was extremely important to me. I see now that I neglected to give any energy to helping my other children to heal or to understand what the divorce would mean for our family.

I thought that everything was going according to my plan. The kids had settled into their schools, and Troy's improvements had made all of our lives much easier. I had read a few divorce books but hadn't seen anything to worry about until one night when eleven-year-old Wesley looked at me and silently mouthed, "Fuck off." I stared in disbelief. A few responses were forming in my head, like, "How dare you! You're grounded for the next month, no phone, no food, no friends, no rides." Instead, I said, "Don't you ever talk to me like that!" She looked powerful in that moment, kicking her sister's backpack as if punting a football. She stomped off, having expressed exactly how she felt, with little more than a slight reprimand from me.

My response was weak compared to the storm her behavior created inside me. I stood in the kitchen wondering how a child to whom I had modeled respect, whom I had listened to with open heart and mind, could so flippantly tell me to fuck off. It was like a slap in the face that woke me up, allowing me to see the faces of three other children who also needed me, who had struggles of their own. I hadn't thought we needed family therapy, but I felt so much pain and anger in her response that I started combing the yellow pages for therapists the very next morning.

I really couldn't afford family therapy, and even though I had insurance, I had already used the entire allotted therapy amount. I called a few places and found a school where students who were ready to get their master's or Ph.D. degree in counseling saw clients as part of their required course study. My money was almost gone by then. Nothing had been settled regarding child support or division of assets, so I easily qualified to pay only five dollars per visit on a sliding-scale basis. We all went for about eight months.

The first thing one of the kids said in therapy was that they were afraid to tell me how they felt because I was already stressed enough. They said that Troy needed me more than they did. They talked, and I heard for the first time how they felt about our lives. Sometimes the kids would see the therapist in groups, sometimes individually, and sometimes we would all meet together. Most of the time I felt like I could have done a better job directing the session, but then I'd probably read more on children going through the divorce process than the therapist in training!

The overall experience was positive, no matter who was leading the session, because it gave all of us a place to go each week to talk about how the divorce felt. In dragging everyone away from their varied activities each week to spend this time together, I'd stepped forward with the declaration that all was not well, that it was time to stop acting like soldiers fighting to survive our first year. It was time to start expressing our feelings. It was time for me to shift my attention from Troy's individual progress to our growth as a family.

The first year after the divorce can also feel like the hardest year of your life, as Jodi, the birth educator whose husband abandoned her midway through her pregnancy, found out. "When I had my daughter, I was out of touch with my parents because they had so strongly disapproved of my husband when we married. I found myself alone and pregnant, and at that point I felt I had to make the decision of whether I was going to live or die. I was pushed out of a job at the religious school where I worked because of the pregnancy. I then moved out of the area where my parents lived to get away from the negative energy.

"Everyone said I'd never make it. I used any resource I could find. I joined a support group, walked into any meeting that looked interesting, attended events listed on flyers that were hung up around town, and talked to people wherever I went. If I met someone whom I thought could better me in any way, I'd establish a friendship. I looked for single mothers who could be mentors for me, then I hung out with them to see how they were doing it. I found many successful, happy single mothers. We're supposed to be stressed and a mess, but I found more women who were growing through the tragedy than women who were falling apart.

"That first year I went through a lot of not knowing. The support groups helped me because they never doubted I'd be a great mother. During that year I got back to myself—I learned to listen to my own instincts. Once I was removed from my parents' world, it was easier to see the truth in my world, my culture, and I came to the realization that my voice was probably the only sane voice I could listen to. In the end I found a therapist who met with my parents and me. As the birth of my daughter approached, I wanted to be around family, so I needed to reconcile with them.

"So much healing has taken place within me over this last year. Really, I'm a much stronger person alone than I was within the marriage. I know who I am now."

Career Decisions

About the time we began family therapy, I started thinking about a career. What could I do to make enough money to support my kids for another year? Because of the abduction accusation, I had to wait a year before I could ask the U.S. court to issue a child support order. Even though I'd written five parenting-activity books at that time, I didn't consider writing to be a career. All of my books were similar in that they described short activities for parents or kids to do. I'd written the first book, *365 Days of Creative Play,* when Wesley was two years old.

The idea evolved out of my controlling nature. I had given birth to my first baby, and I wanted to make sure that everyone—her father, my parents, babysitters, friends, and whoever else was with her—would do things the way I wanted them done! I had a few rules, one being that she was to see no television of any kind. So whenever I left the house, I would leave a binder on the kitchen counter outlining the activities the caretaker could do with her. After about six months friends started asking me for copies of these activities. The binder grew into a book that I decided to publish myself. We sold the first five thousand copies within the first six months. I went on to write a cookbook two years later, then a party book, an after-school activity book, and a book on raising great kids. At that point Sourcebooks, a small publisher in Chicago, offered to publish and distribute all of my parenting books.

Even though I was selling a lot of these books and making a bit of money in royalties, I never considered them real books or real writing. In fact, I thought I was incredibly lucky that people liked my ideas so much. The entire time we spent in New Zealand I was planning a new career in children's book illustration and had decided to go back to school to study illustration.

Whenever I discussed my career dilemma with close friends, they seemed surprised that I didn't see myself as already having a career. Writing a book every two years hardly seemed like a career, and I didn't know how to write anything but short activities. I had a college degree, but it had been seventeen years since I'd worked. Sure, I could have been trained for many of the jobs advertised in the paper, but the pay would hardly be enough to pay for child care. I felt as if I were standing in a deep hole and couldn't find a way out. To support the kids I needed a full-time job, but I wasn't qualified for any of the full-time positions that would pay enough money.

After much deliberation I decided to give freelance writing a chance. I enrolled in at least one writing class each semester and found out, to my surprise, that writing every day, a discipline I practiced for my own enjoyment, had given me skills I didn't know I had. It wasn't long before I had my first article published, and I began writing a new 365 book called *365 Days of Baby Love*. The money did not start rolling in as I had hoped. I needed to ask my publisher for an advance against future royalties just to pay the bills.

I was then faced with the scariest decision so far—where were we going to live? We had to move. I had forty-five days left to live in the rental house, and less than $5,000 in the bank.

Some women determine that the job they already hold will not enable them to meet their family's future financial needs, so they decide to further their education in a new, more profitable area. "I already had a part-time job editing technical books with a high-tech think tank company when my husband asked for a divorce," says Stephanie, a mother of three children under thirteen years of age. "I instinctively decided that I had to go to law school. I needed something important to occupy me, to take my mind off the distress and shock of what was happening. My personal life needed something important and engaging. I guess it was sort of an ego thing. I wanted to say, 'Look, I can do this. I'm not too old. I'm smart enough to take this challenge.'

"Looking back on it now, I see that school was kind of a retreat for me from life. I didn't have time to worry about a social life—I only had time to worry about my kids and school. I've graduated now, and it's time to look for a job. The only other time I've had to hunt for a job in my life was my first month out of college. My problem in finding a job now is that I didn't have time to have a job on the side during law school because I already had a job as mother. I want to find something rewarding and to some degree challenging, but I really have to look at what fits in with my family. Before I had kids I worked for a newspaper. I could easily work a sixty-hour week with no problem, and I advanced quickly. This isn't an option for me now, which limits me in finding a job in the legal profession when I'm competing with twenty-five-year-olds who are able to put in more work time. It's not the end of the world; I'd still choose what I have. It just means that I'm a more difficult person to hire. I've had a few interviews and have found that they expect a minimum of fifty hours per week.

"There is always the possibility of working from home, but I feel it's easier to be in an office where I can concentrate rather than to be at home and be unavailable. The kids don't seem to understand what I mean when I say, 'Don't interrupt me unless it's an emergency.' To me emergency means blood, danger, some sort of crisis they can't solve, and yet when they call for me it is usually something simple like a jar that can't be opened!"

Many mothers find themselves lost, not sure what they are going to do to support their family. Allison, a computer graphics designer with an eight-year-old daughter, lost her job a month after her separation. "I felt the weight of the world on my shoulders," she says. "I was newly separated and unemployed with an eighteen-month-old baby and two elderly parents who I was responsible for. I didn't know what I was doing or where we were going. My dad was just out of the hospital, and my mom was recovering from a broken hip. It ended up that the company I worked for moved to another state and gave all the employees the opportunity to move with them. I decided to move because I didn't have the energy to look for another job.

"We ended up living in a residential hotel for four months, and it was very difficult with my daughter and parents in such a cramped space. I would ask myself what choice I had, and the answer would always be the responsibility I felt for my daughter. Sure, I could have stayed in Nevada and flung burgers for minimum wage, but what kind of life would that be for her? I decided I had to try and give her a life.

"Sometimes I get so tired of taking care of all these other people. I'm in there somewhere, but I get pushed back all the time. One thing I learned in this career choice is that I can rely on myself and on my judgment. This has been a great move, and I like my new life."

Starting Over

My best friend had just purchased a house in Nashville. She was an immigrant from Poland and had no family or friends in that area. Being a songwriter, she and her husband, who was a sound engineer, moved with their new baby from Los Angeles to Nashville. She would call me every week, telling me how beautiful her new house on the lake was, how little it cost them, frequently mentioning that in Los Angeles all they could ever afford was a one-bedroom apartment.

I began to consider moving away from California myself. I wasn't sure how I'd explain that decision to my mom and dad, who had moved from Minneapolis to San Jose to help me, but I felt that my options were very limited. I took a trip to Nashville, visited the schools my children would attend, looked at homes with a Realtor, researched sports teams, and spent the week with notebook in hand, comparing price and opportunity. We could live on my royalties and a few freelance articles a year. I was sold.

I came home and immediately slipped the videotape into the

TV to show the kids what an awesome place it was. The houses were beautiful, the neighborhoods were safe, the school was comparable—I narrated with a huge smile on my face until the tape ended. The kids looked like someone had died. Not one smile, no questions, just blank stares. Finally Brooke spoke up and said she didn't want to move. She asked if we could pitch a tent in one of our neighbors' backyards! Of course I wanted to stay too. I loved the community, the proximity to San Francisco, and my established friendships, but I felt I couldn't afford to stay.

Then something happened that would forever change our lives as a family. Rose, a single mother who had four children exactly the ages of my children, told me that the woman who had been living in her rental unit off the garage for years was ready to move on, and that I could rent the unit. At first I dismissed this option, thinking it would be impossible for all of us to fit into such a small space. I went over to look at it one afternoon to try visualizing how it might work. The rental unit was one room, about thirty feet by twenty-five feet, with a kitchen on one end and a small bathroom with a fiberglass shower, a pedestal sink, and a toilet. I kept thinking, *It's not possible. I can't live like this.*

A few weeks later Rose came by one day with excitement written all over her face. She explained her ingenious idea of turning an old storage room off the garage into a bedroom for the boys. "We could cut a door through to join the bathroom," she said with convincing enthusiasm. I had only thirty days left to live in my rented house and, with so little money in the bank, was beginning to feel panic. I calculated my monthly costs and wasn't even sure I could afford to rent from Rose. She continued with the idea that we could help each other, babysitting for each other so we could each have more time to work, having family dinners with our eight children—sort of like a mini-commune.

I considered her offer for many days and began to believe that if anyone could make this living arrangement work, we could. The idea of working together to help our children through the divorce process intrigued me. There were days in the weeks that followed when I truly believed I was crazy to even think it was possible, but there were also days when I knew it was right. I felt Rose's hands reaching out for me, offering us a place we could afford to rent. I saw a rope, but part of me was afraid to reach for the rope.

We decided that before we reached a decision we needed to put the idea before the eight children in a "family" meeting. Together we told them about the plan: each family would have its separate living space, yet we would also share many things. The kids raised issues of privacy and wondered about having friends over who might not be liked by one of the other kids, and about what their friends would think of our communal living arrangement. In the beginning everyone seemed excited by the novelty of the idea, but as a few weeks went by I heard some interesting comments from Wesley and Brooke. Things like, "No one is going to like me when they find out I don't live in my own house," or, "This is all your fault! If you didn't get a divorce, we would still be living in our own big house."

It was about this time that I started believing in the value of struggle. I have always been pretty good at making the best of a situation. I figured this was my opportunity to teach my children the same skills. Often I would tell myself that the world was changing, that children had to be stronger, that it was better to learn at an early age that we were just as likely to experience pain, suffering, despair, fear, and anger as love, joy, happiness, and success. Then there were days when I would think to myself that most of the world lived in some kind of communal setting. If they could do it, so could I. By then I was sold on the idea of living with Rose and her family, just for the life experience.

As Rose and I started telling friends about our idea, we got an overwhelmingly positive response. One friend said, "I have always been afraid to leave my husband because I knew I would have to change my lifestyle completely. It's nice that you will be able to stay in the community where your kids are comfortable." Another added, "What a great experience for your kids to live a different way." A more common response was, "Are you crazy? Living with eight kids anywhere near each other would drive me nuts!"

Of course, neither Rose nor I could predict how it would work out living on the same property, but we did tell each other that we were committed to dealing with the problems. So when my kids said things like, "We can just move out if we don't like it," we would respond, "No, we'll fix the problem the best we can and all work together until it's solved." From the beginning we told all of them what an adventure it would be.

About three weeks before our move-in date of July 1, 1996, we began work on the studio apartment. Our plan was to put up walls on one end of the room so that I could have a small bedroom inside the apartment. We also planned to convert an eight-by-twelve-foot storage room into the boys' bedroom by drywalling it and putting a door through to connect it to the bathroom. The girls would have a room on the other side of the garage that wasn't connected to the main house or to my studio. That room needed the least amount of work—just a wall added to block off the washer and dryer, some drywall, some painting, and a new window.

First we made a list of materials that would be available for anyone who wanted to work on our project. We scheduled a workday on a Saturday early in June. Four or five mothers from our single mothers group showed up, as well as two carpenter neighbors. With drills, saws, and hammers in hand, we all looked empowered and felt an emotion that is often absent in our society—connection. We laughed, talked, and worked very hard. We let other people know that we were struggling and would appreciate their help. When they asked what they could do, we put a hammer in their hand, let them make dinner for the working group, gave them our children to watch for the day, and borrowed their trucks.

The community helped build a livable space for my family, because we asked them to. They built it because everyone wants to feel part of something, and every human being has a need to give.

The Choice Is Yours

I'm sure there were some people within the community who questioned my decision to move my children into what they saw as a difficult living situation. After all, I could have moved to a nearby town and rented an entire house for the same price as Rose's small apartment. Most of my neighbors would never know how hard it was to make that decision. Although I tried to put a creative spin on the concept, it was the lowest I could imagine myself sinking from where I had been. My income was uncertain. My child support case was unsettled. We had owned a beautiful home, yet here I was stuck with four children in a studio apartment. I felt like I was starting over, but this time without the hope that I could achieve the life I wanted.

Still, the best I could do was to follow my inner voice. I understood from this experience that each single mother needs to make her own decisions about what is most important for her and her children. I had a strong feeling that my kids would do best if I kept them in the community, so I based my decision on that inner knowledge.

Nobody can make these decisions for you. People can offer advice—they can have an opinion—but in the end it is your life. I've made bad decisions, and I've made some incredible life-changing decisions. The most important thing I've learned about the decisions I've made is that people talk about them and judge them no matter which direction I choose, so I may as well live my life the way I want to. So often within a marriage women make decisions from an unselfish place with their husband's interest in mind, or they make decisions based on what others might think. It was a liberating experience for me to have only one adult to consult—me!

"There are definitely positive aspects to being a single parent," says Frances, a journalist with two teenage daughters. "You may receive little or no help, but at the same time you don't have to include or inform the other parent on a day-to-day basis over every issue that arises. The control issues that used to cause constant fights in the marriage are eliminated somewhat. If the girls' father thinks they don't study enough, well, he has a chance to enforce his opinions when they are at his house. When he makes judgments about my choices, it's easy for me to remind him that he has no say in my choices anymore."

The second most important thing about decisionmaking is that you have to know what you want, or you can't make any decision at all. I often ask women who are newly divorced (and who come to me for advice before their first day in court) what they would do with the rest of their life if they could choose any job or live any place they wanted. Starting over isn't ever as easy as a simple daydream. But letting your mind go and imagining what life could be like, given more education or a shift in location, gives a glimpse of hope. It can help a woman move forward with confidence in the belief that her life can and will look better—if she can just be patient.

FIVE

Finding Support

One recent Saturday I had to attend a swim meet, three basketball games, two water polo matches, and a basketball practice. My parents took the swim meet, picked up Wesley, and brought her to her basketball game. My boyfriend took my youngest, Troy, home after his game. Rhett walked home, and a neighbor took Brooke to water polo. I missed the swim meet, made all three basketball games, saw the second half of the first water polo match (and the entire second match), and got to the basketball practice only ten minutes late. I had left the house at nine in the morning and didn't return until seven o'clock that night. On days like that I sink into bed and pat myself on the back for my good fortune in having the most amazing support team imaginable.

Even with this support, there are times when I feel completely alone. When I admit this to my friends and family, they say, "I'm here, I want to help. Just call me if I can do anything." And I do call. I ask my parents and friends to watch my children for the entire night at least twice a month. Yet I feel alone as I realize that the ultimate responsibility for the children is mine. I am the person who works to support them financially, who knows all of their problems, and who interacts with their friends, coaches, and teachers. I check what homework is due, and I sit for hours doing it with them. I make sure that they get picked up and dropped off at school and that they have food, clothes, and a place to sleep. I am the one who wakes up in the middle of the night to hold one of them after a nightmare or to stumble into the kitchen to get cough medicine. I am the one the school calls when they receive a bad grade or get into a fight. I don't think it's possible to give that ultimate responsibility away. My support team can step in and pick up some of the pieces, but I carry my life and four others all of the time.

Whenever I'm overwhelmed with my job as a mother, I feel the strongest urge to give up. I try to imagine their father's face if I were to tell him that I've been responsible for the kids since they were born and now it's his turn. I laugh to myself when I think of him on dinner dates with four children, wondering whether he would even admit that they were *all* his kids. When I want revenge, I envision his perfectly decorated apartment covered with fingerprints, broken chairs, backpacks, fingernail polish, swim bags, and tennis shoes. I imagine him trying to make a phone call or get online between the girls' social calls, and I wonder if he would spend his Saturday night entertaining the seventh-grade class. How I feel about the unfairness of my ultimate responsibility compared to his carefree life begins as anger, then turns to despair as I throw away yet another chance to sign up for a drawing class because it conflicts with baseball practice.

In desperate moments I feel like I have no choice. Then I try to remind myself that I do have choices. I could stop writing books. I could stop teaching art in Rhett's class, or stop doing Troy's speech lessons. I could stop taking writing classes. I could do without the parenting group on how to communicate with and discipline adolescents. I could stop driving kids to swimming, soccer, and 4-H Club meetings. I could miss school meetings, swim meets, and school plays. I could stop making dinner, washing clothes, and cleaning up the house. I could make my life easier and more manageable, but I don't. I already feel guilty that the kids don't have a father who lives with them. How could I give them less of a mother simply because I'm overwhelmed sometimes? That is my ultimate choice. I will keep going because I can, because I have to, and because I want my children to believe that life's tragedies can be lived through and maybe even triumphed over.

When I'm thinking about where I was last year, or even a month ago, and then look at where I am today, I know that my support team is responsible in large part for how far I've come. Family can feel like a safety net. They provide needed child care, allowing mothers like Bonnie to develop a social life. "My family has saved me more than once," says Bonnie, the mother of four whose husband left her for another woman while she was pregnant with twins. "My stepfather, aunt, uncle, and cousin have helped out tremendously. They keep me going. The best part is that they step in without my asking. For a while, when my husband wasn't paying child support, they would show up with bags of groceries. They would just walk through the door, unload the food, and start preparing a meal. If I called crying, even if it was late at night, they would hang up and be on their way.

"They also encourage me to have a social life. I go out at least one night a weekend, and one of them stays with the kids. I don't want to ask them to watch the kids too much because I don't want to be a burden. After all, they are my kids, not theirs. Even with their help and support there are times when I curl up in a ball and just want to die. I manage to get up in the morning and go on, but I have gone days without eating. It scares me to think where I would be now if not for their love."

Finding Other Single Mothers

In the beginning of the divorce process I was confident that my family and friends could offer all the support I would ever need. Then one afternoon I was talking with a friend who had been attending a support group for women who were sexually abused. She said, "You know, I can talk to you about everything. I can see that you feel sorry for me and that you wish you could help me to understand what I'm feeling. But the truth is that you can't understand because it has never happened to you." She continued: "This support group I joined has made the biggest difference. My friends made me feel loved, but this group is helping me to heal and challenging me to move forward in my life."

presence in our community, and people began asking if there were things that the single mothers in our group needed. People started to donate old computers, clothing, furniture, sometimes even vacation time-shares. We began thinking how great it would be if they could get a tax write-off for their goodwill.

"Our group has been working for a while on the idea of using a donated house for single mothers in transition. The mothers would have to pay some sort of rent, based on what they could afford. Many of the women in our group had known the feeling of not having any idea of what to do or where to go in the beginning. Some women hadn't worked in ten years and didn't have a clue as to what they were going to do to make money. Having a group home like this within our community would give women and children a way to stay in the community while they figure things out. The kids could stay in the same schools, and their living situation could stabilize while decisions are being made. We haven't realized this dream yet, but we are all working on it."

Over the years my best information and advice have come not from my attorney but from the women in my support group. My friend Sonja saved me thousands of dollars by telling me how to get my child support case registered with the district attorney. She said that if fathers owe back child support, the DA was required to take on the case for free. Now I work with the district attorney on my child support issues and save on attorney's fees. Sonja was also the one who recently asked me a very important question that inspired me to write a settlement proposal that would greatly reduce my husband's child support arrears. She asked, "Have you ever thought about what you need and want, instead of what you deserve?"

I have frequent conversations with Mary, another close friend, about parenting our adolescent daughters. We laugh at what our daughters do, share stories about our lack of control over them, and generally support each other as mothers. We all share with each other the good and bad experiences with our attorneys, what worked for us in settlement agreements, and how certain judges (and our former spouses) seem to approach the different issues that arise in a divorce. We talk about new relationships,

I was a little hurt by her comment, feeling that I was somehow being excluded from sharing her life simply because I hadn't been sexually abused. I thought about her comments for a while, and then it dawned on me that I was feeling loved and supported by my family but didn't really feel like I was healing or moving forward. After becoming single again, I did spend some time—perhaps too much time—enjoying the extra attention and support that pity can often elicit. I wasn't sure whether moving forward or being challenged was what I wanted.

A few weeks later I decided to attend a single mothers meeting that was organized by my neighbor Rose and was being held for the first time. When Rose invited me, she said she had no idea how many women were coming. I think there were five or six of us at the first meeting, most of whom I had never met. Ours is a very small community; people try hard to keep their personal lives private since it doesn't take much to become the topic of juicy gossip! It felt weird to be sitting in this circle of women, drinking a glass of wine and eating the potluck dinner we had all brought. Were we expected to share our intimate lives and pain with complete strangers?

Rose started off the meeting by welcoming everyone. Then she announced that whatever was said was not to leave the room. We all stared blankly, nodding our heads in agreement. The women began to speak one by one. I was surprised and relieved that I was not alone—they were no longer invited to social events that were mostly for couples either. Their kids felt as mine did, that their world was falling apart. I wasn't the only one terrified about finding a job, and financial pressures were causing stress for many of us.

After the third or fourth comment, I could feel the entire room sigh with a sense of relief—a heavy weight that we all had carried within us was bit by bit being laid on the floor between us. The circle was holding the darkness, and it seemed lighter to me. When it was my turn to talk, I remember sharing a fraction of my dramatic saga and feeling a little like I was wasting their time, wondering why anyone would care. But I realized as all the women spoke how much I wanted and needed to hear what they were saying.

With each story I felt less and less alone. One woman had just settled her entire case in court. She was ordered to go back to work and told that her house would need to be sold. Still, she had a sense of calm about her, almost an air of celebration. The ordeal was over, and in the closing of that door her life was opening. Another woman was in tears as she shared the newly discovered fact that her husband was leaving her for someone else. Then from across the circle came the story of a woman who had already been divorced for five years. Her husband had had an affair and left her with three young children. She shared how she had survived the betrayal, and the other woman, still in tears, hung on her every word. Finally, another woman talked about a financial planning seminar she had just attended to prepare for the reality of single-income life.

The meeting ended two hours after it began. I left with a sense of excitement, having been given the opportunity to build new friendships at an accelerated pace because of the shared pain and the difficulties we had in common. Perhaps I would find the healing and strength to move forward, as my friend had done in her support group for victims of sexual abuse. These women all lived within five minutes from me. Maybe I would have a social life, maybe there were close friendships ahead for me with women who were where I was, maybe there would even be a vacation shared, or help with child care. Maybe my children would make friends who were going through the same thing and see that they were not alone. It was all unknown to me as I walked with my flashlight the three blocks to my house, but I felt myself opening to the possibilities.

Single mother support groups can also be a place to meet other women who want to consider a shared housing opportunity, allowing children and mothers alike to remain in a familiar community while the family adjusts to the realities of divorce. "We lived in our family home for a year before having to sell it," says Martha. "By that time I had Karen living with me full-time, and Chuck had Chad living with him. I was working at a church as a receptionist, so I couldn't afford to rent anything in the area. A neighbor told me I would be welcome to park my camping trailer in her field. So Karen and I lived in the camper for five months.

"I really wanted to move out of the area, to a town where my sister lived. We went to court on this subject, and the judge actually gave custody to Chuck on grounds that I was trying to take Karen out of the area. It was a shock to my attorney, since all the psychologists and court evaluators had advised the court that I should have custody of Karen. Anyway, since I couldn't move out of the area, I started looking for a small apartment. During that time I had moved my office into the spare bedroom in Dawn's (one of the single mothers in my support group) home. She had offered a few times for Karen and I to move in with her and her son. After I took a look around the area at rent prices, I decided to take her up on her offer. We rented two rooms. I also wanted to keep Karen in the same school system, even though Karen didn't want to be there at that time.

"We are still living together a year later, and it has been very comfortable. The house is in our old neighborhood, so Karen feels rooted, there are people in the house when I'm gone, and our dog has a babysitter if we want to take a weekend away! I'm not sure this situation could work for everyone, but for us it has been wonderful. It hasn't even been as hard as I thought it would be. I feel like I still have my privacy. In fact, Dawn is so much better at setting and keeping boundaries than my husband had been. I almost feel like we're on vacation now that we're living in a peaceful place removed from all of Chuck's angry energy."

There are many helpful sources where single mothers can find information and share their stories. "A childhood friend of mine who had gone through a divorce herself sent me a single mother newsletter," says Anna, an engineer in Phoenix. "I enjoyed reading it because it had real stories from other single mothers who were dealing with issues that I was working through myself. One issue talked about how to start a support group, how to establish nonprofit status just by becoming a charter to this national organization. I liked the idea of starting a group because I had gotten so much from the stories in the newsletter. I thought it would be great to have women within my community with whom I could share this process.

"Our group had met for four years before we decided that getting nonprofit status would be a great idea. We had established a

problems with kids, our changing roles as mothers, and our new roles as career women. We laugh with each other, celebrate birthdays, brag about our children, and enjoy each other's company.

Reaching Out to the Community

A big part of getting the support you need is asking for it. People don't read minds. I started off asking for help in little ways, like telling my son's second-grade teacher that I couldn't get to his and three other children's homework every night. I would always try my best, but I was exhausted and felt that I spent most of our family time trying to edit essays, explain addition, and look up words in the dictionary. I told his teacher that our family was going through a rough time and that I was struggling to keep up with everything. I requested that she send homework home only on topics that Rhett did not understand in class. Only twice during the rest of the year did homework come home that needed my attention. What a relief that was!

The first time I filled out a sports form requesting a scholarship for one of my kids I felt humiliated. I knew the man who was in charge of the soccer league, but I couldn't bring myself to call him on the phone and ask for a scholarship. Instead, I wrote a short note at the bottom of the request form, asking for four scholarships and suggesting that he call me if that was not possible. He never called, and the kids were put on teams, all at no cost to me. I was relieved that I wasn't required to explain to him why I needed help.

Then I had to call the school and ask for field trip assistance. It just so happened that the field trip in question was a weeklong trip to the "Gold Country" to experience California history firsthand. The entire fourth-grade class was going. The school paid for Brooke's trip, no questions asked. One time a kind woman who ran the Boy Scout troops for our area actually refunded me the enrollment check with a note saying that she would rather I used the money for something more important. When summer came around, a friend asked if he could pay for the kids' summer camps. One coach paid for Rhett's basketball uniform without even asking me. Other coaches paid tournament fees. The swim club we had belonged to but could no longer afford provided Wesley with a scholarship so that she could continue to swim. The gracious response from schools, neighbors, coaches, and organizations helped me realize that I was still the same person to them and that in saying yes to my requests they felt part of this journey.

One day a friend called up and asked if she could pay for my daughter's ski club trip to Lake Tahoe. My first impulse was to say, "No, I can manage," but I paused a minute, then said, "Thanks so much, I'd really appreciate that." Then I hung up the phone and repeated my new mantra: "I won't need people's charity forever, but thank God for the people who still care." All of these experiences were gifts to me. These generous people in my life may not have known it at the time, but it was their outstretched arms that were holding me up and giving me hope.

We were lucky to be living in a community where extra money was available for this kind of thoughtfulness. However, it was not just money that we were given. People who had kids on my kids' teams volunteered to drive them to sporting events. Neighbors watched my kids after school so I could continue to write. Women from our single mothers group and local carpenters volunteered to help us with needed renovations to the studio apartment that my kids and I first moved into after the divorce. Two things made all of this helping possible: I asked for help, and people in our community responded!

Many single mothers have learned to accept what is available from their community. Sara, who has a master's degree in social work and is the mother of a three-year-old daughter, says, "I was raised in a middle-class environment. I was educated and had worked most of my life. At the time I became pregnant with my daughter, I was thirty-four years old. I had been married previously for seven years, then divorced for two years, and thought that I had finally met Mr. Right. When I told him I was pregnant, he wanted nothing to do with me. At the time I had just applied to graduate school. So I decided to have the baby on my own. I wasn't getting any younger, and I really wanted a child.

"I was accepted to graduate school and thought that I might as well jump in full-time so that I'd be out and working by the time she was fifteen months old. I decided to interview my instructors to see if they would be willing to work with me around the baby's birth. My teachers were so supportive. Susan was born ten days late, so I ended up having her the last day of classes before spring break. She went on an internship interview (with permission) at nine days old and attended her first graduate course at thirteen days old. I took her with me to class for the first four weeks of her life, and it worked out perfectly—*she* got to sleep through most of my classes. A few mothers came up to me the first day I brought Susan with me to class and said that they wished they could have taken their baby with them but they were too afraid to ask."

Some government agencies offer programs to help single mothers. "A friend at work told me about Medicaid after I found out that my ex-husband was no longer carrying me on his insurance," says Sara. "She also told me about the Special Supplemental Nutrition Program for Women, Infants, and Children (WIC). During the pregnancy I was the recipient of all the healthy food. Then when Susan was born, she received formula, baby cereal, eggs, and cheese. I've never been embarrassed about using food stamps, which I qualified for while attending school. When I graduated with my master's degree and started my first job, I was required to send my income information to the county welfare office. I had so many food stamps saved up that I was able to use them for months. Still to this day I stand in line with my Coach handbag and give the checkout person my food stamps. I'm sure the people behind me in line make a silent judgment, but they don't know that the handbag is five years old and represents my old life."

I had prided myself on being successful and independent throughout my life. When I asked people for help, I exposed a part of myself for the first time—a part that I used to consider a weakness. But exposing myself this way helped me to understand that much of my married life had been spent making sure that things appeared a certain way. It was during my penniless stage that I realized that the loss of my marriage, money, and lifestyle had had absolutely no effect on who I was. My friends, family, and community were still there for me, and to them I was still the same person. Some women even told me they admired my determination to stay in the community and to rebuild my life. At a class party a (married) mother came up to me and said, "I've always wanted to tell you what an amazing mother I think you are! You have the greatest kids. I just don't know how you manage it." I felt so good. Not that I'm living my life to get recognition from others, but because of the divorce I've felt that my kids were cheated out of some things. When I'm reminded, as I was that day, that I'm a good mother, despite the difficulties, I'm inspired to keep trying.

When you're a single mom, you may not have another adult at home giving praise and recognition for your small or great achievements each day. Kids are usually less than grateful, and friends don't always know what's going on, so it means a lot to hear that you're doing a good job. Be sure to tell the single mothers around you how awesome they are! This e-mail message from one of the mothers I interviewed illustrates how important it is to let other mothers know that you see their effort.

> You know that after we talked I felt really good. Thank you for telling me that I'm handling things. I think I am. But you know it feels like it's been a long time and I've just been on my own. No one really says, "You're doing well." No one really knows. That's okay. But I've been concentrating so hard on digging my way out of my dark tunnel that I don't even question. . . . I just keep moving forward. So to hear you say, "You are adjusting well, and the things you are going through are a healthy and normal part of the healing process," makes me feel good.

Kids Need Support Too

Kids have always been invited to attend our bimonthly Saturday night single mother support group meetings. All of us believe that it's important for the kids to develop friendships with other kids in the community who are experiencing divorce and its aftermath. This group of mothers and children became an extended family for us.

The meeting would start around 6:00 P.M. with a potluck dinner, all the kids and mothers eating together. At seven o'clock the kids would go off into another part of the house and play games or watch movies while the mothers talked for a few hours. Sometimes we hired a babysitter to make sure that the kids were entertained and orderly so that the mothers could talk freely without fear of interruption or of being overheard. Over time we learned all the kids' names, were able to recognize and talk to them at school or around town, and were sometimes called on to retrieve a sick child, drive to a lesson, or babysit. After all, having several mothers watch out for each child has to be better than one doing it alone. As the old saying goes, borrowed by Hillary Rodham Clinton, "It takes a village to raise a child," and we had created that village.

One night around 2:00 A.M., when I was fast asleep, a child burst through our front door and then into the bedroom. I thought it was Brooke, having a nightmare. It took me a few minutes to figure out that the girl was Wesley's best friend Alanna, and that something was terribly wrong. Alanna's mother, Mary, was in our support group, and they lived only a few houses away. After I got Alanna to calm down, I found out that she and her mother had heard someone in their house, so they climbed out the window together and Mary told Alanna to run to our house and call the police. Mary stayed at home perched outside her other daughter's window with a shovel, watching to make sure the intruder didn't enter her daughter's room.

I called the police and then told Alanna to climb under the covers to get warm since she had run to our house barefoot in her pajamas on a chilly night. We talked, and I assured her that her mother was fine. We waited anxiously for the phone to ring.

We eventually discovered that the intruder had been a huge raccoon on the roof eating a squirrel! Even the police were fooled by the sound they heard, pulling their guns out as they searched Mary's house to find the culprit. We all laugh about this incident whenever the story comes up. Yet I feel an indescribable sense of relief to know that my children have any number of places they could run to in the middle of the night. The door would be opened, they would be taken care of, and help would be on the way.

Children need to go through their own process, to heal, grieve, and understand how the divorce affects them. Involvement with and support from other children living with similar challenges can be an important step in a child's healing process. "My best friend Brittany helped me so much when I found out my parents were splitting up," says Wendy. "We were in fifth grade at the time, and Brit's parents had divorced two years before. She let me cry and yell and say all sorts of horrible things about my parents. I was really angry. If she hadn't been willing to listen and to tell me that she felt the same way when it happened to her, who knows what I would have done. I don't think I would have turned to drugs or anything like that, but I sort of blamed myself for the divorce and hated the way I looked, so my self-esteem was destroyed. She told me that I had nothing to do with it.

"Her mom was great too. She told me I could stay at their house whenever I needed a break. Brit lived with her mother and younger brother, and her house was always so peaceful. My house had been full of screaming leading up to Dad's moving out, and after that it seemed that all my mom could do was cry and complain. It was great to have a place to go where life seemed normal."

Family friends can step in to be a friend and role model in children's lives. "My dad travels all the time, so I don't get to see him very often," says twelve-year-old Bryan. "He does have a very good friend, though, who takes me to a lot of sporting events in our area. The friend doesn't have any children himself, so he says it's really fun for him to take me. We tailgate before football games; sometimes he even arranges to take me to a professional football team's training camp. He shows up for birthday parties and other stuff when my dad can't be there. Actually, even if my dad could be there he wouldn't come because he wouldn't want to be around my mom, but my mom gets along really well with my dad's friend."

Teachers have daily contact with children and can often offer support to a child with problems to talk out. "My eighth-grade science teacher was the best listener," says Mandy. "I'm in high school now, and I still go back to visit her and ask her advice. She approached me right away when she heard my parents were getting a divorce and told me that I could come and talk to her whenever I wanted to about it. She didn't come from a divorced family, so she said she didn't know how I felt, but she listened to me almost every lunch period for what seemed like months.

"I was so distraught over the whole thing. I couldn't study and had a hard time paying attention during class. I lost twenty pounds because I didn't feel like eating. She would tell me that she was concerned about me and asked me a lot of questions to make sure I didn't have an eating disorder, but she always assured me that it was normal for me to feel so sad. She talked to me about grief and the fact that some part of my life had died. Her words really kept me alive."

Sometimes an adult offers encouragement and support to a child for no apparent reason, never knowing how much the attention meant to the child. "I had this awesome coach who kept encouraging me," says Mike. "When my parents separated, I decided to put all my anger into lifting weights. I was in high school and didn't want to be at home that much. The track coach noticed that I was in the gym a lot, so he asked if I wanted some help with a workout. He had been a weight lifter during college. We spent many hours together after school. He was so positive about my potential. We didn't talk about the divorce. I'm not sure he even knew anything was happening, but his encouragement kept me going."

It's important that children see their mothers forming friendships, finding support for themselves, and interacting with their community in positive ways. When a mother can't create the support she needs with other adults, children often feel that it's their responsibility to help their mother through the difficult process of divorce, as Kate did when she was a child. "I'm an adult woman now, but I remember how I felt as a child when my mother's life fell apart," she says. "I felt so responsible for my mom. I was in middle school at the time, and my mom just stopped functioning. She didn't try to make new friends, she didn't want to date, and she didn't care about her career. She started talking to me like I was one of her friends, asking me what I thought she should do and telling me how angry she was with my dad. I ended up moving out and living with my dad for five years because I couldn't handle it anymore. I'm very close to my mom now, but it took me a while to forgive her for being so dependent on me after the divorce."

Professional Help

Even if you have your family, other single mothers, and a community offering you support, there are times when professional help is necessary. Psychologists are able to listen, direct, and see your life from a perspective different from that of your friends. You may be unwilling to bring up certain issues with family but feel comfortable discussing them with a stranger who has no vested interest in the decisions you make or in how those decisions may affect the agenda of those close to you.

"I decided to find a therapist when I heard myself repeating the same things over and over again to my friends," says Beth, the mother of two girls ages two and five. "I really valued my friends and all the support I was getting, but I started feeling like I was leaning too heavily on them, expecting them to solve all the problems in my life. I was afraid that over time all my friends would disappear because I was so depressing to be around. Some days I really felt like killing myself, but there was no way I would tell my family or friends that. They would feel responsible and try to save me.

"My therapist is a safe person for me. She listens, and she doesn't judge me, but she helps me clarify how I feel and goes over choices with me. I know I can call her in an emergency when I feel really down. I didn't have money for therapy, so I almost set the entire idea aside until another single mother said that some therapists saw clients and charged based on what they could afford. I actually can cope with my life with the help of my therapist, and I know that therapy is available for anyone who needs it if they are willing to look for it."

If you are depressed, there is medical treatment available that you may not know about. "My shrink has kept me alive," says Arlene, the mother of a preschooler. "You'd think that I would be able to pull myself together after three years of this, but I haven't been able to do it on my own. I'm taking medication, which is something I felt bad about in the beginning. I thought that medication was a cop-out—instead of solving a problem you pop a pill. Now I can see that medication helps me get to a place where I can actually talk about the pain and deal with the important issues in my life.

"Healing is such a slow process, and I am making great progress. But I have also realized through this therapy that I came into my marriage with issues that I had never dealt with, so only a small portion of this therapy is related to the divorce. It is all related to finding out who I am, who I have been, and why I have chosen certain things. I also think I have learned techniques through therapy that have helped me as a mother, like allowing my son to see me cry when I'm sad. I have never seen my own mother cry, and in a way that communicated to me as a child that it wasn't all right to feel sad, and certainly not all right to show anyone your feelings. I don't think that is healthy. So I'm learning how to have healthier patterns in my life, and hopefully my son will also learn those healthy patterns."

School counselors, drug hot lines, and other resources can be life-saving when there are problems in the family that seem impossible to solve. Hannah's teenage son Samuel "had been experimenting with drugs in the six months leading up to our separation," she says. "But during the summer, when I left the house and Samuel chose to stay with his dad, the drug use started to escalate. I felt so much guilt, believing it was my fault. As soon as I found out about his drug problem, I had him seeing a therapist. We ended up putting him in an outpatient program, but he continued to use, so we put him in a residential long-term treatment program, which I thought would be the only way to save his life. He ran away from that facility, so we found another facility for him. It's been three years of painful personal work and family therapy, but he is on his way to recovery, and I expect him home in the next two months."

Support comes in all shapes and sizes. Going through the process of divorce alone is unnecessary. Communities are full of resources: churches, schools, volunteer hot lines, and professional therapists. Other single mothers are all around you, going through the same process and feeling the same emotions in their own lives behind their own closed doors. The goal is to open up your doors and let people know that you need help and that you need support. Just because you are a single mother doesn't mean you have to be alone.

The Divorce Process

As soon as a woman decides the marriage might be over, it is a good idea to consult with an attorney. It's important to talk through the process and find out what can be expected—that is, how property issues and custody arrangements are likely to be resolved. "When I have an initial meeting, I assess the woman's degree of knowledge concerning her assets," says Lana Norris, an attorney who specializes in family law, located in San Mateo, California. "Then I tell her to go home and copy everything that looks relevant and store the copied documents somewhere safe away from the home. Look for anything with numbers on it; title documents, bank statements, stock certificates, everything. Make phone calls and ask questions."

That day in New Zealand, as soon as my brain registered the reality that I was going to get a divorce, I began to gather the financial information I thought I might need. I hadn't kept track of investments, wasn't sure how to read a tax return, and in general had quite a bit of work to do finding bank accounts and looking into family funds that had been invested in my husband's new business venture. Ron didn't keep any of our finances a secret; it was just that, in our division of household responsibilities, he handled them all.

Even though my emotions were raw, I made myself find the information I knew I'd need later. It was my way of processing the life we had lived together and realizing that the money made during the marriage was earned by both our efforts. I had to know what we had in order to make a claim to it. My instincts later proved to be well founded. Once it was clear that we would no longer be marriage partners, contracts and other important financial information were nowhere to be found, so the computer files I'd copied were our only records.

"There are several important things to think about when choosing an attorney," says Lana. "Look for someone experienced in family law, not a general practitioner who dabbles in family law once in a while. Check if the attorney is a member of a professional family law organization."

I've found that women frequently want to get a settlement instead of going to court—most women don't want to be needlessly inflammatory—so it's important to find someone to handle the case according to your own style. It's also important to recognize your husband's style. If you haven't agreed on anything in a few years and he has to win no matter what the cost, you better find a killer attorney. The best attorney, says Lana, is one "who is committed to settling out of court but who is also willing to stand up and fight if necessary."

It was most important for me to feel comfortable with my attorney so that I could ask questions and have things explained in a way that I could understand. "Also be wary of an attorney who paints too rosy a picture, who promises you too much," says Lana. "In my experience, at the end of the divorce process no party feels terrific about how each issue is resolved. It is a series of compromises that is often gut-wrenching, and nobody feels great."

Once the kids and I were settled, I took the first step of the divorce process—finding a good attorney. I made one big mistake, however: I hired an out-of-county attorney. Because this attorney, whom I'll call Dick, had no knowledge of, or connection to, the county we lived in, he had no personal experience with the judges or the system. Most attorneys I interviewed had no experience with child abduction, nor had they worked on a divorce action out of the country. When we first met in Dick's San

Francisco office, he gave me the impression that he was completely confident and knowledgeable in the area of international divorce. (Mistake number two: he promised too much.) My husband had filed a motion asking the U.S. court to dismiss my case on the grounds that I was a permanent resident of New Zealand with no ties to California. My attorney believed I would win easily based on our U.S. assets and bank accounts, our prior residency in California, and the fact that all of our household belongings and cars were still in storage in the United States.

However, it was obvious to me after the first five minutes of our brief hearing later that month with Ron and his attorney that Dick knew very little about international rules of divorce—we were beaten by my husband's attorney on every count. I lost the motion. The judge believed Ron's testimony—that we had intended to move to New Zealand permanently. The judge was fooled by Ron's declaration that I would be moving to Minnesota, that our house had been sold, and that I was staying in California only to get child support. When I received the judgment in the mail a few weeks later, I was devastated. New Zealand was granted the right to judge all aspects of the case. In the meantime, the New Zealand court had declared that it could not rule on child support or custody until the kids were living there.

I seemed to be stuck in limbo. Neither country wanted to take the case. Dick had given me bad advice. I had asked him to put a hold on our U.S. assets, but he didn't, saying that according to the separation document nobody could move any assets. The day after the court made a judgment, Ron moved all of our assets to New Zealand, and it would be a year before I had access to any money. Dick had also told me to file a child custody case with the New Zealand court so that I would look better regarding the abduction suit. Ron's attorney based his entire case on this request, telling the judge that I had filed the custody case in New Zealand so was therefore in agreement that New Zealand was the correct venue. Had I interviewed other attorneys, obtained recommendations from women in my own community, or taken greater initiative in my own case instead of trusting that my attorney would take care of everything, quite likely the outcome would have been different.

Given the multiple mistakes I made in the beginning of my own divorce process, I asked Lana to share her thoughts on the biggest mistakes that she sees women make. "If you see the woman in the course of the divorce making mistakes, not behaving in a way that is in her best interest, she is generally using the same coping mechanisms that she learned and exhibited during the marriage," says Lana. "I'm always saddened when I see extremely bright, well-educated, accomplished professional women, who appear to have it all together, exhibit very low self-esteem when it comes to the divorce. They seem to be transformed from superwoman to victim in a matter of minutes when dealing with their husbands.

"Sometimes I will recognize that a woman has really been emotionally abused and she can't stand up to her husband. She asks for a restraining order, then she won't authorize it, or we get an order and she won't enforce it. Instead, she allows the abusive spouse to visit her home without enforcing boundaries," says Lana.

Another mistake is to disengage from the process entirely. "My husband first moved into the spare bedroom when we started talking about divorce," says Julie, a CEO with two teenage children. "A few months later he moved into his own apartment. I didn't really think about doing anything legally until there seemed to be some finality to it. I saw no reason to serve him with divorce papers or separation papers. I had a big project deadline at work, so I wasn't able to deal with the extra stress of focusing on divorce issues. I contributed more financially to the family throughout the marriage, even though we both worked, so I thought the best thing I could do was to do a good job at work and continue to bring home a paycheck.

"About two weeks after he moved into his own apartment I received a call from two of our credit card companies. He had charged the limit on both cards. We had not used those particular cards before. The debt was close to $20,000, and all the charges were made after he had moved into the guest room. I decided to find an attorney. In the first meeting I found out that the debt was half mine even though I had not charged anything. She said that if I had served him with separation papers before he made the purchases, the debt would be his alone."

Some women want their attorney to make every decision and handle everything. They repeat the pattern from their marriage, when they gave their husband power and authority, by giving such power to the attorney. This can be very damaging if the attorney they select is the kind who is going to inflame the case. I have watched women turn over everything to their attorney with complete trust. If the attorney doesn't want to settle out of court, the case can be very litigious and costly. By giving an attorney the power to decide the outcome of the case, the woman takes no responsibility for the tone or tenor of the case. "I learned that my attorney was not a rescuer. She was hired to assert and defend my legal rights," says Marsha, a twenty-nine-year-old teacher with twin three-year-old boys. "When I met with her the first time, she gave me an assignment—to think about what I wanted to achieve." As a client you need to be clear on your goals and give appropriate instructions to the attorney. It's a delicate balance of listening to your attorney and following instructions, but also giving the attorney direction without micromanaging the case.

Another big mistake women make is not facing the reality of life after divorce. They don't take steps early enough to get themselves back onto an independent life track, like going back to school or finding a career that is right for them. "Many women are stuck emotionally for too long as they keep running a tape over and over in their minds about what went wrong in the marriage. They need to take immediate steps toward becoming economically and emotionally self-sufficient," says Lana. Finding a good therapist with whom you can talk through fears and anxiety is a great help and well worth the financial investment.

Another thing to be aware of is that every case is unique. "Often women come into my office having listened to all their friends' divorce stories, what they received for child support, property settlement, or alimony," says Lana. "They have a preconceived idea of what they should get based on friends' information, which can be misleading."

Divorce Papers

One day a strange man appeared in front of our house, dressed in old, white, paint-stained overalls. He was cleaning the street (which isn't done in our rural community). I walked out to get the mail and to see what he was doing. He asked if I was Sheila Ellison, and after I said yes, he said that I was being served. I wasn't really sure what that term meant. I walked in the house and screamed aloud when I read that I was being charged with abducting my children from New Zealand.

Falling to the couch stunned, various scenarios rushed through my head. I was terrified that Ron would be able to take the kids back to New Zealand and that I'd have to wait at least a year until the case came to trial in Christchurch before I'd get them back. With an abduction accusation hanging over my head, I wasn't sure if I'd be arrested upon arriving in New Zealand if I went with them, so I called my attorney.

He called back a few days later and told me that according to the Hague Convention (which established laws regarding abduction), the only way I could keep the children in the United States was by proving that one of the following three situations existed: (1) My husband was aware of the plan to take the children to the United States and did nothing to stop us; (2) the return of a child would expose him or her to physical or psychological harm or otherwise place the child in an intolerable situation; or (3) the child didn't want to be returned, in which case the court would have to rule that the child was old enough to make that determination.

My attorney advised me to hire one of the court psychologists to interview each of the children and write up a recommendation as to whether the kids should be sent back to New Zealand. We were thinking that, because of his autism, Troy would be able to stay with me. We hoped the psychologist would also find that the removal of Troy's siblings would cause psychological harm to him, compelling the court to rule that all the children could stay.

I spent five weeks unable to sleep, angry with myself that I hadn't made Ron sign something when we left for New Zealand acknowledging our verbal agreement that I could return to the United States at any time. Thousands of dollars were spent preparing for what might happen. Ron never did attempt to take the kids back to New Zealand, but it was a good strategic move on his attorney's part. His action kept me out of the U.S. courts for two years.

It took me six months to "serve him back" with the divorce papers, because he had no permanent U.S. residence. He wanted the court to believe that he was not a U.S. resident, so he moved between friends' houses. Even the weird street cleaners couldn't find him without an address or work schedule!

Sometimes it takes a few days to prepare and serve someone with divorce papers. Some women choose, as Martha did, to remove herself and the children from the family home at that time. "The night that Chuck was arrested for choking me, Karen and Chad were too afraid to stay in our house. The police had suggested I go to the hospital to document the marks on my neck, and in hindsight I wish I would have done that for the future court battle, but at the time my first priority was to comfort the kids. They kept saying that their aunt would bail their father out of jail and he'd come back to get them. So I took them to a motel that night, and we ended up staying for a week.

"The kids knew their dad was only going to be held for one night, and they were afraid he might show up at school, so they asked if they could miss school that week. During the day I'd be on the phone with attorneys, therapists, and battered women's shelters getting advice and direction. The kids spent their days in the motel pool trying to forget everything. When I thought it was time to return to the house, I called a friend and asked her to straighten up the house so there would be no visible evidence of the events of that night. We also went to the pet store and bought birds. Chad had always begged to have birds, but Chuck forbade it. The day we went back home Chuck was served with restraining orders and divorce papers."

It is possible to get the divorce started on your own, according to Debra, a financial planner with a ten-year-old son. "A friend of mine had recently gone through a divorce and told me how much money she had spent on attorney fees. She was very happy with her attorney but thought it might help if she gave me a crash course on the divorce process. I found out that I could go to the county office and fill out the divorce papers myself. Recently a bill was passed in our county [San Mateo, California] that funds a family law facilitator. She is at the county courthouse every day, available to meet with people who don't have an attorney or who can't afford one. The family law facilitator will help someone fill out the form to file a divorce petition, a motion for support, and other things. Apparently all of California's counties will soon have a facilitator, but I'm not sure about the rest of the United States.

"I called the county office to get this information. I went to see the facilitator, and she explained everything to me that I didn't understand, then told me the legal way to serve my husband the necessary papers. I couldn't serve him myself, so I had to find someone to do it for me. I asked a few of my friends, but they said they didn't feel comfortable with it. One of them said she didn't want him to say bad things about her to anyone in the community. Anyway, I had a neighbor, an older man whom I talked to every so often over the fence. I asked him if he would mind doing it, and he seemed excited with what he called 'detective work.' He was so cute and took the job very seriously. I arranged for him to come over when my son Mike was at soccer practice so he could serve my husband.

"It was great because my husband looked totally shocked. When the neighbor left, I handed him a letter from the woman he had been dating for two years. Since I knew a lot about finance, I covered all my bases before I dropped the bomb. I knew about the woman for two months before I served him with divorce papers, so I already had my finances organized."

Finding and Organizing Records

I remember the day my attorney handed me the list of documentation I would need before our assets could be divided and before any child support amount could be set. Even though I'd done a bit of information-gathering before leaving New Zealand, this request was the biggest assignment I'd received since writing a final term paper my senior year in college. I felt that I couldn't do it, that there was too much work and I had enough to deal with at home. The division of assets didn't feel nearly as important as spending time supporting my kids as they faced daily adjustments in their new lives. On the other hand, I wanted to be responsible, to come up with accurate figures so that I would receive the money I needed to support our life.

I didn't touch my attorney's assignment for a few weeks. Then I went to a single mothers meeting where an attorney was saying that most women want to get the divorce process over with and so don't get nearly what they need or deserve in their divorce settlements. She gave percentages and psychological information about men and women. She claimed that men aren't as emotional about divorce, so they have the ability to keep the divorce process alive, to engage in legal action, and to be less bothered by it. Women, on the other hand, have a strong need to get all the business stuff out of the way so they can rebuild and tend to their emotional needs and the needs of their children.

Her talk inspired me. It described exactly what I was experiencing. I decided to set one whole week aside and do nothing but work on the divorce. I concluded that my future, as well as the future of my children, depended on my organizational skills right then, even though I didn't feel up to it. This process helped me form a clear picture of what assets we had acquired during the marriage. It also revealed how much I didn't know about our current investments, what kinds of life insurance or retirement plans my husband had, where all the bank accounts were, and so on. At the end of the week I was able to have a conversation with my attorney about dividing assets. Without going through this tedious process of researching our records, I could have missed assets that by law were to be divided equally.

"I have to say that finding my records and organizing them was the worst part of the divorce process," says Pat, a forty-five-year-old nurse with an eleven-year-old son. "My husband is an independent contractor, so he billed his time and received most of the payments in cash. When we trusted each other and were living together as a couple, that didn't bother me. It didn't bother me either when we filed our tax returns claiming only the traceable money. But when I had to look for old contracts and work orders to prove that his income was actually twice as much as he was claiming in court, it became a nightmare.

"I have an entire garage full of boxes with records. From the beginning the attorney told me that if I wanted to get what I deserved, it would take a ton of work on my part to put the financial facts together. I worked on finding the records for a year. Every weekend I would go through things and record them in my notebook. In the end there was money missing from our home equity loan account, he had taken part of our retirement to buy a piece of land I knew nothing about, and he had fraudulently signed my name on an apartment building we co-owned, giving him sole ownership. I am very proud of all the work I did. In all I spent four solid months putting the case together. The settlement in court ended up being worth five years' salary for me."

Going to Court

I waited a year, hired a new attorney who came highly recommended, and set out to convince the California courts that it was their responsibility to determine all the issues regarding my children. This time I was prepared. To save money I asked my new attorney if I could write my own declaration and give it to her on disk, to be formatted as the court required. She agreed. I gathered every piece of evidence I could find to prove that we had not moved to New Zealand permanently. The most convincing piece was an article written for a New Zealand national magazine. There was a direct quote from Ron stating that the family intended to be in New Zealand for one year. We were lucky enough to get the same judge who had given New Zealand jurisdiction of our case one year before. When he read my declaration and realized that I had received no child support, that Ron had never followed through on the abduction accusation, and that we'd been living in a studio apartment off of a friend's garage for a year, he had no choice but to rule in my favor.

I'd thought about that judge many times throughout the year. I wondered if he'd ever know the painful result of his first decision, and as I sat there listening to the hearing outcome, I secretly hoped he felt shame over his mistake. I'd finally won. The judge ruled that California would determine child support. He ordered Ron to pay back child support, and then set a current child support amount based on our income and the time that Ron spent with the children.

This was the happiest day of my divorce process. I drove home laughing, crying, pounding the steering wheel to the beat of the music that was blasting as loud as I could stand it. I wanted to celebrate and to call everyone I knew who had encouraged me throughout that year. I felt like jumping up and down, crying with relief for hours, or running madly in my front yard, telling the world that I'd finally won. There is nothing like the feeling of being vindicated.

Many women believe, as I did in the beginning, that going to court will be a fair process, that a judge will see the situation as it really is and rule in their favor. Jodi, the childbirth educator who is also an elementary school teacher, found out that there are many ways for men to fool the legal system. "My husband left us when I was still pregnant," she says. "He just disappeared and abandoned us. I was on top of the world when I graduated from college. We met shortly after that. He did return the day before she was born, so he was there for the birth. It was a terrible experience to have him with me for the birth. That is why I became a childbirth educator, so that I could counsel women not to go through the birth process with someone they don't trust even if they are married.

"Anyway, the first time we were in court I was applying for child support. We got into court, and he pulled out a paper showing that he had filed for disability because he was clinically depressed. The scary thing was how convincing he was. He came to court dressed in a suit, very clean-cut and honest. He said sadly to the judge that he would love to be able to pay but he was disabled. I was steaming. If a woman declared that she was clinically depressed, she would probably lose custody of her child. But he was able to claim it and was allowed to be on disability for five years.

"My daughter did get a very small part of his disability check for a few years, until I received a note in the mail stating that her disability would be cut in half because he had fathered another child. I was already devastated with his leaving us, and I thought that I'd never heal. The hardest thing for me to accept was who he actually was. I felt I'd married one person and he turned out to be another. I was well educated, had traveled, and had many relationships before I married. I couldn't believe my instincts had betrayed me to that degree."

I'm always amazed that nothing about my case was normal or run-of-the-mill. Everything was dramatic. I was given five days' notice before my next court appearance—in New Zealand. In those five days our New Zealand attorneys were working on a mediated settlement. My attorney mailed me something that I thought Ron had agreed to, but he wouldn't sign it.

Three hours before my flight was to depart for New Zealand, I drove an hour to a swim meet where I knew Ron would be watching Wesley swim. I brought the agreement with me to find out if he intended to sign it. He wouldn't sign it and said there were a few things he disagreed with. I had already arranged for my mother to watch the kids in case I had to leave immediately. I drove home like a mad woman to make that flight, knowing that it might represent my only chance for another six months to get before a live person who could make a decision.

I barely made my all-night flight. After landing I took a cab to meet the New Zealand attorney I had hired over the phone. We had just thirty minutes to spare before court was in session. Ron's attorney was shocked to see me in person and asked the judge for a recess so that we could settle out of court. We spent three hours going over the same agreement I had asked Ron to sign the day before. With only thirty minutes left before our end-of-the-day meeting with the judge, Ron signed the agreement via fax. The judge stamped his approval. The next three days I spent finding a real estate agent to sell our house, opening a bank account, and tying up all the loose ends I'd left behind. This was the first time in two years that I had legal access to any of our joint assets. The judge had ordered that the proceeds from the sale of our house in Christchurch were mine.

Sometimes court becomes a game in which one party keeps dragging the other party in with the tiniest cause. "The first time we went to court was for a paternity suit I filed," says Anne, a postal worker with a four-year-old daughter. "We weren't actually married when my daughter was born. He didn't want anything to do with her and wouldn't even sign the birth certificate until after I won the paternity suit. Then he took me to court to get his name put on the birth certificate. Later I had to go to court and ask the judge to sign a medical form for my daughter to get tubes put in her ears. He had refused to sign the surgery form and told the judge the problems were caused by secondhand smoke from my cigarettes. When she was two, he threatened to keep her and not give her back. I filed for a restraining order, and the judge ordered that we use the local police station as a drop-off and pickup point.

"We can't even talk to each other. If one of us wants to change the arranged visitation schedule, we have to send a certified letter. I've talked to other single mothers who have had similar problems, and they tell me, 'If you could communicate, you wouldn't have gotten a divorce!' I do think that all the court stuff promotes more anger and the desire to win. I wish it wasn't like that."

I wish I could say that our situation had been changed by my successful day in the California court when the judge finally saw the light, but it hadn't. Even with a court order in hand I still received no child support. At first we couldn't locate Ron. Then he claimed he was unemployed. By that time I'd spent at least $40,000 litigating the case and had no money left to pursue him. A friend suggested I go to the district attorney's office and fill out what seemed like a book of forms. Out went my costly attorney and in walked my lesson in patience and perseverance.

Three months later I got a call from the district attorney and my all-important case number. Five months after that I discovered that Ron had been working for many months. The Franchise Tax Board got involved and started writing letters, putting holds on his bank accounts, calling his friends and family, and generally trying to make his life miserable. It had taken a year, but we finally located his employer, ordered him to show up in court, and in the end received a court-ordered wage assignment so that child support would be paid directly by his employer.

Ron had seen the kids a few times during that year but would usually show up at the house unannounced, or he would have a friend pick them up so that he wouldn't risk being served. He refused to give the kids a phone number or address because he knew we were trying to find out what was going on. I was almost embarrassed at my single mothers group meetings to report the progress of my case over that year. I'd always hated the complaining victim view of life. I felt I was doing all I could, but everything was taking so long, and I couldn't hide my continual disappointment.

The other women would offer advice and ask if I'd tried this or that, but in the end we had all been frustrated and disappointed in our divorce processes. I had lost all faith in our legal system. It seemed to me that something as straightforward as child support would be easy to collect, especially from a successful working man. Boy, was I wrong.

Restraining Orders

One day after school Rhett didn't come home. He usually walked home and was generally on time. I knew there were many parents who also walked with their kids that same way home. I decided to call my closest friends first, feeling a little embarrassed that I didn't know where my son was and not wanting to alarm anyone. The fifth person I called said she saw Rhett picked up in a red sports car.

I didn't even know that Ron was in the country. I confronted Ron when he returned Rhett, and his response was that it was his right to see the kids whenever he wanted to. I felt there had to be some way to legally set a boundary that made me feel I wouldn't be guessing every day of my life whether or not he might show up at our front door. I wanted some sort of court order that prevented Ron from showing up in front of our house unannounced, honking the horn, expecting all the kids to drop what they were doing to run out and spend the evening with him. I filed a restraining order requiring him to give me notice before approaching the house or the kids.

He was insulted, acting like I'd accused him of beating someone, but all I wanted was to have a sense of order in my life that hadn't been present in our marriage. I was trying desperately to find a balance between the kids' having a good relationship with their dad and my being able to create a safe, sane, and predictable environment in my home.

Sometimes restraining orders have to be used when letters sent from attorneys and other requests are ignored. "I've never liked the idea of a restraining order," says Brooke, a computer programmer with two boys. "My former husband was not a violent person at all, but I couldn't get him to stay away from our house. It seemed that every time he picked up the kids he would walk in the front door, come into the kitchen, look in their rooms, and generally act as if he still lived there. Sometimes he'd even open the refrigerator or ask the boys to get him something to eat. The kids liked to show him things in their room, so sometimes he stayed for up to an hour.

"I asked him repeatedly to stay outside the front door and said that the boys would be out as soon as they gathered their things. I didn't want to make a scene in front of the boys or scare them, so I rarely said anything once he was in the house. My attorney wrote several letters to his attorney, and the response was an apology and promise to change the behavior. One of the reasons I wanted a divorce in the first place stemmed from his inability to respect boundaries. After six months of dealing with this, I asked my attorney to serve him with a restraining order. It was really hard to get because he had not done anything to hurt any of us, but I continued to feel violated. He knew that I didn't want him in the house. The judge gave us the order after we showed him the many letters and requests that had already been made."

A little legal advice on restraining orders. "It's very important to be careful how you start the case, what actions you take, and what actions you authorize your attorney to do to start the case," says the family law attorney Lana Norris. "Sometimes at the outset it is necessary to give an immediate order to remove a spouse from the house. In too many cases women file an emergency order and put insulting accusations that can do nothing but inflame the case at the onset." In my case I filed an emergency order to get Ron to respect the boundaries of my life—to call before appearing on our doorstep and to let me know when he would be taking the kids from their school. I did put a few insulting accusations in that order that did inflame the case. After a few weeks, when I had calmed down, I realized that it wasn't necessary for me to put all my thoughts on the matter in the declaration that was served on Ron. I could have achieved the same result by being factual without being insulting, but at that time I took every opportunity to voice my feelings about the case.

Mediation

A friend who is just starting the divorce process called me the other day. She asked for the name of a good mediator. I gave her a few names but told her I couldn't recommend the process one way or another since I had no personal experience. But I did give her this advice from Lana Norris. "Mediation is absolutely wonderful in the appropriate case, but it isn't right for everyone," says Lana. "It works well if both parties are proceeding in the spirit of compromise, as opposed to one side wanting to win it all."

"We have never had to go to court," says Hannah, the mother whose son had drug problems. "I started by doing research and reading self-help law books. I then realized I needed some help, so I looked in the phone book for an attorney and saw a woman's ad that appealed to me, so I called her. She was great because she allowed us to be in a process. It took two years to finalize the agreement. We would meet several times, then six months would go by and we would be arguing on the phone and trying to settle things. When we were far enough along on the issue we were arguing about, we would make an appointment with the mediator.

"When I look back on it now, I think that if I had hired an attorney I would have gotten a better financial settlement. In mediation we were dealing with emotional issues, and I didn't really have anyone to fight for me, so in that way I gave more than I might have had someone said, 'Hey, what are you doing?'

"My biggest financial loss was to agree on a price for our home as of the date of separation. Within the two years of the mediation the housing market went crazy and the house went up substantially, so I lost a lot of money. Another mistake I made in mediation was to accept a child support amount without finding out what I would have been owed by law. An attorney would have told me that the house should be valued at date of divorce and would have worked out a support schedule based on state law.

"The benefit in choosing mediation was that I felt like it kept third parties out of my personal life. I think the process helped me do some emotional healing work so that I didn't get into the fighting aspect of things. It also required that I really listen to my ex and what his concerns were. The process kept communication open, although we did have our share of phone slamming! Mediation allowed us to make exchanges. I owned a music school at the time and had a music CD. He agreed that I could have the school until I told him I planned to sell it. He had some retirement accounts that he wanted because he was ten years older and they were important to him. I didn't want him involved in my creative projects, and he didn't want me to take his retirement, so we compromised."

There needs to be a level playing field emotionally. If there is a history of one person being emotionally dominant and one person always giving in, then it can't work. There needs to be a level playing field financially as well. If one party is very knowledgeable and the other party is in the dark regarding family finances, the latter will be taken advantage of. Cheryl, a freelance writer, says she had every intention of settling her divorce by mediation. "We both started out so positive, putting the kids first, working on visitation arrangements, and agreeing on most of the issues having to do with the kids. When it came time to determine asset division, how much child support would be paid, and all the other financial factors, the mood changed completely.

"We both had attorneys we were consulting on the side, so we had a place to bring our mediation work and have it checked. We had already decided on the time-share arrangement with the kids. Then my husband realized that the amount of time I had with the kids greatly affected how much money he would have to pay me. After this realization, he wanted everything changed. We had agreed before the proceedings started that I would have a few years at home with the kids before I started looking for a job. In the financial part of the mediation my husband demanded that I start working immediately or said we'd have to sell the house.

"This was all so shocking. I guess he had no idea how much money he'd actually have to pay me. When he found out, he panicked. He told the mediator that he needed some time to think. We did come back in a month's time and settle most of these issues. The mediator had suggested that we both consult our attorneys and get a good idea of what the law would require of us. I found out that I would be required to work at least part-time if we went to court, and he found out that he would most likely get 30 percent visitation with the kids. The mediator told us that 'fair mediation' means that both people feel like they have lost."

"There has to be an underlying trust in the other side's honesty," says Lana. "There is no formal discovery or tracing of assets in mediation, so you better believe the other party is telling the truth."

"My husband and I both agreed to get divorced, and we were both very saddened by the loss of our marriage," says Brenda, an art teacher with two adolescent children. "The one thing we talked about right from the beginning was that we didn't want to spend a lot of money on the process. We had two children to put through college in four years' time, so we tried to focus on them.

"The first time we met our mediator, we told her that we wanted to settle everything in three meetings and pay $1,000 or less for the whole divorce. She was supportive of this idea and sent us home with an assignment. We were each asked to write a settlement proposal, including how we thought assets should be divided, how much money would be needed for child support, what the custody arrangements should be, how holidays would be handled, who would pay for health care, and so on. She told us not to discuss our agreements with each other, but to come prepared with our proposal and our reasons for wanting what we wanted.

"The next meeting she proceeded point by point, letting us read what we had each written. She started out by saying that we would each get half of what we wanted. There was give-and-take on each of our parts, *and* we settled our divorce in three meetings using less than $1,000. The mediator said we were very unusual because we still respected and trusted each other and we each had our kids' best interests in mind."

There are many variations on this mediation theme that might work. Each party can have his or her own attorney who sits in on the mediation. A very effective new form of mediation is called collaborative law: each party hires an attorney, but everyone signs an agreement in the beginning that they won't go to court. If issues cannot be settled and going to court is necessary, then both parties have to hire another attorney for representation. This constraint forces people to make a commitment to solving their case outside of court. Collaborative law also offers the option of hiring a private judge. Although this sounds more expensive, it may actually cost less. The hired judge is more available for a quick resolution. It's also possible to hire a judge for one particular issue. So if the mediation goes great except for the alimony portion, you can hire a judge to decide that issue.

Every person has a unique way of dealing with conflict. Every relationship has a history that will definitely repeat itself during the divorce process. Finding an attorney and a way of settling the divorce issues, whether in a courtroom, through mediation, or through collaborative law, is the first step in getting on with the journey that lies ahead.

Is There an End in Sight?

We all want to get on with our lives, and yet it seems that some aspect of the divorce process keeps jumping back into our laps. He wants more time with the kids, there is a change in jobs, someone gets married, a child wants to move in with another parent, there's a birthday or holiday visitation problem, and so on. In the beginning it is overwhelming to think that this kind of interaction with our former husbands may go on until the last child turns eighteen! It is possible to find creative solutions that make the process easier.

Knowing what you want is half the battle. Karen, the mother of three grown children, says that she survived this stage of the divorce by taking each problem as it was presented. "In the beginning I lumped all the issues together and would sit staring out the window each day, unable to pick a direction to go. When I learned how to work on the immediate problem at hand, my life was much simpler, and I became a more effective negotiator."

I use the word *process* because each woman I interviewed seemed to start out with an idea of what divorce would mean for her. Then, after months of agonizing, preparing information, and deciding what would be "fair," some decisions were reached. A year later the process would start up again because another issue had arisen. This time their husband wanted more time with the kids or claimed to have a decrease in salary. Family life would be thrown into the air again, and issues that seemed to have finally settled into the gentle rhythm of daily life would be open for rearrangement.

Most women grew stronger and more able to accept the process over time. They learned how to handle each new crisis without letting it disrupt their life or emotional balance. Many said they gained personal clarity and genuinely liked themselves better after divorce. "I definitely would not have chosen this path as a way to discover my talents and strengths," says Sonja, "but this process has taught me to stand up for my rights and to believe in myself."

What Is Best for
the Children?

Christmas morning had just passed, the presents were opened, and everyone was putting away new prize possessions, opening boxes, assembling Tinkertoy models, plugging in stereos, playing Nintendo games—until I said the words, "We have to pack."

My own childhood Christmas days were long, lazy, and without any schedule, but for my kids postdivorce Christmases involve getting packed up and going someplace with their dad for a week. This particular Christmas they would travel to Washington, D.C. I usually have the kids during the week leading up to Christmas—a time that is far from relaxing, with the present buying, card writing, and, of course, helping the kids get all of their homework done before leaving on vacation.

The day before Christmas I had asked Wesley to do the dishes, to which she replied, "I made the photo albums." Then I walked into the living room and asked Rhett to vacuum the hallway, to which he replied, "Brooke hasn't done anything." It was at that point, after spending the day running from store to store finding everything on their typed and itemized Christmas lists, containing no less than thirty items, that I broke into temporary insanity. Through clenched teeth and in a voice I didn't even recognize, I decided to pick on the inanimate objects throughout the house. The swim bag was greeted with, "This bag is always sitting here—move it," followed by a kick. Next the books, backpacks, and dirty clothes. As the kids stared at me with a mixture of fear and laughter on their faces, I stormed out of the house to finish the shopping. I returned to find a very clean house: the dishes were done, and the vacuuming was finished. All the while driving I had raged and shouted, "Those little brats! Don't they see how hard I work for them?"

I thought about Christmas and what I wanted it to be for our family. I remembered the promise I made to myself back in October—to have the shopping done before Thanksgiving—and I felt a deep sense of regret that what my mind could create my body couldn't produce. There isn't enough time. Not enough time to teach them what giving is about. Not enough time to have them make their presents to give to others so they can feel that sense of pride. Not enough time to hold them, to hear their dreams, to put together their toys—then they're packed up and gone.

The kids didn't like it either. The boys had only had a few hours to play with their new toys. The girls were torn between wanting to spend time with their dad and having a little vacation time to spend with their friends. They voiced their complaints with a sort of resignation as I shoved clean clothes into their bags. I watched the car drive away. Rhett's head turned to look over the back seat—I blew a kiss and received not even an acknowledgment of the gesture. Troy was facing the back window with earphones on, listening to something. I waved, but he just stared straight ahead. I wondered if I would see them again. My stomach hurt with worry. Would anyone be holding Troy's hand in case he dashed across a busy street while visiting the Lincoln Memorial? I remembered hearing Brooke cough the night before, and I worried that she'd be sick and I wouldn't be there to take care of her.

Now they were gone. I had the break I so desperately needed, but I was left with the urge to reorganize my life—to make time to spend alone with each child. To not become so upset when an extra swim bag, a pile of books, or a pair of dirty shoes tripped me in the hall. When I'm alone, I feel a sense of order and peace. I'm able to finish my work assignments without cooking breakfast, making lunches, cleaning the house, doing the laundry, driving to sports practices, correcting homework—so I have the time and space to visualize the kind of mother I want to be. But the truth is that it's so hard to be that mother. My kids act like all other kids do—being concerned with themselves and their lives—and I react as most moms do—crying when I feel exhausted and unappreciated.

If just for a moment they could imagine our lives as a stage production: I play all the parts and at times spin dizzily to the floor, unable to get to each part of the stage fast enough to avoid disaster. Sometimes the curtain doesn't open—for instance, when there's no food for school lunches. Often I have to miss a performance, or they have to walk to a practice. I'm sure that they sometimes think I don't care about them at all and that each one suspects that another one is my favorite. All the while I'm running to focus the spotlight on the right child, to say the right lines, to order the costumes, to generate the revenue to keep the theater open.

Now that they were gone for the holiday, I felt the peace that I still hadn't figured out how to feel when they were here.

Ending the War

Although you may be coparenting effectively, you may also be disagreeing over legal issues, custody arrangements, visitation schedules, and so on. Finding a way to communicate that works for both of you can certainly be difficult. I always had mixed feelings when Ron called and talked to the kids. I wasn't sure whether I should try to talk to him myself about divorce issues, since he never called to discuss them with me. He had made it very clear that he did not wish to talk to me. Even when I really needed to discuss something with him, I would immediately hand the phone over to the kids. I was afraid that if I forced him to talk to me, he would hang up or not call the kids at all.

As I write this book, it's been four years since I initiated our divorce. For most of that time we have been in a state of what I would call war, with each of us fighting for our own positions, views, and rights. I felt that I should get what I deserved according to the law. The longer Ron went without talking to me the less human he seemed. It was hard for me to feel compassion toward someone who, even though I had loved him with all my heart for fifteen years, had become a symbol of my pain.

During a conversation with my friend Sonja, something shifted in my point of view. I started thinking about what I *needed*, instead of what I *deserved*. Instead of thinking about how much support the court awarded us, I began to think about my children and how I could get their father to move closer to them, from across the country. I knew if given a choice my kids would forgo extracurricular activities if it meant they could see their father weekly. I started believing that maybe we could all get what we wanted—the kids could have their father, I could have some time off, and he could participate in raising them. Instead of sticking to what I had fought so hard to win in court, I began to see that my court orders were not giving me what I needed. Instead, they were adding ammunition to the war. The questions became, "What can I do to end this war?" and "What would bring peace to our lives?"

"We actually spent months in reunification therapy, which was something I had never heard of until Chuck was charged with parental alienation," says Martha. "I'm sorry to report that it didn't work. The purpose was to put both our kids in a safe environment with a therapist who could listen to them and not put negative thoughts about either parent into their heads. I guess that one hour each week was not enough to overshadow the many messages my son received from his father on a daily basis. I kind of knew intuitively that Chuck was too attached to the war he had created to accept the idea of a peaceful life with all of us living in harmony. I know that there is no chance for my son to voluntarily walk back into my life until he is out of his father's grip. He's fifteen now, so maybe when he goes to college. There is only one short meeting left with the reunification therapist, so I guess the only thing I can ask is that the therapist share with me what is happening in Chad's life."

Personal beliefs can be a source of strength for women who are trying to remain true to who they are even if their spouse is picking a fight. "My spiritual beliefs have helped me to act from a place of peace even when Dwight wants to fight," says Joanne, the woman whose husband received his law degree and is trying to keep her from seeing her sons. "There have been many instances when my attorney told me that we could go to court and win, that I don't have to pay him as much as I do, and that we could get a court order that my boys have to spend time with me. I don't want my children to be ordered to see me. I don't want them to have to move out of our condo because their father doesn't make enough money to support them. I am happy to contribute to their lives, and I am comfortable with what I have. I want my boys to remember how much I love them and how I have been there for them in the past.

"I have complete faith that given time my loving attitude will triumph over his angry, hateful one. I will not lower myself to his tactics. It is more important for me to be true to who I am at all costs. I believe that my boys will have the whole picture one day, and in the meantime I will keep loving them any way I can."

At one point I was hopeful that I could reach some agreements with Ron based on my decision to get what I needed instead of what I deserved. I negotiated for close to three months—releasing any claim on back child support in exchange for his commitment to take more responsibility as a parent in the kids' lives. However, the entire time we were negotiating to reduce his child support arrears in exchange for signing over to me a co-owned piece of property, Ron had already received the money from the property that we were negotiating over. He somehow had talked the attorney into paying him three months early so that the district attorney couldn't put a lien on it. He was going along with my suggestions and agreeing to search for a job in the area just to buy himself time. For the second time in the divorce process I had to decide whether to press criminal charges.

I still crave an end to this fighting—I want peace for myself and for my children—but Ron continues to make choices that hurt my kids. He's been in contempt of court twice; when a bench warrant for his arrest was issued, I asked the district attorney to set it aside for the sake of my children. This time, I wondered, should I let go of the situation and do nothing to prevent the legal consequences of his behavior from happening?

I know that the only way to end the fighting is to fix it for him, to erase all of his arrears, to drop all charges. If I do that, he will probably move to the area and see the kids regularly. Some days I want to let it all go, but the people I trust believe that Ron's choices and behavior have to have consequences. Everyone tells me I need to tell the kids the facts—not to make any judgment about Ron as a person but to report unemotionally what has happened. But I don't want them to know even just the facts because they will worry. What will happen to us, and what will happen to their father? Would knowing the facts make the kids feel better, or would they then believe that their father doesn't care at all? What would I gain by telling them the truth?

I've spent years thinking about what it means to protect my kids. Is it better to pretend that their father has done nothing wrong just to protect them from embarrassment or pain, or is it better to tell the truth and let them know what they can expect from their father as they go through life with him? I haven't decided what to do. In my heart I know that Ron and I have to call a truce before we can move forward in our lives as parents and as human beings. I'm just not sure how many sacrifices to make or how much to give away. My goal is to give my children a good life full of opportunity, but I don't believe I can do that without Ron's presence in their lives—his financial support and his emotional interaction. When I think of their future, I find it difficult to wave the white flag.

Custody

Child custody and all the related issues cause most of the problems once the divorce has occurred. Couples get divorced for many reasons—they don't communicate well, they don't like the lifestyle of their partner, they don't like the decisions their partner makes, their partner could be more responsible, they don't feel loved. Not surprisingly, the same list carries over into the child-rearing arena: the other parent doesn't care about homework, the child is left at home alone, there is not enough discipline, the kids are being brainwashed, the kids aren't being given the right values or morals, and so on. Two people who for various reasons have chosen to be apart, who may not want to have anything to do with each other, must still raise children together.

I remember that first day in court, trying to work out a visitation schedule with Ron. The family services officer was trying to get him to commit to a dependable and regular schedule. At the time he traveled across the country and never knew when he'd be in the area. The best we could come up with was that I'd get seven days' notice before each visit, or if he came unexpectedly and called I had the option of letting the kids go with him or not. I asked that he at least be required to call once a week. He said no to that as well. I'm sure that Ron wanted to talk to his children as often as he could, but since the request came from me, he felt the need to fight it.

Over the years the kids received postcards from locations all across the United States. I envied his ability to have no responsibility, to go out when he wanted, to have no homework to help with, no extracurricular activities to drive to, no one but himself to worry about. Sometimes I'd make myself so mad thinking about the unfairness of my life compared to his that I'd feel sick with self-pity. On those rare occasions when he took the kids, every place he took them was fun—nothing was ordinary; everything was perfect and spectacular. Life with me was ordinary. I consisted of the mundane things that make up a day, like washing cereal bowls, helping fold laundry, bouncing on the trampoline, walking home from school with friends, doing homework, sharing stories of the day, walking the dog. On good days I felt lucky to share so much time with the kids, to know their friends, to be able to watch them play sports, act in plays, and finish school projects. On bad days I wanted Ron to have them full-time, to feel the stress of having no time to himself, to struggle with all the responsibilities and decisions that he knew nothing about.

"Shared custody has gotten much better over time," says Stephanie, the mother who decided to apply to law school. "In the beginning my heart was broken. I was so unaware that this could happen in my life. When I realized that he had been seeing someone else, I wanted him to lose the right to see the kids completely. I started seeing a therapist immediately, and we also had a family therapist for the kids.

"I was very lucky. I had many friends that I could vent to, so I didn't have to vent to the kids. I think that it is very destructive to dump thoughts and emotional issues onto children. I would let them see that I was upset, I would cry, but I wouldn't say bad things about their dad because I didn't think it would help them. The kids are very loyal to him, but sometimes I hear resentment when they say, 'Why can't Dad help with that?'

"From the beginning the kids stayed with their dad two days each week. It's been a few years, and we are still on the same schedule. I think that he is much more there for the kids now than he was during the marriage. Occasionally he will even help work on a school project. Last week a gigantic project that Pete had started with my oldest son was dropped off at my house. I panicked, thinking there was no way that I could finish it since I had a paper due myself. Pete surprised me and showed up to help my son finish it.

"An old pattern during the marriage was that Pete would start something and just leave it so I would have to finish it. When we were married, he never played sports with the boys, but he did a lot of sports himself. Now he occasionally will go for an hour bike ride with my youngest, and that is like gold for that kid. When Pete does make these efforts, I praise him to the skies—how much it means to the kids and on and on—because I really want to encourage it. It makes me gag a little, but I have a goal in mind. I guess we are better as unmarried partners, but I'm still the general partner and he's the limited partner."

"I was awarded full physical custody of my kids, but we still have joint legal custody," says Patty, a journalist with a fourteen-year-old daughter. "Our daughter Peg has been diagnosed with depression. She began seeing a psychiatrist after the court-appointed psychologist, whom we hired to determine what the custody arrangement should be, suggested she needed help dealing with the divorce. My ex-husband, Rich, was angry that I was given physical custody, so he is trying to exercise his need for control by refusing to sign her medical release. The psychiatrist has determined that Peg needs to be on antidepression medication, she is fourteen years old, and I'm scared that she might hurt herself. Rich doesn't believe in drugs, so he has convinced Peg that we are trying to make her into someone else instead of letting her express her feelings, or get her so dependent on drugs that she has to go and live in a mental ward. So now Peg herself is refusing any treatment, even though she has admitted being afraid of her intense negative feelings.

"My issue is that Rich rarely sees Peg because she chooses to spend most of her time living with me. Sure, he takes her out to dinner a few times a week, maybe shopping or to some sports event on the weekend, but he doesn't have to live with her every day. One day when I'd had it with both of them, I suggested that Peg move to her father's for a while. My thought was that if he could see how depressed she was, how difficult it was for her to deal with everyday things like homework, then maybe he'd change his mind. It didn't work. He basically left her alone, carrying on with his life as he did before she moved in. A week later she called, begging to come home.

"I hate it that we have shared legal custody. I don't believe that Rich makes decisions based on Peg's best interest. He makes decisions based on what he perceives as my losing. If he knows I want something, then he goes against it on purpose just to make the point that he still has some sort of control over our lives."

From the beginning I've had full physical custody of my kids, but Ron and I also share legal custody. That means I'm supposed to contact him when any medical, educational, or other important decision has to be made about the kids. Since Ron refuses to talk to me, discussing any course of action is impossible. Troy was in the hospital with pneumonia for two days before I was able to locate Ron. When he called the hospital, he was furious with me for not reaching him. I have no address, no phone number, and an e-mail address that he changes regularly.

There have been many times when I've had a big decision to make, such as where to send the kids to school, and felt that Ron was the only person who could give me insight. Other people can listen, they can give me great ideas, but they don't have the same connection to my kids as Ron. I have made my decisions alone even when I was afraid to, and although I would prefer shared custody and the shared responsibility that goes with it, I am gaining courage to navigate the parenting journey alone.

Two Houses, Two Sets of Rules

Often parents may have disagreed about some of the house rules while they were married, yet they still worked together to present a united front. Once divorced, parents may take the opportunity to structure home life around their own values and rules. While we were married, Ron and I *always* argued about what the kids were allowed to watch on TV. I wanted the TV off when they were awake if there was a chance they might see news updates of people being shot, adult programs, and advertising. Ron thought I was being overprotective, that they needed to experience the world as it really was, not as a sort of fantasy.

After the divorce, when I set up my house, I decided we were not going to have a TV. The kids thought I was being terribly mean and told me that I had made them the most unpopular kids at school because they couldn't discuss a popular program with their friends. It wasn't that bad—we actually had one TV in the house so they could watch movies—but we had no connection to broadcast or cable TV. Ron took the opposite stance, becoming even more permissive about their viewing habits. He let them watch whatever they wanted on TV and took them to movies that I refused to take them to.

It is still very frustrating for me. I will tell the kids they aren't allowed to see a movie, and they respond, "Dad will take me, and there is nothing you can do about it!" Sometimes when we are visiting friends, I'm at a loss for words when Troy starts telling the kids the names of the violent, R-rated movies he's seen. Friends think that I should step in and tell Ron what he is allowed to do, but in reality the kids follow his rules and values when they are with him.

Sometimes having a different set of rules becomes a way to get back at the other parent or to make a subtle statement about the other parent's values. "Things were easier in the beginning when my husband's girlfriend didn't want him to see our four kids," says Bonnie. "She wanted him to prove that he loved her more than the kids. For the first five months after he left, when he wasn't seeing them, my oldest daughter was a different girl. She screamed all the time. She is in counseling now, which I have to pay for even though he is responsible for half. Now he sees them, and the oldest is definitely daddy's girl, which bothers me sometimes. He buys them candy, and I make them clean their rooms. Sometimes they say, 'Daddy lets us do this or that!' But I tell them that I don't care what Daddy does; this is our house and this is how we are going to do it.

"If my ex-husband knows I don't like something, then he's the first to do it. My nine-year-old is a little boy-crazy, but I think she is too young to be getting phone calls from boys, so I don't allow it. But the boys are allowed to call whenever they want at his house. I absolutely hate for them to see scary movies, because they often have nightmares, but he has rented more horror films then I have seen in my lifetime. I try not to let his decisions bother me and often remind myself that I am only responsible for my own behavior."

Even though some parents are angry with each other, they basically agree on parenting issues and are able to put the kids' needs first. "We are lucky that we both think the kids are more important than our differences," says Stacey, a fifty-year-old homemaker who has two teenage daughters. "Maybe that's because we married a little later, so we were older when we had our children. We have similar rules, which makes the transition from one house to the other easier for our kids. We both value school and expect the kids to do their homework immediately after school during the week and early Sunday afternoon on weekends. We have similar TV rules: only one hour each weekday and five hours total on weekends. Phone issues are the current problem. Our youngest daughter just started high school, so she spends hours on the phone. We are working to establish some expectations in that area. Generally we talk to each other and try to come up with something we both think will work."

It has amazed me how easily my children can move back and forth between our households, as different as they might seem. They have learned that life with their dad has some advantages, like more independence, exciting vacations, board games played until the wee hours of the morning, and tasty meals planned well in advance. Life with me has its advantages too, like predictability. I know their friends and their teachers very well. And though dinner may not be restaurant quality, it's on the table night after night. They can count on my support in their everyday challenges as I help with homework, discuss a problem with a friend, or talk about a goal they would like to achieve.

I'm sure that Ron and I have different rules, but the kids are very careful not to tell me too much about life with their father. When I ask, they are vague. Sometimes I get a clearer picture when they talk to each other. When they came home from Washington, D.C., after visiting their father's apartment for the first time, they couldn't stop talking about how beautiful the view was, how his furniture was so cool, and how nice everything looked. When I heard that someone spilled juice on the suede couch and a coffee table broke when one of the kids leaned on it, I felt a secret glee. The kids said that he couldn't believe how rough they were and that he planned on buying furniture covers for everything before they visited again. I laughed quietly to myself, thinking how quickly he had forgotten what it was like to have dirty fingerprints on the walls, to have kids wrestling and playing, bumping things—how easily four children can make a house look very used. His beautiful castle now had the markings of family life, just as my house did.

Visitation

The following is a note I received via e-mail from Brooke while she was visiting her grandmother in Seattle.

> I really miss home. I just talked to Dad and he said he is coming to Seattle in a few days so I have to stay until the night before school starts—which I really don't want to do! We've been here two weeks already. Please help me get home.

It was technically her dad's time, so there was nothing I could do. When my children are far away, when they are in their father's care, when they need me and I can't be with them, I feel helpless. When vacation plans are changed in midstream, when kids don't show up on scheduled airlines, and when homework is left undone—who is ultimately responsible for making things right?

One school vacation Rhett was to spend five days in Los Angeles with his father. After he left I called the number I had been given three times a day for a few days, leaving messages to return my call. When my calls were never returned, I started feeling that something was terribly wrong. Just when I was about to call the police, a friend from Los Angeles called and told me that Rhett was in St. Louis. Ron decided to take a cross-country trip! This trip was the best experience of Rhett's year. He loved having this exciting time alone with his father. They traveled Route 66 together and visited every state's tourist attractions along the way.

One of my goals since the divorce has been to facilitate as much visitation time as possible. I would have completely supported this trip had I been told about it. Instead of enjoying my week knowing that Rhett was having the time of his life, however, I sat by the phone and wondered what had happened to him.

Over Christmas vacation I thought the kids were skiing in Lake Tahoe when I found out a week later that they were stuck in Salt Lake City. They were three days late returning because they'd taken a train to get there and the train tracks were covered with snow. Ron had decided on the spur of the moment to give the kids a train adventure—eating in the dining car, sleeping on the train, and waking up in Utah. Surprise!

Ron wasn't trying to be malicious. He just didn't want me to have any control over his time with them. Our agreement stated that I had to agree to any out-of-state trips and be given a telephone number where I could reach my children. During all of the trips the children took with Ron in the first few years after our divorce, I never had a number or any way to reach them. My daughters would sometimes call me collect from the ladies' restroom to let me know where they were and to tell me how everything was going. Before they left I would give them phone cards and beg them to call. Their response reflected Ron's attitude, and they couldn't understand why I had to know everything or why I needed to talk to them when they were away. They would tell me that it was Dad's time and that he didn't want them to call me. Sometimes the boys would tell me before they left how much they missed me and how they wished they could talk to me, but they were too afraid to ask their dad. They thought he'd be mad at them for missing me.

Ron successfully created an atmosphere in which I didn't exist. Over time my kids adjusted to this strange arrangement, but I couldn't. My family would see the distress I felt wondering about my kids, not being able to talk to them. Their advice echoed my attorney's—don't let them go on these trips. Maybe that is what I should have done, but I knew how much the kids loved their dad and how desperately they wanted to see him. I also knew that if I told them they couldn't go, I wouldn't hear the end of it for months. Before each proposed trip I'd threaten not to let them go unless I had all the information about it and a promise that I would be contacted. Then for a few days the kids would say, "Please let us go. We'll be okay. We never get to see Dad, and if you make him do all these things, he'll never want to see us." In the end I sent them every time he asked. Ron usually returned them when he said he would, but it sure would have been nice to have had contact with them while they were with him.

Most mothers seem to feel that it is their job to ensure that their children have a solid relationship with their father. Monica made a decision that many of us can understand: she flew with her two young girls out of state to visit their father even though he was neither paying support nor showing interest in his kids' lives. "We were separated off and on for a few years before I actually filed for divorce," says Monica. "My husband was living in a different state at the time of the separation; I had taken a few weeks off work as part of a severance package between jobs and decided to take the girls to visit him in Colorado. I'm not even sure why we went. I'm an idiot. He wasn't sending any money for the girls, and he was driving a vehicle that I was paying for. But I decided to go anyway for the girls' sake.

"We were in the car one day driving to a park when he asked the girls if they wanted to stop at Starbucks to get a brownie. He pulled into a handicapped space to the side of the store. It occurred to me for a second that something was wrong, but I didn't follow my intuition. The girls were begging to go in with me, but he told them I would just run in and we'd be on our way. I came out of the store a few minutes later with the brownies, and they were gone. Thank God, I had my purse, although I had left my phone in the car. I called the police. When they arrived, they said that they couldn't help me because I was married and he was the girls' father. It took a bit of convincing, but I told them he was from Tehran and that he had their original birth certificates in the car and had just taken passport photos recently.

"Early on in the marriage he had tried to choke me once. I was able to grab the car keys and drive to the police station to file a report. So the police were also able to locate his record, which showed the assault charge. I had the police, the FBI, immigration, and his probation officer involved. My family was at home faxing and copying, looking through records for me, and doing everything they could to help. I didn't change my clothes for four days, and it took two days before I realized I hadn't even brushed my teeth. I spent all my time at Kinko's sending papers back and forth. The manager actually came up to me after hearing what I was doing there and said they would print everything for free—posters and letters, whatever I needed.

"My husband was on the run throughout Colorado, changing cars each day so he wouldn't be found. I went to malls, restaurants, and parks, everywhere I could think of believing that I might run into them to steal them back.

"Four days later I got the girls back. They looked like homeless rats, with filthy hair and ketchup all over them. They were wearing each other's clothes. We had three suitcases in the car, but he had gone through all of them, returning things in paper bags. I found out later that he had copied my entire Daytimer. The girls said they sat in the car and ate Oreos when he went to make copies. When they asked for me, he told them that they were with him now. He went through all of my clothes and threw away all my underwear.

"While this was all happening in Colorado, I had hired an attorney at home to file divorce papers and apply for temporary orders. The orders ended up requiring him to take random drug tests and allowed him to see the girls one hour at a time in a counselor's office. He was also allowed to call them three times each week. He stopped calling after a few months. Now he is taking me to court, claiming that I don't allow him access to the girls on the phone. My goal is that he never sees them alone. I'm still afraid he might leave the country with them. He wants a court evaluation, but that will cost $2,000, so we haven't done anything yet."

I have spent the last four years doing my best to keep to myself my anger toward Ron for his absence from the kids' lives. I remember what it felt like to crave Ron's attention, and how I felt when he chose other activities over spending time with me. I watch my kids suffer from the same kind of rejection as they wait for a phone call assuring them that he will be in town for the father-daughter dance, or that he will be able to see them on Christmas, only to be disappointed by his lack of availability. Then my heart breaks.

Sometimes I've thought to myself that their lives would be easier if he were dead. I think it hurts more to be ignored when you know that the person is alive, well, and capable of making a phone call. Yet I still believe that my children need to have as strong a relationship with their father as possible, so it's my job to put my own feelings aside and do what I can to make visitation happen.

Coparenting

You're no longer living together, but you still have to parent together, and it isn't always easy to set your own wishes aside in order to put the needs of a child first. In general, I believe that I'm more in tune with what my children need in their lives because I live with them every day. I become very defensive when Ron offers suggestions because I feel he's criticizing my parenting choices. At other times I resent how easily he offers advice on how to do something that he's never around to do himself.

After watching one of Rhett's basketball games, Ron called to tell me that Rhett should be in a better league with better coaching. What he said was true, but signing him up in a better league would have entailed costly coaching fees and driving further to practice. Instead of thanking him for his suggestion, my response was, "Why don't you move out here and coach his team yourself!"

Not as mature a comment as I would have liked, but old feelings run deep, and it's difficult for me to change my pattern of responding defensively.

I have this belief that Ron needs to earn the right to make decisions about his children based on the amount of time he devotes to their lives. This may not be fair since, as their father, he has a right to have a say in their lives as much as I do. But I still resent him for his freedom to live exactly as he pleases without accepting many of the everyday responsibilities, joys, and (sometimes) drudgery of parenting. I guess I haven't matured or healed enough to accept his right to choose the direction of his life, just as I am choosing mine.

"It really took me a long time to figure out how I would parent alone," says Mara, a mother of two girls, ages nine and thirteen, who went back to work as a teacher's aide. "My husband used to do homework with the kids at night so I would have a little time to read or relax. Now I have to do both our jobs when the girls are with me. I didn't want the divorce, so whenever I talk to him to arrange something for the girls, I feel this pang of longing for him.

"There are things I wish I could control, like his having his girlfriend over when the girls are there. I brought it up to the judge, and he said that it is healthy for him to get on with his life and to start forming new relationships. When the judge said this, I started to understand that coparenting has two components. The first is that you try to work together to coordinate your children's lives and to make joint decisions in a positive way. The second is that you really have nothing to say about the way the other parent lives their life."

Another single mom, Gloria, a forty-year-old homemaker with three children under twelve, tells me, "What I hate about this coparenting arrangement is that the school's teachers, the kids' coaches, and most everyone else thinks I'm responsible for everything. When my daughter misses a soccer game because her father makes last-minute plans, the coach calls me. When I explain that Pam is with her dad, the response seems to be one of annoyance at my inability to have more control over the situation. If Pam is with her father on a school night and doesn't get her homework done, the teacher calls me. So in a way I still feel I'm responsible for her father's parenting decisions, even though I have no control over them."

I know that my kids would love it if Ron and I could talk to each other, show up at their events, stand together, and act like other divorced parents they know. I wonder sometimes about the example we are setting; I worry that, as they grow up, they might model our way of dealing with conflict—if you have a disagreement with someone, you cut them out of your life completely. There have been times when I've had to ask the kids to locate their father and find out information like travel plans, or to make simple requests like, "Please return the kids' ski equipment." Usually the kids dislike doing this and make comments like, "You need to ask him yourself. I'm not going in between." Whenever the kids miss Ron, they tell me that he doesn't live in California anymore because he doesn't want to live anywhere near me. That translates into, "Mom, it's your fault we don't get to see our dad."

There have been times when I wanted to attend a family function with my children but chose not to because of the scene my presence might create. When Ron's brother died, I wanted to be at his funeral with all my heart. I wanted to help my children say good-bye to the uncle they loved. Ron's family called and asked me to attend, but the kids told me that their father had said he would not be there if I went.

Over and over again I find myself making parenting choices I believe are wrong because I want my kids to feel at peace. I make choices I wouldn't otherwise make—like not attending the funeral, or letting them go on a vacation without any knowledge of where they're going—just so they will experience less conflict. I do explain to them how I feel and why I'm making a certain choice, but I'm still afraid of the message I'm sending—that Ron can act however he wants, refuse to follow agreed-upon rules or court orders, and still get exactly what he wants.

"I am lucky to have a great 'parenting' relationship with my former husband," says Amanda, an interior designer who has a twelve-year-old son and a fifteen-year-old daughter. "I have to say that he goes to as much trouble as I do to make sure that he is available to drive them, to attend their performances and sporting events, and to meet with their teachers and attend school events. My daughter has often said that our ability to be civil to each other has really helped her accept the divorce. We don't sit together or act like we are still married, but we can be in the same gym or on the same baseball field without feeling uncomfortable. We talk once a week on Sunday night at an arranged time to go over the week's schedule. He contacted the school to make sure that all the school information was sent to him as well. We also try to be flexible with travel plans and schedule business trips or vacations when the other is available to be the full-time parent. There are still lots of things we disagree on, but I think the bottom line is that we both respect each other's role as the kids' parent."

I was doing an interview on my book *365 Ways to Raise Great Kids* for a radio station in Los Angeles when the talk show host asked how long I'd been married. When I said that I was divorced, his response astounded me. He said, "How can someone who couldn't stay married write a book on how to raise great kids?" I almost hung up in the middle of this live interview, especially since this man had been rude from the beginning, but I didn't. Instead, I ignored his comment. The next question was almost as bad: "Do you think working mothers try to buy their kids since they don't have time to love them?" Talk about a distorted point of view! My answer was easy. "I don't think it has anything to do with whether or not a mother is working. It's more a parenting style. Some parents give their kids more material things than others do. The working mothers I know are wonderful mothers, skipping lunch hour to make a child's school performance, forgoing promotions so that they are available to pick kids up after school, and sacrificing in many ways that most men would never consider!" He responded, "So you're saying that your ex-husband isn't as good a parent as you are?" He was tiring me out! "No, if I said anything I'd have to say we parent differently."

I was wondering if his intention was to embarrass me or if he had some point to make. He did go on to talk about my book and about teaching kids. "You stated in your book that kids learn more from a parent's actions than from their words. So I was just thinking that if children see their parents as unforgiving, judgmental, or unable to work together as parents, it would be hard for the child to learn how to be any different." His point made, he then ended the interview.

I hung up the phone and thought about his words for a few minutes. I hadn't even experienced coparenting since my divorce because at that point Ron refused to speak to me at all, except through our kids, a mutual friend, or his attorney. I knew that our behavior affected the kids' lives. After this interview, I decided that I had to set up some new rules, the first being that Ron would have to talk to me or e-mail me directly instead of sending messages through our children. I accepted the fact that I could control only my own actions, but I also began to see that there were things I could do that would help both of us move in a more positive direction.

Child Support

I received a fax from my husband's attorney a year after our separation that read: "Sorry, Ron won't be able to make this month's child support payment. He's too depressed with a failed business venture to deal with it." I read the fax a few times in disbelief. I couldn't quite see the connection between writing a check so that his four kids could eat and the fact that something didn't go as he had hoped. I stomped around the kitchen for a few minutes drafting a letter in my head: "Sorry for the short notice, the kids will be arriving on the next flight for a month's stay. Sheila isn't up to watching them." I sat at my desk, looked out the window, and wondered if there would ever be a time when my ex-husband would cease to affect my daily life. Had I known in the beginning that it would take another year to enforce that support agreement that he so easily disregarded, two years to divide family assets, and three years to start receiving monthly child support, I would have given up.

That day marked the first time Ron decided not to pay child support. Since then we've gone twice without child support, for eight months each time. The court ordered that the medical and dental bills be split between us, yet Ron has gone three years without reimbursing me for those expenses. I have found ways to pay my bills—sometimes I live for months on credit cards until an article I write is published, sometimes I take money from our home equity loan, once in a while I have to borrow money from family or friends.

The hardest part for me is not being able to pay for things my kids want to do. It infuriates me to know that if Ron were keeping up with his part of the bargain my children would not have to be missing out on lessons, camps, and other activities. I'm the one who has to live with the disappointment on their faces as I tell them that they can't take a class trip, or attend an out-of-state swim meet, because I can't afford the airfare.

I realize that these things are not necessities in their lives. All I should really feel responsible for is providing food, shelter, clothing, education, and a safe and loving home. That list in itself is incredibly difficult at times, and yet I blame myself for not doing better. When I qualified for financial aid at a local Catholic high school, I was required to pay half the tuition and Wesley was required to work for the other half. She worked part of the required time over the summer. But when the second semester started and I found out she would have to work in the lunchroom instead of eating lunch and socializing with her friends, I wanted to go to the school and ask if I could work in her place.

Ron doesn't have to live daily with the result of his actions, with the tears, with the humiliation and explanations that the kids have to face. I do, and sometimes it takes all my effort not to scream like a mad woman my feelings about Ron's lack of responsibility. When I know I'm losing my composure, I try to focus on the image of a bullfighter holding a red blanket. I see myself with the blanket holding it to the side as I visualize Ron as the bull charging toward me. As he attacks, I gracefully lift the red blanket and step aside.

One day when I was furious with Ron, a friend told me to push against her arm. As I did this, she went with my motion and I fell past her. The Eastern system of self-defense called aikido is built on this principle. I'm learning to go with the force pushing me instead of fighting against it. I may not have the power to change the problem or the situation, but I can change my response to it.

Cheryl, the freelance writer, says that she couldn't handle her husband's demands for constant accounting of child care—they had agreed that the hours added or deducted from the visitation schedule would affect support amounts—so she decided to make her life easier. "I wanted to know that I would receive a set amount of child support each month and that I'd receive it for three years at that set amount. It was taking too much of my time and energy to record and prove everything. My husband liked this proposal because we also agreed that he wouldn't have to report every penny he made to me. My attorney said I would get less than what I deserved, but that extra money wasn't worth my time and peace of mind."

Money isn't the only kind of support that is important. Yolanda, the mother of three boys, says that she would trade the money she gets for time off from her kids. "Sometimes at the end of a month, when I've had the boys full-time, they haven't spent any time with their father, and I've worked thirty hours a week, I really believe that I can't go on. I love my boys, but the weight of constant responsibility really gets to me. Scheduling every doctor appointment, attempting to make all the school functions, taking care of our home, and giving energy to my career, all this leaves no time or energy to spend on myself. I don't have time to see friends, I don't have time for a love life, which is what I really need! The feeling I have when I fall into bed every night is that I am completely alone in raising my boys.

"Their father spends fun time with them once in a while, but he doesn't bother with the serious stuff, all the things that determine what kind of character a person will have. He thinks it's funny when they burp in public, are rude to each other, or lie. Or better yet, he tells me they are just being boys. I've never understood how it's okay to misbehave just because someone is male.

"Anyway, what I would like more than money is two weekends off each month when I could start to build my own life, have some time to myself. I'd love to have the emotional support of their father calling the boys and checking up on things like homework. I do have family and friends who offer to help, but I feel so indebted to them since it really isn't their responsibility. The only time I can completely relax, knowing that I don't have to hurry home to relieve a babysitter or my family, is when the boys are with their dad."

Ron's choice to support his children sporadically has had a surprisingly positive effect on our family. My children, who were at first horrified and embarrassed at the thought of looking poor, grew in ways I never imagined. Wesley once said to me, "I thought I'd be really unhappy not having a lot of things, but this has been one of the best years of my life." Brooke commented, "I think I'm stronger than a lot of my friends, having lived through this. I'm not so afraid of my future anymore. If I can't get a job after college or have to live in a small apartment, I know I can still be happy."

Having to pack up all of their belongings into only one box each when we moved into the studio apartment definitely introduced the idea of simplifying one's life to my children. Once we experienced this simplicity, a certain strength emerged as we all discovered how to live without things we once thought were absolutely necessary. Costly trips to the movie theater were replaced with a rented movie and homemade popcorn. Sleeping outside on the trampoline, moon walks, and nights telling stories around a fire replaced expensive vacations. Taking turns using the bathroom, living in the same room with many siblings, getting ready for school without waking everyone up—all taught my children to be sensitive to others. We've grown closer and stronger.

Even with all the disappointment, the depth of love my children have for their father astounds me. It doesn't matter if they see him ten days a year or one hundred, whether he pays thousands toward supporting them or nothing—he lives in their every thought, and they love him. The unconditional outpouring of love they have for this man, even when it isn't returned as they might hope, has shown me the fragile, open nature of childhood. The faith kids have in their parents and perhaps the unconscious knowledge that they are half of each parent helps them to love and accept a parent for who he is, even if he hurts them.

Sometimes this realization makes me want to steal my kids away, to shield them for as long as possible from the truth of their lives, and to make sure that I am financially independent so that Ron's lack of support will not affect their lifelong opportunities.

As I've watched them over the last four years, I have marveled at my children's strength, at their ability to see the truth, to feel the hurt, to work through it, and to triumph over it.

EIGHT

Grieving the End

Children and Their Loss

The other day, as I sat watching Rhett's basketball game, I felt what I call my "repeated sadness." I looked around the gym at the fathers offering words of encouragement to their sons. I was sitting behind the bench and cheering the team on myself, but I felt in that moment that if I hadn't wanted a divorce Rhett's dad would have been there too.

The first day Troy started baseball I noticed that all the other boys already knew how to throw and catch a baseball. Troy wasn't even sure how to hold his mitt. As each new sports season approaches I try to get out in the yard and review ball skills, but I admit I'm a sorry substitute for their athletic father. My basketball defensive play makes Rhett laugh so hard that he can't even shoot the ball. I'm afraid of being hit with a baseball, but I don't pitch well enough to stand more than ten feet away, so the moment I pitch the ball I fall flat to the ground to avoid being knocked out. What I can't offer in athletic knowledge I make up for in comic relief! But no matter how many games I attend, performances I sit through holding bouquets of flowers, or school functions I chaperone, I can still see the pain in my kids' eyes as they look around the park or gym with the hope that just maybe their dad will be there.

"In the beginning I was most upset by not having my dad around on a daily basis," says Hank, a twelve-year-old boy. "I still look at old pictures and home videos and feel sad that things aren't the way they used to be. But right now the hardest part is that my life is so divided. I have stuff at my mom's and stuff at my dad's. I want to wear something or bring a book to school, and I don't have it. The schedule is always changing, so I'm not sure whether I can ask a friend over that weekend because I'm not sure where I will be. Sometimes I feel like I'm constantly on vacation packing suitcases and going from one place to another. I can get really angry about it too. Both my parents are trying to make what they call 'this transition' easy, but I know that this is forever, not for some transition time. It's hard for me to accept this new arrangement and let go of my old life—it was so much easier before the divorce."

It's even more complicated when a child chooses not to see one parent. "After she was attacked by her father, Karen had no desire to see Chuck ever again," says Martha. "Chad, on the other hand, wanted to talk to his dad the next day. However, I have to say that even before the police incident it seemed our family was divided. Karen and I spent more time together, and Chuck and Chad spent time together. There were times when I would reprimand my son for a behavior and Chuck would step in and accuse me of abusing him. Chad would come to me first with most of his needs, but he picked up his dad's attitude that something was wrong with me and with our relationship. Chuck wasn't warm to Karen. He was afraid of her in a way, but he knew boy stuff. So, it didn't surprise me that Chad would want to be forgiven and make up with his dad the next day, especially since Chad felt responsible—it was he who called the police. I could feel Chad taking his dad's side when he would say things like, 'Dad owns the house and you don't, so where are we going to live?' Or he would go around the house and ask, 'Who does this belong to?'"

Martha's son didn't want to see her. "Over the course of a few months my son refused to see me," she says sadly. "It seemed like he was getting brainwashed. It has been two and a half years since I have spoken with or seen my son. Over time and after many lies by her father, Karen chose not to see her father. I'm heartbroken whenever I think about our circumstances: that my son has lost his mother and sister, and my daughter has lost her father and brother."

"Sometimes parents don't realize what has happened in the child's life," says Susan Shapiro, a Los Angeles psychologist. "Think of how you feel as an adult when a friend doesn't call you back, your social life has ended as a couple, everything has changed. You have to think about that for the child as well. Their safe environment doesn't exist anymore."

Kids' grief may be reflected in all sorts of changed behavior. Your child may not want to talk about anything with you, may not want to go to school, or may experience a change in eating patterns. Any change in the way kids usually act may be a sign that they need help. Your nine-year-old might start sucking his thumb or wetting the bed, or your teenager, always a C student, suddenly starts to get straight As. These might be signs that you need to find professional help.

The most important thing is to acknowledge that something has been lost. Weekly I would try to bring up how sad I felt and try to talk about what a hard time it was for all of us. Sometimes the kids would respond, "Well, then, why did you get a divorce?" I tried to answer all questions and comments with a statement that brought the focus back to whatever feelings I thought might be behind the comment. I kept bringing it up because I knew we all wanted to pretend that everything was all right when it wasn't.

"It is incredibly difficult on the child if the parent is leaning on them for emotional support, telling the child adult information and feelings that the child has no business hearing," says Susan. "Finding a happy medium, where there is a space to talk about how life is different while at the same time assuring the child that you will still love and care for them the best you can, will create some sense of stability."

Sometimes it's difficult to see the problems your children might be having because you are in the middle of your own grief. I made a point to talk to my kids' teachers, the mothers of their friends, and their coaches, to let them know I needed their help in identifying any problem. I also called the school counselor and asked her to pay special attention to my kids, to talk to them whenever she saw them, and to let them know that she was available if they needed a friend.

We used to go on vacations together as a family. The kids still take great trips with their dad—to ski in Utah, to Atlanta for the Olympics, to Arizona to hike the Grand Canyon, to Seattle, to Washington, D.C., to Hawaii. I experience the fun only through their brief retellings of their experiences as we drive home from the airport. I haven't taken the kids on one family vacation because I've yet to figure out how to financially support their daily lives and also save money for such grand, expensive leisure.

I do, however, spend the time they are on vacation worrying about everything, since I'm not there to control what they do or monitor their safety. When they left for New Zealand for a three-week trip with Ron, I must have given Wesley and Brooke pages of instructions on what to do in case of emergency before I unwrapped my arms from around them and watched them walk with the stewardess down the walkway to the plane. I felt a stab in my heart when Rhett looked at me before he left with tears in his eyes and said, "I'm afraid Dad will keep me, and I'll never see you again." Every few steps Rhett and Troy looked back, smiled a slight smile, and kept walking toward the plane's entrance. I waited until they couldn't see me anymore before bursting into tears. What had I done to their lives, to their sense of security?

Whenever I hear the kids reflect on the divorce, I wish they could have been more removed from the drama. I wish they hadn't known how hard I had to fight to keep them from being sent back to New Zealand without me. I wish they hadn't heard their father's accusations that I stole them from him or the names he called me. They were too young to carry the burden of all the information they were given. I wish I could have changed the circumstances and given them back their innocence, but I couldn't. Instead, I gave them the phone numbers and addresses of all my friends in Christchurch in case they needed anything. I taught them how to call me collect. I told them what to do in case there was no one to meet them in the Auckland airport, how to do Troy's therapy, and repeated (to calm myself) that they would be just fine. Still, I felt helpless and sad at their loss.

My children are moving through grieving to acceptance just as I am. The difficulty is that we're all doing this at the same time, so it's hard for me to work through issues with my kids when I am struggling to heal myself. There are times when I look at my children's behavior, at their hurt and confused feelings, and wish I had stayed married. Then I think about who I am now, and I know that they are experiencing a new and improved mother. My ten-year-old son Rhett said recently, out of the blue, "I haven't seen you cry in a long time." Over time I hope my children will see that they are better off with one happy parent at a time than with two unhappy, bickering adults modeling the wrong way to have a relationship. With time I hope they will work through their grief, understanding that the pain will become less and less.

Personal Loss

Mostly I feel like I'm grieving out of order. When I fled New Zealand for the United States, I felt relief. I grieved often during the last five years of our marriage, somehow anticipating what was to come. The grief helped me to be honest with myself and to let go of my relationship one piece at a time. During the three years after I left, my anger over my husband's behavior kept me from feeling anything but rage, disgust, and irritation. Everything changed when he called me recently and actually talked to me in a kind way. He asked me about how the kids were doing in school and our summer plans, and we even discussed health insurance policies. I hung up the phone and said, "I can't write this book. He's become a human being." I've been grieving ever since, wishing I could go back to the time when he was too mean to trigger any compassionate feelings in me.

I was unpacking boxes about a week after that conversation when I found the box I'd marked "Memories." There were pictures of Ron and me when we were eighteen years old, the kids as babies, wedding pictures, and years of family Christmas pictures with a child or dog being added to the group each year it

Grieving the End • 135

seemed. I started crying, and then I began yelling at a picture of Ron: "Why couldn't you love me? It was all so perfect. Look at these beautiful kids. Look at our lives. Why did I matter so little to you? What could I have done differently?"

A week later I was driving home with all the food and presents for Troy's first communion party. I had a heavy feeling of loss, knowing that we wouldn't be sitting together in the church pew as a whole family. I was crying again, feeling guilt over my decision to divorce, wishing it were different. Then some sense of self-preservation stepped in and said, "Don't do this. Think about what it would actually be like if Ron were here today. Would he be helping you prepare the food, clean the house, get Troy dressed and to the church? Or would he be playing golf, working in his office, or doing something else that he had planned, only to show up looking spectacular at the church to hold Troy and feel the glory? Would you still be alone?"

I had to answer yes, and that made the tears stop. Yet I knew that the kids, who don't understand what goes on behind the scenes in adult relationships, wouldn't have cared whether he had lifted a finger to help with the preparations for this special day as long as he was there with them. Part of my grieving is for me, but an equal part is for what I've taken from my children.

Once you've ended the relationship, it's easy sometimes to forget the desperation and loneliness of the person you were during the marriage, a person whom you wouldn't recognize today. Sometimes waves of grief wash over me, making me wonder why it was so hard to make the marriage work, because from this place, away from the pain of the relationship, I have new strength that perhaps could have carried me through many years of married life. That is when the doubt, the questioning, the looking back and wishing for different outcomes, creeps in and I have to remind myself that those options didn't exist in the relationship. But the pain lives on, sometimes for years—the pain of remembering when I look at pictures, the pain of hearing his voice and knowing exactly what he is feeling just by the tone or rhythm of his speech. The shared life and shared memories that drift through me with the words from a song on the radio, a trip to a restaurant, a look on my son's face that is so Ron that my heart breaks. In those moments I forget the intensity of my anger and the days when I thought that if I had had a gun I could have killed him.

This pool, this gentle pool of mixed feelings, this rough and rugged sharply cutting knowledge and remembrance—this grief. It still lives, but it is my choice in the moment to move past the fantasy thoughts that make me believe I've ruined everything and instead to move on to the reality of how it was. I know that our marriage would be no better if we tried again today.

"The hardest part was trying to understand why he left," says Amy, the woman who had moved to her husband's hometown and was left when she was six months pregnant. "We saw a therapist for three months together. Then our daughter was born. Two months after that Brett told me that he thought we could work it out, but there was one problem: he was gay.

"I had spent months rejecting all the things that made me happy—my career and my friends—because I felt guilty, believing these things were ruining our marriage. I was trying to modify my behavior so that I could get him back. The whole thing was just so shocking, and it happened all at once. I lost my love relationship, the plans we had made as a family, and my dreams for our future. I lost sight of who I was. For a while I believed that I had done something to make him gay, since it was during our marriage when he made this discovery.

"It was my daughter who helped me heal from the total loss I felt. It was so great to have this little life to provide for. I felt this tremendous responsibility. I was completely on my own with no family living in the area, so from the beginning Brett was an active participant in our daughter's life. It took some time, but I was able to forgive Brett for the pain I felt. I'd known him for so long and simply came to the conclusion that he couldn't help it that he was gay. He's been there for us no matter what, but I still feel like I lost the life I wanted."

I've found that whatever time I spend centering myself, enjoying myself, laughing, being creative, is time that goes directly back into my family. The kids often reflect my mood, so the more often I feel good about myself, the better the family dynamic seems to go. They benefit by having an active, involved mother who wants to learn and grow. I have greater energy and more interesting experiences to contribute to our discussions when I feel good about myself. They are able to feel more secure when they see me rebuilding my life, since they know their future depends on my stability. Sadness and grief may be necessary, but they are not emotions I want to live in for extended periods of time. I try to remind myself often that it is my own choices and actions that determine my life.

What Is Positive About Grieving?

For most women the grief process begins the moment they know the marriage is ending. Once the papers are filled out, the research has been done to divide assets, and the divorce papers have been signed, all that is left where the marriage once stood is an empty, grief-filled space. You may have an overwhelming feeling of failure: the grand plan that you formed in childhood and partially carried out through the experiences of marriage and motherhood has been forever changed. Self-doubt replaces self-confidence, and guilt invades your mind. Often you experience a kind of embarrassment, a feeling that some explanation is needed, that you should offer the world some reason as to why you made such a choice, why you "failed."

How can any of this grief be positive? We learn most about ourselves when life hurts. We gain courage, we learn to be vulnerable, and we become more human as a result. At some point we start wondering what we need to do for ourselves to recover our sense of purpose and joy in life.

Grieving helps this healing start. I'm not sure if a woman can ever totally get over the loss of her marriage. It might be a sadness that surfaces throughout the years at recurring events like kids' birthdays, graduations, and weddings. Maybe there will always be an empty space in my heart where the love I had for Ron lived for so many years. That doesn't mean that the space the divorce created can't be filled over time with new relationships, a challenging job, renewed energy as a mother, hobbies, and a full life. The point is that, no matter how successfully you grieve, no matter how sure you are that the divorce was the right decision, there will continue to be moments of sadness.

Finding ways to be kind to yourself during these periods of sadness can be a gift. Some friends have told me that I try too hard to be positive in my life, that I should be weeping, moaning, and letting it all out. One thing I do is to give myself a time limit to feel the sadness. I started this idea expecting that thirty minutes would be enough time to feel sad. Then I'd feel like a failure when I felt just as bad twenty-four hours later. Now I give myself one day. I look at the clock and let it be all right to feel sadness, for one day, over whatever thought has pushed me off balance. Even after the thought leaves my mind I intentionally think about it a few times over that twenty-four-hour period to make sure I've adequately felt it so I can let it go.

If the sadness wants to hang around longer than a day, I pull out a card in the top drawer of my desk that says, "Choose yesterday or choose today." This reminds me that what is done is done and that there can be no going back to redo (or to undo) my life. Sometimes I even write positive things on index cards by my bed so I can read them first thing in the morning. I always feel much worse when I wake up in the morning, when I lie in bed and think of all the things I have to do that day and dream of a different existence. These little positive thoughts have helped me get out of bed many a morning.

All of the above I call my "positive reinforcement voice." My plan to take a day to feel sad doesn't always work, but at least it keeps me focused on the idea that there needs to be an end to whatever sadness I feel. If I can't establish some sort of control over how I feel, then I find that I can't work, I can't care for the kids properly, and in a sense I sabotage my chance for recovering from the divorce.

"I attended a divorce workshop one weekend about six months into the divorce process that made all the difference for me," says Amanda. "I didn't know that the entire weekend would focus on grief, or I probably wouldn't have signed up. We went through the stages of grief, starting out with stage one, denial. I was past that stage but remembered when I didn't believe that my husband was actually going to leave. I was in a state of emotional shock. I actually acted like it wasn't happening, telling our kids that Daddy was on a business trip. At that stage I remember thinking there was some mistake, that he would come home to us.

"The next stage we worked on was anger. I was still angry, so angry that the day before the workshop I had packed up my husband's belongings that had been left at our house and given them away. Most of my days my mind was preoccupied with methods of revenge—how I could hurt him as much as he had hurt me. When I heard the other people at the workshop share their feelings, I started to realize that it was a normal part of the process and that it was possible with time to get through the anger stage. I still couldn't help telling all my friends what an ass he was and am embarrassed to admit that my angry stage lasted months after the workshop ended.

"The third stage was called bargaining. One woman shared how she dyed her hair, lost twenty pounds, and starting jogging daily, promising her husband that if he would take her back she would change whatever was wrong. I think my anger kept me from going through this stage. My husband remarried a week after the divorce was final, so I guess I knew from the start that there was nothing I could do to win his love.

"The fourth stage was letting go. I think that is the stage I am in right now. One of the homework assignments from the workshop was to write a letter saying good-bye to some aspect of your life. My letter included everything I could think of that I was losing—good-bye to our house that we had to move out of, good-bye to our relationship, and good-bye to the kids' father. I've actually written a few of those letters because they really help me when I'm feeling depressed. I have also written one letter where I said good-bye to the negatives, like his keeping me up every night with his snoring!

"The last stage we discussed in the workshop was acceptance. Many people shared how they were feeling more emotionally alive, that they were ready to be independent and to be involved in a new relationship. I have gone on a few dates, but I don't think I have totally accepted my loss yet.

"The best thing about that workshop was that it outlined some of the experiences I might go through. That has helped me to understand that I'm not going crazy and that there will be an end to the grief at some point."

"What helped me most in the grief process was accepting the layers of grief as they came flowing through me naturally without avoiding them," says Frances, the journalist with two teenage daughters. "I didn't stuff it. Not that I walked around the house wailing either. I tried to acknowledge the feelings for what they were so I could move ahead and not get stuck in the process of grief itself. I'm sad and I hurt, but I still have to do the dishes, I still have to get the kids to school, and I try to live my life with love and joy even though I'm grieving.

"Rituals have helped me to work on letting go. I visualize I'm sitting in the lap of the great mother and she has her arms wrapped around me holding me like a child. I sit in the comfort of her arms and allow the sadness to wash over me. After I feel the emotions of grief calming down, I imagine a great light source above me, and I allow that light to surround me."

"I play music that I love when I start to feel depressed," says Vickie. "I move around and dance and act like I'm happy and alive even when I don't really feel it. I also believe in exercising. When I exercise, I don't have any energy left to be angry. I also remember someone telling me that looking great and being successful and happy would be my greatest revenge, so I refuse to look dumpy. I don't believe it's necessary to go and buy new clothes and redo your entire appearance just to make a new beginning. Those credit card bills can be depressing later. I guess I try to look like I'm to-gether even if I feel bad, and often my actions influence how I feel.

"To help me let go of the relationship, I have all sorts of mini-conversations with myself. I say that families are being redefined, that I haven't screwed up, that I am a great mother, and that a wife is basically a fancy housekeeper, family accountant, and man's helpmate. I'm not afraid to use whatever tricks I can come up with to help get through the pain."

Loss of a Lifestyle

My husband had been a professional athlete. That fact seemed to define our lives in many ways. We lived in a large, rambling, ranch-style house in northern California. The walls of the house had floor-to-ceiling windows that looked out onto our beautiful garden full of tulips, daffodils, and flowering cherries in the spring, and in the winter past the bare trees to the creek that lined our property.

I had spent years working on each room so that the design reflected our family's personality. There was a huge playroom that I covered with eight-by-ten photocopied black-and-white pictures of each person in our family doing the things he or she liked to do. The hall surrounding the kitchen had a hand-painted Indian scene, and in the master bathroom I hand-painted rose vines climbing up one wall. I did everything myself, enjoying every minute spent painting, sewing, and caring for this building that contained my life. It was my home, the place I put my creative energy into, hoping it would be a lifelong investment.

When we first arrived back in Portola Valley, I avoided driving by our old house even though it meant taking a longer route. One day the kids begged me, after hearing from neighbors that the new owners had cut down "our beautiful oak tree," to take them to see the house. I agreed to drive by, promising myself that I would be unemotional. I turned down our old street and for a moment could imagine the girls three years before riding their bikes in dress-up clothes up and down the street. I remembered walking across the street to the swim club to read a book while I watched the kids swim on hot summer days. We'd order dinner from the snack bar so I wouldn't have to cook, then walk home just in time for baths and storytime. My life was so much easier then—I had leisure time!

My office in this house was more like a craft or sewing room except for my computer, which sat untouched for weeks on end until I felt the urge to write or had a new book idea. I didn't have to work. Whatever I wrote came from a place of inspiration, not an editor's deadline. Money was not a problem. I can't even remember thinking about a career. The inspiration for book ideas came directly from daily interaction with my children and all the activities I liked to do with them. At the end of each sports season we took a vacation wherever we wanted. When the kids needed new clothes or I was registering them for expensive summer camps, I didn't even think before I wrote the check. I took art classes a few afternoons a week and had no problem fitting in an hour here or there to exercise. I had part-time childcare and cleaning help. Days slid by with no real pressure. I had simple purposes in life: to take care of my children, to take care of our home, and to be the best wife I could be.

Divorce has completely changed my lifestyle. My choice to work at home allows me to be there for the kids and to adapt to family needs, but that flexibility also has its downsides. What I notice most is my increased stress level. I have to worry about generating writing assignments, making enough money to pay our bills, and finding the time to meet my kids' physical and emotional needs. Radio interviews inevitably get booked during orthodontist appointments, and media tours fall on a birthday or championship sports game. The kids complain constantly about the events I can't attend even if I miss only one out of six! I rarely have time to talk on the phone or meet a friend for lunch, and my exercise program consists of yoga once a week if I'm lucky.

It's not just my loss. We all work harder, whether it's keeping the house clean, cooking meals, or helping with homework. The hardest part of "wearing all the hats" in the family is that I can't give my children as much of my time as I would like. I feel guilty that my two youngest have had few lazy days with me when there was nothing I had to do. Sometimes I remember the easy lifestyle I had during my marriage and feel very sorry for myself and jealous of all the women around me who have partners to share the responsibilities. Feeling sorry for myself is my way of grieving the loss. Nevertheless, even though I may not always like it and it often causes me pain, this new lifestyle is mine, and I'm trying my best to make it work.

"I used to attend all the kids' functions," says Stephanie, the mom who went to law school. "I hate missing them, but it hurts that the kids show no recognition that I'm missing them for a reason. Their dad can miss things, and they seem to accept that he is at work. There seems to be no understanding with me. They say that I don't have enough time for them and that I like school better than I like them.

"My sisters took the kids to my law school graduation. It meant nothing to them. When their dad rides a bike nine hundred miles, they are really excited. He's a better self-promoter. I guess I have to start being my own PR woman. My son did a poster for school featuring Peter's bicycle trip. The teacher was so impressed with the accomplishment. No teacher has ever come up to me and said, 'Your daughter said that you are going to law school. What a great accomplishment!' I wish the kids could be aware of me as a person and see what I've achieved and be proud of me instead of taking everything I do for granted or complaining that I'm not doing enough. I felt much more love, acceptance, and connection to my children before the divorce, when I was able to play a more active role in their lives."

"Our lifestyle has changed a lot since our arrival in the United States," says Jenny, the artist whose husband abused her. "Now we live with my parents, and I'm still in the process of meeting people and trying to establish a social life. I continue my painting when my daughter is at preschool, so I am going forward with my career.

"I've found so much joy in simple fun. Sometimes we go to street fairs on the weekend. I love seeing other artists out selling their creations. My daughter likes to get her face painted, to listen to the street musicians, and to taste the various foods. We feed the ducks that live on a pond near our house. We go for walks in search of flowers to press between telephone books that we will later make into pictures. We put music on and with old scarves in our hands dance around the room with the scarves floating above and around us. I'm much more emotionally available for my daughter now. I laugh more and look for moments each day to play and have fun."

Slowly I came to terms with what I perceived as a permanent change in lifestyle based on decreased finances. I would listen to the kids talking wistfully about the vacations their friends were going on, surfing camps, trips to amusement parks, and how boring their summer would be. I thought about my childhood and how our house was always full of people. There were six kids in our family, and I didn't remember a whole lot of "purchased" fun. I remembered hours spent riding horses in the creek with my best friend, flag football with neighborhood kids, the county fair, and Sundays spent with my family at various lakes around where I had grown up. I began to feel that it was my job to make up for the pain of the divorce by buying a life my kids would be thrilled with. Yet I couldn't find a way (or the money) to meet their high expectations. It seemed that everything they wanted had a price tag attached.

The day I stopped buying into my failure to create a life for them comparable to what the neighbors had was the day the fun began. I focused on one goal: to make our house a fun place to be for the kids and their friends. Whenever the kids ask to have friends over, no matter how many, I try always to say yes. We live close to their school, so I encourage the kids to bring friends home after school. We bought a big metal fire pit so that we could have campfires on the weekend, complete with marshmallow roasting and songs. We've always had a huge trampoline, so I encouraged the idea of outdoor sleepovers (much to my neighbors' regret!). We make beads out of clay, have game nights, take night hikes, and go to drive-in movies, always filling every leftover seatbelt with an extra friend.

I know all of my kids' friends and enjoy having a house full of activity. Of course there are many times when I feel tired and uninspired, but I try to put those feelings aside and remember what I want to create. The goal has been to change the mood in our house from "We don't get to do anything fun" to "This is the coolest place to be." I easily accomplished this as soon as I shifted gears and decided that a little sacrifice on my part (peace and quiet, a clean house, time to myself) could go a long way toward creating the family life I wanted.

Working daily to create what I want in my life has given me something to hold on to through my own grieving process. Walking any direction that is forward keeps a woman from sinking into endless grief, whether that direction is volunteering at your kids' school, finding a part-time job, enrolling in school, or taking daily dance classes. Pick any goal, it doesn't really matter what it is. What is important is to move your energy forward and begin to visualize the life you want to create. To do this you will need to find other single mothers who can offer you their support, friendship, and shared experiences.

NINE

Who Am I Now?

Once everything has been stripped away, there is empty space. It is black. I am alone. I'm falling down some dark passage with nothing to hold on to. I hear only my own cries. Will anyone recognize me? Where am I? What happened to my life? The fall takes too long. Then all of a sudden there is a thud, and I hit ground, not sure whether I can breathe or move. Am I still alive? Everything hurts. In mythology I remember the heroine's journey into the underworld. Is this what it feels like? Maybe I've fallen into that underworld. And now I sit at the bottom of this dark pit, scratching the slippery walls for something to hold on to, wondering whether I will live or die. Do I have the courage to gather up my life, which has been stripped of everything familiar, and rise from the ashes like the heroines I remember?

There were many moments on my journey downward when I had glimpses of who I was. When I heard a song and was moved from someplace inside to get up and dance with arms floating and tears flowing, feeling really alive. When I was making love and lost myself in the feel of our bodies, the smells, sounds, and movement, as if nothing else existed. When a bulb I had planted survived the winter and blossomed into the brightest daffodil while everything else remained gray. When I sat beside my children's beds and listened to them breathe, placing my hand on them as I cried softly, an apology for my mistakes and their pain. When something I wrote passed straight from my heart into words without any thought. Those moments kept me going. They reminded me that I was still alive even though I lay under a pile of rubble and could only peek out at the world whenever I had the strength.

I was sure many times throughout my divorce process that I had hit bottom—you know, that bottom that everyone seems to mention whenever they talk about grief and healing. I remember saying with a laugh, "Well, things couldn't get much worse!" Then a month later they would get much worse. I had no idea it would take so long to hit the lowest point. I fell in love while I was still on my way down, but even that couldn't change the direction of my fall, because the journey I was on, even though I didn't recognize it at the time, had nothing to do with physical experiences. I was learning who I wanted to be.

On the way down, the pain was about letting go of my self-image, accepting my dark side with all its imperfections, letting the failure in, seeing the fragile spaces within myself that I had been too strong to acknowledge in the past. By the time I reached the bottom of that dark pit, letting go of one piece of myself at a time, there were only a few thoughts left in my mind. Could I still love myself? What was left of my family? How could I start to rebuild my life? Was it possible to climb back up to the surface?

Finding and Loving Yourself

I had an idea when I was sitting at the bottom of my pit that if I could only find my old self, the girl without so many scars, that I could love that person. I thought it would be like finding a lost watch. Once it was in my hands, I could simply put it on and wear it. In reality, I've had to find myself dozens of times since my divorce, and I've had to learn to love myself in each new discovery.

This quest to find myself is what I call my soul work. The journey is a spiritual one, not because it has anything to do with religion, although it might for some, but because it is about moving Spirit from one place to another. My spirit started the divorce process—unrecognized by me, cast aside by my anger. Now, five years later, I can wrap my arms around my spirit. The process seemed more like a birth into my existing "self" than a birth into any God. But as my mind opened up to new ideas, the world seemed friendlier and I began to see past the problems that had kept me pinned under my pile of rubble.

I first recognized the awesome presence of Spirit in nature. I think I had unconsciously closed all channels of feeling within myself in order to avoid feeling pain. Then one day I was standing in the front yard of the cottage I had just purchased, feeling overwhelmed by the weeds and dead grass. I looked up to Windy Hill, a majestic open space preserve we can see from our front yard, and I cried softly, "There you are, Great Spirit. God, you are still here!" From that point my life slowly moved from black-and-white glimpses of feelings to breathing and beating in full color—to feeling the wind, touching the dirt, laughing aloud, and engaging once again in life's dance. I was reintroduced to Spirit through the senses I had closed.

One afternoon shortly after my Windy Hill experience, I attended a talk titled "Finding God in All Things," presented by an older Jesuit priest. I will never forget the looks on the faces of his listeners (I was by far the youngest in the room) when he started talking about fairies, leprechauns, and the spirits of the earth. I had just experienced his message clearly in my own life: "Open up your mind to 'Spirit' around you. It's everywhere." I felt like standing up and dispelling the disbelief I saw in the room. "Really, you have to hear this! The spirit of a flower or an old redwood may be the closest thing to the creator God that you will ever touch!" I sat there moved by this little man, who stood as a priest yet was willing to risk presenting ideas that were not easily accepted by society, in order to share his own unique experience of Spirit in the world.

So the question "Can I love myself?" was answered as I found these pieces of myself, and as with a puzzle, I began to place the pieces into a picture that was me. Standing in the weeds that day in my front yard, I was able to feel the beauty, the majesty, and the presence of something more powerful.

This finding of self happened gradually over time as I regained my ability to feel the world around me. When I sat on the grass and saw Troy in his baseball uniform for the first time, walking with such excitement as he swung the bat to warm up, I was able to feel nervous, excited, tearful, and proud all at once. There was this sense of "Wow, I'm here in this moment, and these feelings are mine." At Wesley's eighth-grade graduation I listened as she addressed her class on what it meant to be a leader in the world, my mind racing through the events of her life over the past four years. Somehow she had managed, during our most difficult years as a family, to become class president and to receive awards for community service and for being an outstanding athlete.

And those were just the obvious, outward rewards. As she walked past me during the procession, she turned her head to smile at me in what felt like slow motion, and in that moment I forgave myself. Not just in words, which I had done many times before. This time forgiveness washed over me, and I felt my grip loosen on all the ideas that I had held on to so tightly—things I felt guilty for, all the "could haves" and "should haves." By the time her face with its acknowledging smile turned away and I could no longer see her eyes, part of me had healed. Another part of the puzzle slid into place—I was a good mother. I had done the best I could, and my best had been good enough.

In the beginning of the divorce process many women feel, as Bonnie did, that they don't know who they are anymore. "My attorney keeps asking what name I want to be called, and I keep saying that I'm just Bonnie. I guess my attorney is frustrated because I can't decide if I'm going back to my maiden name. That name hasn't been mine for fifteen years, and my four children have my married name. Part of finding myself is deciding what I want. My parents can't understand why I would keep my married name after all that I've gone through, yet my kids are my greatest accomplishment and love in life, and I want to have the same name as they do. I've always tried to please everyone. This is the first time in my life I can actually remember asking myself, 'Bonnie, what do you want to do about this?'"

Sometimes finding yourself means confronting a past fear, or doing something you've never done before. "Before I tell you this story, I want to say a few things about myself so you can see the significance of my action," says Lauren, a CPA with three children under nine. "I have been what most would call a 'good girl' all my life. I don't drink, have never done drugs, and have had only five sexual partners in my life. I was sexually molested when I was twelve by my soccer coach. He was a college student, very cute, and I had a crush on him. So when he started paying attention to me, asking if I needed rides home or if I'd want to go get ice cream, I was thrilled. The first time he kissed me I was so excited, but as he pushed further I felt scared. I asked him to stop, but he didn't, convincing me that it would feel good. It did feel good, but after that I felt ashamed. I knew that he had raped me in a way, but I liked him and wanted him to still like me. I ended up in therapy during college because I had such a hard time trusting men or having a relationship.

"After my divorce I went with my closest girlfriend on a vacation. I talked to her about how I was always afraid of wearing what some might consider sexy clothing. I think I'm attractive, but I was always afraid to attract the attention of men, thinking that if I were raped or attacked it would look like I asked for it. We had a few glasses of wine one night, and we were taking turns telling each other what would be the scariest thing we could imagine doing. I told her that being on a stage and stripping would be the worst.

"To make a long story shorter, she convinced me that we should both go to the strip joint that was in the town where we were vacationing and ask if we could do one dance. I thought she was nuts, but she said that it would be good for me because I would be expressing my sexuality and the men watching would not be able to hurt me. It's a good thing she is ten times as brave as I am because I would never have done it.

"We arrived at the club. It was dark inside. There were probably thirty men sitting around and strippers on the stage. My friend told the manager that we were journalists writing an article for a national magazine and that we wanted to talk to some of the strippers and experience it ourselves so we could write about it. I admit that this was the scariest thing I have ever done in my life. The manager agreed to let us do one dance on the stage at the same time. There was one other woman who would be dancing with us, and she said we should just follow what she did. It was a totally nude strip joint, but the manager said we could take off whatever we wanted to. My friend and I agreed with each other to strip to our underwear.

"When the music started, I looked out into the audience and saw unfiltered lust on the faces of the men. I began to move to the music, and I actually enjoyed taking each piece of clothing off, bending over, shaking my breasts, it was so freeing. I had spent years in therapy discussing my sexuality, how I wished I could be more expressive, how I thought that part of myself had been lost when I was twelve. I actually ended up taking off all of my clothes even though my friend, who was laughing as we danced, kept her underwear on. I can't exactly explain how this happened, but I swear I walked off that stage a completely different person. I had done something that terrified me and survived it, and I had fun with my sexuality without feeling threatened by a man. Since that experience I can wear whatever I want without feeling afraid, I can flirt without feeling I owe anyone anything, and I feel more like a woman instead of a child."

Sometimes finding yourself means admitting you have a problem and taking the steps to do something about it. Patricia was an alcoholic when she became pregnant with her son. "I was strong enough to quit drinking while I was pregnant," she says, "but after my son was born and my husband asked for a divorce, I went back to drinking. Sometimes when my husband had the baby at his house, I would wake up with an empty bottle lying next to me in bed, and I couldn't remember what I had done the night before. There was a woman at work who I had heard spent some time in jail. She approached me one day and asked if I had a problem with drinking. We started meeting at a restaurant before work in the morning to have a cup of coffee and talk. She talked me into going to Alcoholics Anonymous with her.

"Part of the process for me was forgiving myself, forgiving my husband, releasing the anger, and understanding my victim attitude. Before I joined AA I was religious only because I was raised Catholic and was supposed to believe. I didn't pray or respect God outside of church. This group has given me a place to go, a place to share who I am, a place to find out who I am. I don't think I have ever really loved myself. There is love and support in this group that I wasn't lucky enough to find in my family while I was growing up. When I'm really on edge now, instead of drinking I pray. Prayers always help me, they don't cost anything, and most of mine have been answered. I may not have the white picket fence, and my life may not be what I expected, but at least I know who I am now and I know where I'm going."

Start Rebuilding

One night while doing the dishes I took another step toward the surface when, with no thought or warning, I understood that every choice I made was mine. I didn't have to become someone for somebody else. I was free to decide who I was. I was free to create my life. I didn't owe anybody an explanation. My sole responsibility was to my children and to myself. In that moment things became simpler.

It dawned on me that the disappearance of the person I knew (me) over my twelve-year marriage did not kill me. My spirit was still alive! I began to wonder—what is life, and where is it stored in a soul? Is life like a painting, something that is created layer by layer as each new color is added? What are the colors for me that make a painting (or life) that I can live with forever? What is the life picture I'm trying to design? Have I given myself time to think, feel, and take in the ruined canvas, the picture that I spent twelve years painting that lies ripped from its frame on the floor of my life? I thought its colors were vivid, I thought I could feel their peace and harmony. But the picture was an abstract—shapes that never fit, pieces floating alone on a sea of white.

How will I know next time that it is my soul speaking and not just a need to be part of a picture, any picture, that can decorate my life and fit the wall and the available space in an acceptable way? As I did the dishes that night, I let myself want more. I let myself dream. By the time I finished wiping the table, my mind was floating. I envisioned future success, a love that nobody else had ever felt, passion unmeasured, a life marked with original brush strokes.

I've been told many times throughout my life that I want too much. Maybe my mom's words to me when I was sixteen were right. She said that I expected the extraordinary and either was disappointed when I couldn't find it or, when I couldn't find it, worked without distraction to create it. I had received a letter earlier that day from my best friend from high school, Carolyn, who said, "You've always been able to take tragedy and make from it a thing of beauty." She called it "Sheila style." Her words reminded me of who I had once been, and who I might be again.

When rebuilding a life, it is important to think about what you want, how you might earn money, and where you need to devote your time. Vickie, the broadcast journalist, knew she had to leave the marriage, but it took ingenuity to find jobs that fit into her mothering schedule. "It didn't take me long to figure out that Tom had a girlfriend," she says. "After the night when he walked out telling the girls I was a fucking idiot, we went to counseling for a while. He came back home for a few months, and I found a suspicious number on our phone bill. I called the number, and a woman answered. I told her that her number showed up on our bill twice and asked if she knew Tom. She denied knowing him, so I called the phone company. The next day the woman called, crying and saying that she didn't know that he was married. I asked her to explain the nature of their relationship, and she said it was her personal business. I then said, 'If my husband is in your bed naked, then it is *my* personal business, and I want some answers. For the rest of their lives my two girls are going to come from a divorced family, and I want to know what kind of character would do that.' She hung up.

"Three months later that same woman called and apologized for her actions months earlier. Tom had told her we were almost divorced. She went on to say that now that we were divorced (we hadn't even filed), she did not want me to interfere when they got married. I later found out this woman was an intern at the station just out of college. Their relationship ended, and so did ours.

"I hadn't been working that much when all of this happened. I immediately started looking for jobs. I found little jobs all over the place—on-camera work, some writing and producing, sometimes a commercial here or there. I also started teaching a kids' commercial acting class and also a dance and gymnastics class.

"Tom makes fun of me, saying that I'm a loser with no direction. But I really like all the jobs I have and am bringing home paychecks even if they are inconsistent. I took theater classes in college and dreamed of being an actress. I feel a freedom that I didn't have within the marriage, living with his judgment and expectations. My name may not be lighting up the big screen, but I have fun in my work, and it's all kind of acting-related. If I have to work, if I have to rebuild my life, I figured that I better start over doing something I liked."

My thoughts inspire me, but ideas have always come easily to me. Putting my ideas into action, the actual rebuilding of myself, has been the challenge. It can be exciting to start over, strip away old patterns, and take on new roles and responsibilities—like remodeling an old house that no longer fits the family's needs. When you remodel the kitchen, you might take out the old (your making dinner every night for your husband, your buying all the groceries, your doing all the dishes) and install the new (shared meal preparation, a chore chart, and family shopping night). In the bedroom out goes the old (arguments over the frequency of sex, the television, and the pile of newspapers your husband reads while you're trying to fall asleep) and in comes the new (that stack of delicious novels, a stereo system, a new bedspread that fits *your* personality, and sex with a man who likes it). This is fun. In the office out goes the old (getting no pay for working eighteen hours a day, that part-time job as a waitress, that full-time job as a maid) and in comes the new (a chance to reeducate yourself, a new career, mental stimulation). You get the idea.

Keep asking the question, "Now that everything has been stripped away, what do I want and how can I start to rebuild?" Get excited about the possibilities, brainstorm, and write all your dreams down—give yourself something to hope for. Who do you want to be? For just a moment stop reading this book and try to answer that question. It is really important, because if you don't know the answer, you can't replace what was stripped away with something new.

Rebuilding a life is not as easy as just wanting something. Discovering who you are can be the task of an entire lifetime. Some people think life is just fate: if something is meant to happen it will, and others are simply lucky. Some people wait until they feel better, hoping someone will knock on their door and give them money, a relationship, or a job. It takes serious soul work when the task at hand is traveling from the darkest place in your life toward the light. It also takes tremendous vision—an ability to imagine the light even when you can't see it.

New Definitions of Family

As I was waking up one morning when we were living in Rose's studio, I heard these words booming from our shared (by five) bathroom. "If you're a boy, go outside!" The amazing thing was that I could laugh—loud and long—at this seemingly impossible situation. Four children and me, in an eight-hundred-square-foot room, with one bathroom and few private spaces. We'd lived there for fifteen months, but we were moving out soon. We had survived it and, in the process, grown in ways we never imagined.

Just as I had struggled to find pieces of myself, we had all lived through new experiences, fears, and challenges as we tried to redefine ourselves as a family. The anger the kids felt toward me for "causing" the situation had subsided. They had stopped asking me to drive by our old house. And every once in a while one of the kids would even admit that our little space was cozy. What I had thought would be a very lonely journey—my children and I struggling to fit into the community—ended up being filled with loving people. The single mothers group had become one layer of extended family who gave the kids a chance to spend time with other kids going through the same struggles. Living on the same property with another family was another layer, helping all of us open our minds to the possibility that there were many ways in this world to live as a family.

Now as I look at the possibility of remarriage in the near future, we will be experiencing yet another version of family. For me the rebuilding of my life in this area was the easiest, maybe because I knew how broken my marriage to Ron already was even as we were within the relationship. The kids, on the other hand, seemed completely surprised by the divorce and felt the deepest loss. As mothers we have an intuitive strength that tells us we have to go on and adjust to the new arrangement, but kids (even after many years) may fantasize about their old family being reunited.

I asked my girls if they could remember how they felt just after leaving New Zealand. Wesley said, "I hated you because you were the one who took us out of the country, away from Dad. It took me a while to accept the fact that you guys would never be married again, but you move on—things happen. I don't really know how I did it. I guess over time things just felt different. My definition of family changed the most when we lived with another family. Now I am more open to accepting people into our family and making them a part of my life. I learned that family doesn't have to be the people you are born with. It can be anyone who loves you, who participates in your life and takes care of you."

"I didn't even know why we left New Zealand, but since we were going to Disneyland I was pretty happy," said Brooke. "I don't remember when I figured out what was going on. I was so used to my dad being gone it didn't seem that different until I got older, and then I missed him when you wouldn't let me see him. There didn't seem to be anything I could do about the situation. I was mad at you especially when you went out with another man."

The definition of family can change over time to include neighbors and friends. "In the beginning I spent so much energy beating myself up over the breakup of our family," says Jessica, the mother of three children under twelve. "It's been five years now, and in that time my idea of family has changed dramatically. I would be lying if I said that my kids' lives are better because of the divorce. We weren't a couple that fought or had any really disturbing behaviors that the kids would notice. Their father is a great dad, so they really missed him when he wasn't living with them every day. What surprised me was how easily the kids and I established a comfortable family unit that was as much a family as when their father lived with us.

"I also think that my children formed excellent relationships with other people in our community and extended family, which they might not have developed without the sadness of the divorce. Holidays like Christmas now include many nonfamily members and their children in the celebration. We've opened up and created an extended family that is more like a tribe than a blood family. I'm not saying the divorce was a good thing, just that I did the best to make my family feel whole."

Ultimately the most important thing that defines a family is love. "My kids don't have a father because their father left us years ago and hasn't been back," says Alex, a thirty-five-year-old waitress. "I didn't have a college degree. I worked two jobs, one as a grocery store attendant and the other as a waitress. My three kids had a very hard life, but I loved them very much, and they knew it. Sometimes I think that too much attention is put on what kids have and what they don't have, the horrible things that happen in their lives that have this terrible effect on who they become. I would tell myself whenever I felt like I was failing my children that the one thing every human is striving for in life is to be loved. I believed that if I could love my children, be there to emotionally support them, and be honest with them, then I would have given them more than a house, more than new clothes, more than a fancy car. Sure, we had a broken home, we had a broken life—there was nothing I could do to change that. At least I know they don't have broken hearts, and they feel good about who they are."

Climbing Back to the Surface

In 1994 my mother gave me the book *Women Who Run with the Wolves: Myths and Stories of the Wild Woman Archetype,* with the inscription: "You are running in the Spirit of all the wild women of the Earth. Feel their power, joy, and laughter! You are free." When I read the book, the stories were entertaining and I learned quite a bit, but I didn't know what power I was supposed to feel. And I definitely didn't feel free. Recently I picked up the book again and read the first few chapters. My heart was beating with each of Clarissa Pinkola Estés's words. How could I have completely missed the essence of what she was trying to say the first time I read it?

Defining *wild* as "natural," Estés argues that women need to find a way back to their instinctual nature. In using stories to illustrate what captivity feels like, she describes my married life with astounding accuracy. With each myth I read, I felt a yearning to be more instinctual, to go with my initial response to a situation, to make decisions from a heart place instead of a "should" place. I so desperately needed to hear her message in l994, but I couldn't—I wasn't ready.

Sometimes it's hard to measure how far we have traveled because we have forgotten where we started. If I remember the day when I stood screaming into the face of God, "Where are you, you incompetent Being?" and then look at myself now, the progress is remarkable. What steps did I take? What layers did I drape across my naked soul that protected me and gave me the courage to continue the journey to the surface?

My spiritual journey alone would fill the pages of a book, and yet as I look back over the last three years, it's hard to separate my everyday struggles from my spiritual journey because somewhere along the path the two became one. It was the arguments with my children, the frustration over divorce papers and court dates, the grieving for my old life, and the ordinary human struggles that taught me the nature of the divine. All through the process I thought that I had lost my *faith,* when in fact I'd simply changed the word to *hope* and was living with complete faith as I made one difficult decision after another. I remembered from my college classes the ideas woven into the fabric of all the world's religions: acceptance, truth, grace. These ideas were definitions for me in the past, but now they have living meaning based on my own life experiences.

My son Troy taught me how to let go of expectation and accept life as it unfolds. I did everything I could to "fix" his autism. Initially, after the diagnosis, I just couldn't let go of one of my core beliefs—that if I worked hard enough, I could change the outcome, make it perfect. Then one day I just got tired—tired of all the therapy, tired of endless hours of speech, tired of the lack of balance in my life. In that moment of exhaustion, when I had no energy to fight for him anymore, I understood that my son was perfect, a whole person just the way he was. Not that I decided to stop helping him learn and working with his siblings to help them understand his view of the world. It was more of a change in thought process: I lowered my expectations of myself

(I had only so much energy, time, and ability) and accepted my circumstances (I had a child with special learning needs).

Truth was another concept I needed to learn. My first attempt at this had a painful outcome. A close friend and I were working on a writing project together. I worked very hard to get the project sold, but it kept getting turned down. The rejections had something to do with my friend's contribution, but I was too afraid she would be hurt if I told her the truth, so I kept working with the project, trying to present it differently and hoping that a publisher would accept it. When I realized that the project was never going to be accepted, I decided to tell my friend the truth. She hasn't spoken to me since.

My sorrow over losing a friend I loved has made me think about the importance of truth as a way of life. Had I told her the reason for the negative response I was getting in the beginning instead of trying to protect her, the news of rejection would not have hurt her so much. As a result of this incident, I found myself wanting to be more transparent, to be more real, to tell the truth and to be able to let go of the outcome.

The word *grace* has always haunted me. I thought of grace as an experience that just happened, as a gift from the world (divine, God, or universe) that we don't work to get. For a while I thought, *What have I done to have so many bad things happen to me? Why can't my life be more full of grace?* I couldn't see the little gifts I was receiving, even in those dark times, because I was looking for the winning lottery ticket, a huge career success, or some other obvious, visible, life-changing event. Now I understand the mystery of grace as I watch the little gifts I received being transformed into life-changing events.

When we moved in with another family, it seemed like a temporary means to survival. But that experience grew into a family-like relationship that made divorce seem like an adventure instead of a funeral. When a friend told me about a one-bedroom cottage for sale in our community, I was thrilled to be able to buy it but worried about my ability to afford it over time. That cottage has become a home with bedrooms for everyone and a shared beginning for our new family unit. When I fell in love, I wasn't sure whether I would ever be able to commit my life to another human being again. The relationship is more alive with each day. I now understand what the word *partner* means and am contemplating remarriage.

My children have often been my teachers in life's most important lessons. Six months ago Wesley and her best friend Alanna decided to hold a meeting about spirituality for our mother-daughter group. It seemed an odd topic, considering that the past group discussions had covered topics such as friendship, dating, stress, and homework. I had no idea what they were going to talk about, especially since Wesley had recently declared that she didn't believe in God at all. The girls started off the meeting by instructing everyone to write a eulogy. "Pretend that you have just died, and write all the things that you would like someone to say about you." I looked across the room at Mary, Alanna's mother, with the question written on my face: Wasn't the topic spirituality?

I wrote my eulogy in silence. When the mothers and daughters had finished, Wesley and Alanna asked everyone to read what they had written. Wesley then drew the most profound conclusion I have ever heard. She said, "Whatever you have to do in your life to live the life and to be the person you just wrote about—that is spirituality." They hadn't exactly explained to the group the steps they might take to become spiritual. They skipped all the traditional definitions of faith, forgiveness, prayer, and meditation. But somehow their thirteen-year-old minds already knew that spirituality is in the process—that it is in the living of life that soul is born.

To get from the bottom of my pit to the surface I had to build a ladder toward the light one rung at a time until I could touch a new life that was completely my own. Sometimes it felt as if I were carving each rung out of huge, hard wooden logs, with only a stick for a tool. Other times I would be carving one of the logs and feel internal stirrings like a soft wind brushing across my face, reminding me to look upward and to hope. The first rung was "I do love myself." The second was "I know what I want." "My family is still whole" was the third, and the fourth was "I can choose who I am."

From this quiet, internal place, our hearts begin to heal. Life might not look different yet, but our minds are becoming aware of a sense of purpose, wholeness, and worth. Aspects of ourselves that disappeared during our failed marriages begin to resurface. The seeds of an idea are being planted in our minds: we can remake our lives by choosing our own direction and become fully the person we imagine ourselves to be. We begin to take the broken pieces and put them back together in a completely new way, with guidance from a Spirit that is partly outside ourselves, yet also within ourselves.

....

On Your Own

I walked through the front door one evening, carrying a gallon of milk in one hand and a paper bag full of bread, chips, and cereal in the other. I heard the soundtrack from *Grease* blaring on the kitchen CD player: "You're the one that I want, you are the one I want." Then the shower turned on, the toilet flushed, and I heard the sound of water splashing on the floor as the voices on the CD faded. The kitchen sink was full of Comet, and a pile of crumbs sat in a neat pile in the middle of the kitchen floor. I set the groceries down, then jumped as the kitchen wall vibrated with a loud thud, from what I assumed was the vacuum cleaner running into the boys' bedroom wall with repeated fury.

I couldn't believe my eyes. The night before I had been fed up with the kids and their inability to clean up after themselves, so I cried for twenty minutes while I stormed around the house cleaning what I could and complaining loudly as I came upon any mess I felt they should have noticed. In the end, after my tears had subsided, I called a family meeting and asked for help. I told them that I was working as hard as I could and that although I would love to have a maid myself, I simply couldn't be theirs. My tearful message—"Things have to change around here."

Kids with New Jobs

The morning after my "clean house" experience, I woke up feeling guilty that I had burdened my kids with adult tears and helplessness. I feel sad that my children have to take on more responsibility than other kids their age. What I really wish for them is a carefree childhood free from worry—about whether we will have enough money to buy Christmas presents, or whether I will be able to afford their college education. When Brooke says that she wishes she could buy clothes without having to work for them, like other kids, or when Rhett says that he really needs a new pair of basketball shoes by Saturday's game, I feel like I've let my kids down. When Wesley asks for a ride to water polo and I tell her she has to ride her bike (six miles) because I have an assignment due and can't spare the time, I feel like I'm failing at my "mother job."

Since the divorce, that unconditional "loving mother" concept—the idea that I'm available for the kids whenever they need me—seems to have vanished. When Brooke said, "You are my mother. Who else am I supposed to ask to take me to get poster board?" there was nothing I could say but, "Get in the car. Let's go." When Troy (then seven years old) announced proudly to a group of my friends that his job was to clean the toilets, I looked around apologetically until someone broke the ice with, "That's great! Even my husband doesn't know how to do that!" I wish I didn't need their help so much, but I do.

In the beginning of the divorce I felt terrible over assigning new responsibilities to the kids, and they felt burdened by what they perceived as my demand for "slave labor." Brooke made a poster-size sign one night and left it on my bed. It read:

THE DECLARATION OF DISHES

We the people declare that every person under the age of 30 should not be allowed to do dishes *at all*. It is harassment! Doing the dishes should be banned from doing. Whoever orders people to do dishes is officially declared a SLAVE DRIVER! People think that the world's greatest problems are war and pollution but I declare dishes is up there too.

Thank you.

At least her words made me laugh. I took a photograph of her sitting on her bed holding that sign and told her that I planned to give her the photo on her wedding day!

It took a few years for all of us to adjust to the added chores we had to do every day. I began to appreciate all the new life skills the kids were learning. Over time they forgot how life was before the divorce and perhaps began to think their new responsibilities were simply a part of growing up. There was a sense of pride in their voices when they talked about how their friends couldn't scramble an egg. I would then pat myself on the back and remind myself that feeling competent in life raises a child's self-esteem as much as succeeding academically in school or athletically on a sports team. I would listen to other parents say how resourceful my kids were and begin to let go of my guilt.

I don't want to paint a picture of my children scurrying around the house with smiles on their faces, happily doing every chore I assigned. They were still the same grumbling children I started off with! What changed was their attitude of acceptance—they understood that I desperately needed their help and responded to my plea.

"When I started asking my kids to do a few of the jobs I was doing daily, it became very evident how out of balance our family had been," says Susan. "Maybe I was playing supermom to impress my husband, get more attention, or show him that he needed me in his life. When he moved out and I was emotionally exhausted, I began assigning jobs. I used the same approach I used at work, talking about the team effort we all needed to show. It's the best thing I've done. Now I don't feel so much resentment toward my family for all the work I have to do."

"I hate the way my mom gives me all the jobs that she should be responsible for," says Dan, a fourteen-year-old. "This has been going on for five years. I have to babysit my younger brother when I'd rather be at a football game or hanging out with my friends. I don't know anyone who has to do the family dishes every night or clean bathrooms. Sometimes I tell my mom that she shouldn't have had kids if she didn't want to take care of them. She chose to get a divorce, so she should just stop complaining."

"My mom did me a great favor when she assigned me household responsibilities when I was eight," says Kate about her childhood. "It helped me learn to be a responsible person. When I graduated from high school, I was able to move out on my own, get a job, and care for myself. I knew how to do laundry, cook, balance a checkbook, go grocery shopping, and pay bills. I went on to college and have been very successful in the business world. I guess I have an attitude that nobody is going to do anything for me. If I want something done, I do it myself."

New Roles and Responsibilities

No matter how helpful or helpless your husband seemed, he was still an adult body with the capacity to take on some of the household responsibilities. Single mothers change their hat repeatedly each day. The garbage disposal breaks, and on goes the plumber's hat. Kids need a ride, and it's a chauffeur at your service. When the grass needs to be mowed, Mom becomes the gardener. And in her spare time she's the cook, carpenter, laundress, counselor, garbage collector, decorator, correspondent, and breadwinner. Family life is tiresome and stressful even when two adults pitch in. When one adult is no longer present, the burden shifts to one person, requiring that the whole family adjust to a new system.

Working full-time was the biggest adjustment for me. Because I work at home, I thought that the kids could handle some time on their own after school as long as I was close by. The rules had been discussed: I would greet them after school, get them a snack, start them on their homework, then go back and work for two hours. It looked good on paper, but I forgot to figure in all the sports practices, after-school play dates, class projects, and long field trips. They would forget to tell me something, or need a question answered, and then there would be a knock on the door, interrupting an interview or a paragraph I had just started. On the days when the system did work and I emerged from my office at five-thirty, I'd hear that someone had written on someone else's school project (just to take a phone message) so the whole thing had to be redone. The kitchen would be a complete mess, nobody's homework was finished, and inevitably there were cookies that needed to be baked for a class party by morning.

I decided I had to hire someone. My attorney had already told me that, according to California law, Ron had to split the cost of work-related child care. When I called a few agencies in my area, I was shocked. With four children, the minimum hourly rate was fifteen dollars. If I expected the help to make dinner or to do housekeeping, that person would have to arrive at least one hour before the kids arrived, since the agency believed that it was too difficult to watch children and prepare food at the same time. When I mentioned Troy's disability, the rate immediately rose to twenty dollars per hour. I would also be responsible for paying household employee taxes. It seemed to be an impossible spiral. I would have to make at least $700 more per month in order to pay my half.

I felt stuck. I needed to make more money to support our family, but it seemed that the majority of the increase would go toward child care. I resented Ron's ability to work as long and hard as he wanted, visiting the kids after homework was done. I felt sorry for myself when I imagined his ability to make more money each year while I sat restricted by time and a sense of responsibility to the kids.

I interviewed many people, but I didn't hire anyone. Over the weeks of interviewing others, listing the tasks that needed to be done and describing what I expected, I decided that nobody was equipped to handle the chaos. I also discovered that I wasn't ready to trust someone else with the few hours I had with my kids each day. So I still don't have any help, and I still get frustrated when I have an article due and can't find the time to finish it. I still like to think that I can work in my office when I need to and that the kids will leave me alone. They still bother me, and I still don't like it.

But I do feel a sort of peace with my decision. I don't make as much money as I could. There are days when I wish I could leave the house at nine, have lunch with a co-worker, return home at six, and receive a dependable salary with health benefits. But on most days I remind myself that I like being the first person to greet my kids when they walk through the gate, that I enjoy hearing all the school gossip as they make their snacks, and that I like knowing all their friends who wander in between school and sports practices. I guess I've found a sort of balance between my career and my job as a mother that works most of the time.

"I've always worked," says Amy, "so the real responsibility for me was dealing with a baby. Now that Rebecca is eight, I realize that I spent so much time focusing on work and on her that I haven't had any time to think about me. How are my friendships doing? What are my hobbies? How am I growing as a person? I feel like my personal life has been cut off as I do everything just to keep my head above water.

"I want to leave the company I work for—I love the work, but it is so crazy. I'd love to have another child, but I've come to the realization that there is a high chance that I won't. I have regrets about the time and focus I've placed on work. I think that work has kept me from being where I ultimately wanted to be. It's kind of a bittersweet success. On the one hand, I have made a lot of money and have this incredible ability to live wherever I want to live and never work another day in my life. But that dedication cost me finding a fulfilling long-term relationship, and I missed a lot of Rebecca's childhood."

After the divorce many women find, as Stephanie did, that they have a new responsibility to manage the family's financial future. "My husband had done most of our financial planning," she says. "After the divorce I felt that it was now my responsibility to secure the family's financial future. When the shit hit the fan in my personal life, I decided to find a financial adviser. I didn't want to have to sell my house, but I was committed to going to law school and didn't want to be strapped to uncertain payments. I had enough uncertainty in my life already. It made me really angry that my husband didn't have to get the house ready to sell, he didn't have to move anything, and he got half the profit.

"When I met with the financial planner, she told me I really needed to think about retirement since I was in my forties. I felt so nervous, as she worked the numbers, about whether I would be able to afford a house at all. She told me exactly what to do. I had to sell my house, move out of the area, and buy a much

smaller and more affordable house. She used my projected income and my lack of income during law school and gave me a
road map to follow during my uncertain times. I have followed it
exactly, and it's been a source of stability for me. Knowing exactly where I stood financially helped me make the moves I
needed to secure my future. Had I tried to hold on to the house,
I would have exhausted all of my savings."

People Will Talk

Not only will people talk about you as you struggle to design a
life on your own, they will also judge your decisions. If a single
mother is making it on her own and looks successful and happy,
she may be perceived as a threat to family structure, encouraging other unhappily married women to consider divorce. If she
is struggling, missing the opportunity for a good job, or having
to move in with her boyfriend to make ends meet, then she is
selling herself and making poor decisions regarding her children. What I try to remember is that what people are really talking about is how society is changing and how threatened they
feel. There are more and more divorced families every year, and
as women pioneer new roles, as they design new life pictures,
people want to discuss what it all means and come to some conclusions.

My first experience being the center of this type of "community discussion" made me feel like packing up and moving out of
town. A friend came over and said under her breath, so the kids
wouldn't hear, "Were you arrested for drunk driving?" My heart
sank as I replied weakly, "Are you kidding? Where did you hear
that?" My friend told me about a rumor going around my children's school that a teacher had reported to her. I wondered
how I, of all people, could become the subject of anyone's conversation. I spent most of my days at home, with a social life that
I considered nonexistent.

Then I thought about every possible cause of such a lie. A
month before I was supposed to drive Brooke's class on a field
trip. Troy was sick with the flu, so at the last minute I called to

say I couldn't drive. I offered my station wagon to the teacher so she could drive. Maybe the other mothers thought I had lost my driver's license, as happens to anyone charged with drunk driving. Another thought was that the woman who bought our house might have started the rumor. I heard from a few people that she was angry about the way Ron had left the house after hosting a party the night before moving. I couldn't imagine that the house was left in such a mess that she would start a rumor for revenge.

My whole evening was ruined. I called my mom, my boyfriend, and a friend and told all of them the story. I felt an overwhelming urge not to live in a place where people would talk about me.

My next move was to tell my children about the rumor. I didn't want them to hear this lie from someone else. I started out by asking them if they knew what a rumor was. Rhett replied, "It's when someone says something that is not true about someone, like if I'm taking a vitamin C at lunch and someone says that I'm taking drugs." *Great,* I thought. *At least they know what I'm talking about.* "Well," I said, "I heard a rumor today that I'm very upset about." I told them the whole story, and thank goodness, they all started laughing. "But, Mom, you don't even drink!" I felt better—at least I had a small army of children ready to defend my honor!

I wondered if this rumor would have started if I were still married. Maybe people did talk about me when I was married, but at least I'd never heard anything. I felt vulnerable and sad. I imagined that somehow my single life was more visible for all to comment on, whether those comments were true or not.

"There was a little gossip, but not as much as I expected with Tom being a sort of public figure as a news anchorman," says Vickie. "People thought we had this perfect family. Everyone thought he was so charismatic and funny. People were surprised and curious, but nobody really pointed a finger. Before our divorce there was another divorce at the girls' school, and everyone felt so sorry for the little boy. I decided I wouldn't do that 'poor me' thing, and I didn't want anyone hugging my girls and feeling sorry for them. I did not want to be a victim. Whenever anyone asked what was happening, I'd answer, 'My husband thought it was okay to have a girlfriend, and I didn't.' I'm sure that started a few rumors, but deep down I wanted everyone to know that it wasn't my fault."

Organization Is Survival

I was talking to a neighbor recently who asked me how I find time to exercise. I told her I don't exercise alone. I do yoga in the middle of the living room with a few of my kids so we can talk about the day. I walk, water plants, and clean the car with at least one child at my side. We turn the music up loudly and dance while we do dishes together. I have my own pair of roller blades, and I recently learned to shoot a basketball so I can help Troy practice. Who needs to exercise anyway, with grocery shopping, retrieving laundry, leading classroom projects, and working all day? All I have to do is fifty sit-ups each night to have hit every muscle group!

What she really wanted to know was how I hold everything together. Not just the exercise, but getting my kids to all their practices, working, having a boyfriend, and all the other stuff. She told me that I make it all look so easy. I had to laugh. If only there were a camera in my bedroom as I fall into bed each night exhausted!

What I do have is incredible organizational skills developed out of necessity. I learned them from my mother as I watched her juggle six children while earning her college degree in art. For a single mother, organizational skills can be critical for survival. The great thing is that organizational skills are easy to learn. There are tons of books that offer various systems to help organize work, home, and personal activities.

In order to organize your life, you have to know what you want to do with your time. That usually means writing down goals of some sort. Each New Year's Eve I like to give myself a few hours to look back over the past year. I list every little thing I can remember about my year, using just one or two words. This reminds me that I really did get something done, and usually much more than I give myself credit for. Then I think about the upcoming year and decide on three big things I would like to accomplish, such as finishing the remodeling of the house, planting a rose garden, or writing a book proposal. Next, I make a list of all the other things I would like to do during the upcoming year. I then write my ten-year goals. That list helps me to remember that I have lots of time left in my life to dream. I also write down my short-term goals on a weekly basis, and I really enjoy checking things off my list as I go!

In order to turn a goal from your list into reality, you must have the ability to set boundaries, to say no, and to stick to your schedule. Once when a cousin was visiting from New Zealand for a month, I walked into my office and there was a letter on my computer screen addressed to her mother. I admit to reading a few lines—"I can't believe that Sheila is so busy that she has to make appointments with her own kids. I'll never be like that when I'm a mother." At first I felt guilty, but after thinking about it for a while, I still thought that making appointments with the kids was a good idea. Otherwise, my time seemed to evaporate before I'd spent it the way I wanted to.

I also try to stick to my daily schedule. If I plan to write from nine to twelve, then I sit down to write at nine. I don't finish the dishes or clean out the drawer with all the pencils sticking out or return phone calls. I just write. I find that there is so much housekeeping and child management to do that I could fill every hour of the day with chores. So occasionally we have a house that's messier than I would like because I have only thirty minutes a day allocated on my schedule for straightening up. Something has to give!

The idea is to devise a schedule that works for you and to use it to guide your time. If you are asked to do something and you can't fit it on your schedule, say no. A few ways to create time: delegate jobs that can be done by someone else, limit the number of after-school activities for each child, turn off the TV, and use your answering machine to screen calls.

"I have several calendars," says Vickie, "one for the kids, one for myself, and a work calendar. I try to look at my week on Sunday and look at the spots where I won't be available to take one of the girls to a scheduled event, sometimes because of work appointments but often because they have sports games or birthday parties that occur at the same time. I call other mothers and ask if they could help out. I do favors for people all the time, volunteering to pick up their kids, or take them home, or watch them after school. So when I need help, it is pretty easy to find.

"I've also changed my idea of what a clean and organized house is. I would rather spend time with the girls than cook dinner, so I order in pizza or buy precooked or frozen meals. I don't feel guilty about that anymore. I also have a laundry method that we've all gotten used to. I wash and dry the laundry then dump it onto the couch. It never gets folded; we all know where to find our clean clothes. Every so often I fold them, but it doesn't matter if I do because there are more important things in my life."

Single mothers like Bonnie, a mother of four, work hard to find creative solutions to organizing a house full of children. "I have to be at work by 8:00 A.M., so I have had to devise ways to get everyone out the door on time. I actually dress my twin babies the night before. I give them a bath, then put their clothes on, including their shoes. On weekends they wear pajamas. My other two girls dress themselves, make their own lunches, get their books together, and help me feed the babies. We are a well-tuned machine!"

Accepting their own limitations helps mothers like Brenda, a twenty-two-year-old accountant with a two-year-old son, understand that they can only do so much. "I recently threw away my 'to do' list because it always made me feel that I was behind schedule," she says. "I now have a 'done' list that I fill out each night where I briefly list the things I did. That way I go to sleep each night feeling good instead of feeling guilty."

Having a Social Life

I admit it—I brought it on myself by watching *Melrose Place*. As I watched those impeccable men and women living their perfectly sex-filled lives, I felt left out. My last attempt at a romantic night started with a bottle of red wine, a few minutes of heavy kissing, then ended abruptly when we heard the children start coughing, followed by the sound of feet stumbling into the living room. And finally that dreaded request: "Mom, there're monsters in my room. Please come and sleep with me." A quick good-bye, followed by, "Sorry. Maybe we can have dinner together next week." No chance of risking a kiss with an audience!

I woke up the next morning, lifted Troy's small leg off my stomach, and wrestled to repossess my nightgown, which was anchored under his body. I crawled over Rhett, who must have joined us sometime during the night because he was afraid to sleep in his room without Troy, and got out of bed feeling triumphant that nobody woke up. I looked in the mirror at a few new wrinkles I was sure I hadn't seen the day before, and I felt tired. After a two-minute shower I sat staring at a closet full of wonderful clothes and thought to myself, *Why even bother?* Whatever I put on would be stained by jellied hands, dirtied with mud from a ball mistakenly thrown at my feet, or colored with paint from a picture thrust at me after school. I passed my makeup table without stopping. I could slop on some blush, dab some color on my lips, and brush on mascara so I appeared to actually have eyes, but why? By nine o'clock everything would be smeared from kisses and grimy little hands massaging my face.

I stumbled into the kitchen, turning the teapot on before driving the mile down the road to pick up Wesley from swim practice. By the time I returned with Wesley, everyone was up. Troy was in the kitchen, trying to pour waffle batter onto a cold waffle iron. Rhett was finishing a fairy tale that was due that day, and Brooke was yelling at the mirror because the ponytail she was trying to create kept having bumps in it. I was clearing the kitchen counter so I could start the lunch orders when I caught a glimpse of the empty red wine bottle and was reminded of the previous night's frustration. It seemed impossible that romance would ever have a place in my life again. This was one area in which I was not on my own—I was one plus four.

There are many fun options for social interaction. "I have such little time in my schedule for a social life, I'm sure not going to wait around for a man to call and ask me out," says Dawn, a forty-year-old secretary. "I go out with girlfriends. Sometimes we go dancing; sometimes we just go to the local bar and have a drink. In the beginning it was hard because I didn't have any close girlfriends, but I decided to really make an effort in that area. Now if I want a date on a Saturday night, I have lots of friends to choose from. Men are overrated as far as fun goes. Not that I don't want one in my life sometime. I just refuse to let my life pass me by waiting."

"I joined a coed volleyball team last winter," says Haley, a forty-three-year-old attorney. "It was so much fun. I haven't played any sport since high school, but one of my neighbors told me about the sign-ups and encouraged me to be on their team. I thought that it would be all couples, but there were a few single people. The team was organized by our community, which mostly consists of families. I wasn't great in the beginning, but I did improve over time, and I think the kids had a good time coming to the games to watch and to play with my team members' kids. I made many new friends and had something to do on Friday nights that involved other adults."

"I joined a dating service," says Anne. "None of my friends know that I did this because it sounds pretty stupid, but I really wanted to meet some new people and go out on dates. I received fifteen calls the first week my ad was in the paper. It was fun to write a description of myself and then be able to describe the type of man I was interested in. I hadn't really thought about it, so having to condense my dream man into a few lines took days.

"The good thing about the personal ads is that you don't have to go out to bars or other public places and try to attract perfect strangers. It's also nice to be able to list your life situation up front so there isn't any confessing to do on the first date. They already know you have kids. Some of my dates were boring, and I couldn't wait to get home. Other dates were really fun, and I've continued to see a few of the men."

Make Time for Family Fun

With all the business of reorganization, new responsibilities, and new expectations, it's important to reconnect as a family in fun ways. If life becomes all work and no play, your kids will hate being at home! Creating a home environment that my kids considered fun gave me a sense of accomplishment when the rest of my life seemed to be out of my control.

I looked for ways to incorporate inexpensive family entertainment into everyday life. When our family moved into our friend's studio apartment, we had no cable connection, so we had no television. The kids hated it. I loved it. I never had time to watch TV anyway, and it was nice to watch the kids choose other activities or be forced to interact with each other!

It truly amazed me how much time we had when the communal box was unavailable. I felt relieved when I would come home to see children playing cards at the kitchen table, with new clay projects drying on the windowsill or homemade holiday decorations taped to the wall above our couch. Anything was better than walking in and seeing four heads staring at a box. I still believe that you can't be tempted by what isn't available! We made clay beads, learned how to macramé friendship bracelets, made up plays, learned a little sign language, improved our drawing skills, and played outside. Every once in a while I'd hear them say there was nothing to do, but it didn't last too long.

Sharing common interests helps family relationships to blossom, as Martha and Karen found out. "Our family used to go camping quite a bit together," says Martha. "When Karen and I went by ourselves, it was a little challenging at first. We took our kayak, which is a sport we both love, our camping gear, and the dog and headed toward a national park with redwoods and a running river. We clumsily set up camp, trying to figure out how the tent poles fit through the loops. That had always been Chuck and Chad's job. When it was time for dinner, the camping stove we brought didn't work, so we had to rely on the campfire. I guess all my years of Boy Scouts with Chad helped, because we actually had a working fire for every meal. We had a blast! It was so much fun that the next time we went camping we decided not to bring a stove at all. Well, we couldn't light a thing and ended up eating in restaurants the entire time."

I experienced a major shift in our family entertainment. The kids still had a chance to go on vacation, take ski trips, and enjoy times with their father that were similar to our predivorce excursions. I would hear about their trip to the Olympics, the Final

Four basketball tournament, or the limousine ride on someone's birthday and feel like the life I offered was so boring in comparison. They would often come home from a visit and ask me why we never did anything fun, or why I never took them on a vacation. I missed having vacation time with them, and I resented Ron's ability to be larger than life in their eyes—the father extraordinaire!

Over time, however, we all seemed to settle into a more everyday sort of entertainment. Sleeping on the trampoline, going on moon walks, and cooking marshmallows around the fire pit became a tradition that the kids could depend on. In the wintertime we had game night, movie night, and bowling. Throughout the year I encouraged the kids to invite friends over, to have slumber parties, or to plan dances in our garage. When I bought an old drum set and we moved the keyboard into the garage, the idea of a band was born. When Halloween rolled around, we constructed a haunted house together on the front porch. I encouraged the children to design their own bedrooms, to pick a new paint color (and to paint it themselves), and to work within a budget to create the space they wanted.

I began to see that they were no longer comparing the kind of fun I was orchestrating with their father's fabulous trips, but appreciating it for what it was—a way of daily living. I had achieved what I wanted: a family that could play together.

....

ELEVEN

Feeling Good

If it is true that you never stop being a single mother, that it becomes a lifestyle, then learning to feel good even amid the chaos
might be your most valuable learned skill. Everyone I knew gave
me the same advice: "You do too much. You have to get more
balance in your life and learn to rest more, to have more fun."
Easy for them to say! To me balance was a question of whether I
could make a salad, correct the homework, and get ready for a
school meeting all at the same time. I didn't have time for fun.
Feeling good, I thought, *what a concept.*

It was only after I had weathered the most difficult years of
the divorce and moved away from survival mode that I could
see how out of balance my life was. How easily I would say yes
to the kids—a ride here, a ride there, sure I'll help choreo-
graph that dance, of course I can chaperone the field trip—but
I rarely said yes to myself. I didn't sit down to read a novel. I
made no time for exercise. I rarely went out with friends, and I
hadn't taken an art class for five years. The ridiculous thing
was that I was the one who was creating these rules. I was the
one who believed I didn't have enough time or energy to take
care of myself.

Then one day a friend who was sick of hearing me complain

suggested that I make a time wheel representing one day's worth of my activities. She wanted me to see where I was wasting time. I made the wheel by drawing a circle and putting 8:00 A.M. at the top of the circle. Then I made twenty-three notches around the circle so that I could draw pie shapes to represent my hourly activities. When I looked at the finished wheel, I resented my children even more. My complaints were warranted—only thirty minutes on that daily time wheel really belonged to me.

I stared at the wheel for days, trying to figure out places where I could make more time to enjoy my life. This wheel painted a perfect picture of how out of balance my life was. I started thinking about my motivation. Somewhere along my life journey I had begun to believe that the most important daily measurement of my life was how much I could get done. My "to do" list never got shorter, but I was unwilling to lower my expectations and simply enjoy some of my time. I was the one who made my own schedule, yet I was harder on myself than any boss would have dared to be.

I decided to make a new wheel. I called it my "dream wheel." I made it exactly as I wished my life looked. There were even unscheduled time slots available for me to choose what I wanted to do. The hardest part was to determine what I wanted to fill the unscheduled spaces with! Everything I listed seemed frivolous, without direction, purpose, or goal. I looked at my dream wheel for another few weeks, afraid to fill in the blanks, not wanting to commit to something that I couldn't carry out. In the end I discovered that the problem was not that I lacked time, but rather that I hadn't decided whether I deserved to enjoy my life.

I began to look at the areas in my life I had shut down in order to conserve energy and make time for the divorce. Physically, I had stopped exercising. Emotionally, being consumed with ending my marriage and healing my pain had left minimal space for new relationships. I had little energy to learn anything new, so I was also mentally unchallenged. In my spiritual life I'd been riding a love-hate roller coaster with my soul. *Balance* . . . I kept focusing on that word. I tried to remember daily that I wanted to feel good, that I wanted to feel whole.

Feeling Good Physically

Two weeks after my first child, Wesley, was born, I was back taking my weekly dance classes. Wesley would sleep in her baby carriage, no matter how loud the music played, as my classmates (between leaps across the floor) commented admiringly on her good disposition. By the time Brooke arrived fifteen months later, I could no longer make my dance classes and had shifted instead to a health club that provided child care. The health club's policies allowed me to leave the girls for only two hours at a time, and some days I skipped exercise class altogether just to sit in the sauna or whirlpool, do my nails, write letters—anything just to have those two hours of peace. When Rhett arrived two years later, I was lucky to find fifteen minutes to prance around the living room while watching an aerobics tape on TV. Along with Troy's birth came the end of my regular exercise attempts.

Troy is nine years old as I write this, and I still haven't been able to get into the swing of a regular routine. Mothering is an exhausting job with little free time to engage in "frivolous" activity (like exercise), I told myself! This steady decline in the attention I pay to my physical well-being and health has become a pattern in my life as I continue to put the needs of my kids and my family first. I am still struggling with how to fit everything into each day. For example, this morning I promised myself that I would do yoga for at least thirty minutes before I started to write. But then I walked into my office, looked at the clock, and started to panic. If I chose yoga, I knew I wouldn't get everything done. So here I sit typing away, neglecting my physical self once again. Physical renewal has not been one of the more successful areas in my life!

Luckily, a few months ago I came up with an exercise routine that I think will work for me. I had been reflecting about all the times when I started something only to quit a few weeks later, feeling like a failure. Doing the same exercise over and over again bores me, especially exercises like jogging, which, although healthy, is one of my least favorite activities. So I made a simple agreement with myself. Each day I will do thirty minutes of some type of exercise, but I'll reserve the time simply as "exercise," without deciding ahead of time what I'm going to do. One day I run. The next day I walk or hike. On the third day I ride my bike, or whatever else I feel like that day.

Over time I've extended the idea to include less strenuous activities like gardening, yoga, dancing to the radio, jumping on our trampoline, shooting basketballs, even roller-blading with my kids. This plan has been much easier for me to stick to. I don't get the benefit of developing runner's legs or a biker's buttocks, but at least I'm doing something—and that's a start. I notice that on the days when I stick to this agreement with myself I feel less stress and more of a sense of accomplishment for having taken time out to improve my health.

"After the divorce I decided to take up swimming again," says Lucy, a forty-six-year-old fashion designer with two teenagers. "I was a great swimmer as a kid and had so many fond memories of summer swim team, but I stopped swimming when I didn't make the high school team. I guess I never went back to it. When I was feeling down after the divorce, a childhood friend of mine happened to be in town on business. We went out to dinner, and he started telling all sorts of funny stories about swim team, things I had forgotten. It felt so good to laugh. I remembered writing the team's name all over my body with permanent Magic Markers, forgetting that our eighth-grade graduation ceremony was just days away. My dress was sleeveless. I tried everything, including nail polish remover, to get the marker off my body, but the best I could do was to lighten it. When I walked up the aisle to get my award, the swim team kids, who were younger than I, started clapping and chanting. I was so embarrassed, but at the same time it was fun.

"While we talked that night, I had silently promised myself to visit the pool. I still lived in the same area, so it was easy to drive by one day after work. I couldn't believe how many adults were in the water. They told me about the masters program, and I started immediately. You know, there was actually a woman there who was on my team when I was young. We weren't good friends then, but now that I've been swimming three times a week for five years we are like sisters. The physical activity and the people involved gave me something to look forward to. It gave me a way to rebuild myself in a form that I had control over. It brought back memories of a time in my life when I knew how to play. I really think that finding swimming again helped me more than anything else in getting through the divorce."

"One thing I did physically that helped me reclaim who I used to be," says Chelsea, a fifty-two-year-old professional, "was to give away all the clothes I had that reminded me of my husband. When we met, I dressed with what many called a creative flair. I didn't follow the fashion of the day; I used my clothes as an expression of myself. I even designed my own outfits, picking fabric in colors that I loved. I didn't care if I looked like magazine models or anybody else for that matter. I was also creative with my hair, which is long. I would wear my hair a different way each day.

"After we had dated for a while, Brad started telling me that I had no style. He'd say that I was so pretty but could look much more professional in more subdued colors. I wanted to impress him, so I started wearing browns, blacks, tan, and gray. I looked the same as every woman I passed on the street. I started wearing my hair shoulder length and parted on the side. He said I looked classy. The problem was that I didn't care whether I looked classy, I wanted to look like me, and I was much happier dressing like me.

"We were married for twelve years. After the divorce my sister was visiting from Seattle, and she started talking about how much she used to envy my sense of style and expression when we were younger. Something clicked in my mind, and we did the craziest thing—we went through my closet together and laughed, yelled, cried, and in a way ritualized the end of his presence in my life. It was very freeing. Now I dress like me."

As much as we would all like to believe that beauty is on the inside and that the physical body doesn't matter, we all know that isn't reality. So much of what we believe to be true about ourselves as women in this society comes from media images. When paging through magazines, I often chuckle to myself imagining the sleek model transformed into a mother, with one child holding on to her leg, one in her arms, and one tugging at her hand. I'm sure her hair would not be blowing carelessly in the wind, she wouldn't dare to wear that $500 outfit for fear of drool, and her breasts would no longer be so perky!

Work with what you have. I've watched too many of my friends declare that they won't go on a date until they lose twenty-five pounds. Three years later they still haven't been out to dinner with a man. Not that getting a man back in your life is the goal—it's just an example of the barriers that many women set up that make them feel not good enough.

I've interviewed many men on the topic of sexual attraction, and they aren't as critical of women as we are of ourselves. Most say that a woman's attitude about her body is most important. If she gets out of bed after making love and can't move without covering everything up, or talks endlessly about the stretch marks on her breasts, then the man will notice. But if she walks around like a goddess communicating, "Hey, this is it, and I'm comfortable with it," a man doesn't notice the extra weight. He's too busy thinking, "This is going to be fun!"

Make a daily effort to have a good attitude about your appearance, even if you don't like the way you look right now. Don't make the mistake of putting your life on hold while you "self-improve." Last piece of advice—throw away all fashion magazines!

Feeling Good Emotionally

When I was married, I didn't spend time developing friendships outside the marriage. I was busy with the kids and believed that my husband was also supposed to be my best friend. During the healing time after my divorce, however, the women in my life became very important. I valued the new conversations I started having that didn't relate to children or men but to me as a person. My friends helped me rediscover the fun parts within myself that I had lost, simply by giving me a place to be fully myself, with no fear of being judged.

I also found that my emotional healing came in waves: some days I couldn't name one good thing in my life, and other days I seemed to dance with promise. It felt safe with my new friends and in my single mother support group to talk about the emotional roller coaster I was riding. Sometimes I was afraid to express my true feelings, thinking that no one would understand or that my friends would jointly decide that I'd lost my mind. But something inside told me that I had to keep talking, that it was important to clear my heart and my mind. Some simple things helped on those low emotional days, like inspiring music or books on tape, which gave me something to look forward to while spending time in the car as a shuttle service.

I had spent many hours in therapy before my divorce, so I felt I had a base of experiences to draw from. I remembered the reason I initially visited a therapist: I wanted someone with whom I could work through the issue of whether to have my tubes tied. I knew I didn't want more children, but I was only thirty years old and the procedure scared me. I thought that one or two therapy sessions would help me to work through my feelings surrounding the issue. Four months later I was still sitting through tearful sessions mourning the fact that I'd never nurse another baby.

What surprised me the most was how much healing was needed before I could make what I thought was a simple decision. At the end of the four months I did decide to have the surgery, but instead of going through all the feelings after the fact, as many women do, I had worked through them before and was comfortable with my choice. I knew from this experience how long it took me to reach peace and wholeness on that one emotional issue. I knew I still had many things I had to let go of. So I expected that my emotional healing would take longer than my physical, mental, or spiritual healing.

What I had missed most in my marriage was the feeling of emotional connection with a person who understands and relates to what you say. It seemed that the longer the marriage went on without this connection, the less connected I felt to my own feelings. The only place where I practiced sharing my thoughts was in my journal. The experience of connecting, of feeling heard, and of hearing others put me back on the track to feeling good emotionally. Shared dinners, morning hikes, yoga classes, concerts, and telephone calls from friends reminded me that I had much to look forward to in my life. I found great pleasure in relating to others.

My children inspired me as I devoted myself to helping them find success in their lives. I learned a tremendous amount through Troy's therapy that I was able to apply to everyone—

most important, the significance of creating fun in your life. I spent time watching each of my kids to discover their special interests and the activities they were good at. Much of my own healing energy came when I took time to do things I liked and was good at, like painting, design work, and gardening. I wanted to encourage my kids to find that same protected space so that when life felt too hard they would know how to engage in something that felt good. For Wesley it was swimming, for Brooke drama and dance, for Rhett drums, and for Troy crafts and bouncing on our trampoline.

Children have the same need as their mothers to move toward wholeness after divorce. The issues may be different, but the children's world has been torn down, and they also need to build themselves back up. Their lives feel different, and sometimes life feels empty. These interests gave my kids something of their own to fall back on, something to fill the space in their lives that was created by the divorce.

Part of emotional healing is the ability to put things into perspective. "I think in images a lot when I get into a difficult emotional space," says Hannah. "I think there is a tapestry that you weave when you live with someone. You weave it together, and it is your life. When you separate from each other, you have to undo all of that, and it takes a long time. When you leave abruptly, there is no resolution. It is like someone taking a scissors and cutting the tapestry in half instead of taking the time to unravel it one row at a time.

"It's been years since my divorce, and I feel great in so many ways. I have a love relationship that is a true partnership, I'm doing work that is also my passion, and my son is healing from his drug use and will be coming back to live with me any month. Yet I find that sometimes I feel terribly sad. It hits me from out of the blue—which is when I use my image of the tapestry. I try to visualize myself moving the threads, unraveling instead of making my grip tighter. I try to go with the process and realize that it took a long time to create my married life and that no matter how great I feel there are still parts that are unraveling."

Recovering from an abusive relationship can be an incredible drain on a person's emotional energy, as Martha found out. "We had lived together eleven years before we were married; I was only fifteen when we met," she says. "I feel like I'm starting out for myself for the first time in my life, and I'm in my forties. I went straight from my parents' home to living with Chuck. Neither one of us went to college but instead worked in the family business together for the length of our marriage. The business did become successful, and we were able to buy a home in a very nice area.

"I know now that we could have done better if both of us had been emotionally healthy. We both had issues from our childhood that kept tripping us. I was dealing with my issues then in therapy, and I'm still in therapy working through them today. You have to go back and turn over every rock, then find a way to get to the other side. In all those years of working side by side with Chuck I hadn't realized how incompetent he made me out to be. When I decided that I had to find another job, I was terrified because I believed that I had to be perfect, that I couldn't make any mistakes or they would fire me. Chuck would get furious if I ever made a mistake.

"The first job I took was part-time as a church receptionist, which I got from a friend. This was great because it put me back into the work environment, and I found out it could be fun. I decided on a part-time job because I wasn't emotionally ready for a full-time commitment. I still wanted to be around after school for Karen. About six months after that job started Karen told me she wasn't afraid to be alone after school anymore, so we talked about my working full-time.

"I now have a full-time job in an attorney's office. This isn't work that I can put my heart and soul into, but it is helping me to heal emotionally. I have found out that I am amazingly competent, that I have a lot to contribute, and that I can do anything I put my mind to. I'm learning about the person who disappeared because she was afraid. I still have many issues to work on, but I like who I am now, which allows me to interact with the world in a much healthier way."

Feeling Good Mentally

I have a younger sister who is an attorney. When she calls me, her energy is infectious. She talks about the fabulous books she's read, always recommending at least three that I have to read immediately. I ask her to talk about what she learned from the books, because I know that I won't get around to reading them. It's so much fun to talk to another adult who has information to share. As a full-time writer, I don't work in an office or with other adults. I'm alone most of the time, just thinking up ideas. Whenever I receive an article assignment for a magazine, I look forward to researching the topic and learning new information. In the beginning of my divorce I had little creative energy to write and no inclination to learn new things. As each piece of the divorce is completed, my brain recovers space for learning.

My newest idea is to learn to play the drums. Rhett and Troy started drum lessons a few months ago, so I've had a chance to sit through lessons and to watch them practice. I asked Rhett if he would mind teaching me whatever he learns. I would never have imagined myself enjoying this instrument, but after pounding on our drums to music from a CD player, it's like spending a few hours in therapy. Maybe it's because for a few minutes I am letting myself explore a new creative space, free from my everyday thought patterns.

I also read a lot about herbs and their uses. One of my goals is to plant a huge herb garden, to learn the medicinal effects of each plant, and to be able to use them in everyday life. I recently joined a women's finance club so that I can learn about investing. We meet once a month and discuss what we've researched that month. Everyone has an assignment and is required to come prepared to present the information to the group. I've found that this group forces me to learn what I intended to learn anyway.

The great thing about classes or groups is that you are accountable to someone for what you learn. Recently I also attended a seminar on improving memory. I was inspired when I realized that my memory is bad for a reason—I never work on it. With the little time I have left each day to learn new things I might be a grandma before I can carry out some of my goals!

What matters most to me is the energy I get just from thinking about what I want to learn and the fact that I feel alive enough to take in more information.

For most single mothers the one thing they can count on for mental stimulation is the career they choose. The time following a divorce may be the opportunity to train for a new career. Many of my single mother friends went back to school. A few asked the judge if they could have career counseling so they could pick a job that would make them the kind of money they needed to support their kids.

My friend Sonja was working as a real estate agent when she decided that she just didn't want to do it anymore. Her new plan will require living with her mother for a few more years and taking out loans to pay for school and living expenses, but she is glowing with excitement. She is going to the Culinary Institute in San Francisco, where she is studying to be a chef. At first I was surprised at her decision, because I know how little child support she gets and what an effort it will take for her to start over in a new career. But I admire her clarity of direction and her determination to choose a career that she will enjoy.

"My time of mental stimulation comes each night before I go to sleep," says Pam, a thirty-five-year-old broker with two young boys. "I can't tell you what a relief it is to crawl into bed alone to read a great book. For so many years the bedroom was full of such conflict and struggle. We'd fight after dinner. I'd do the best I could to get the kids in bed early so that I could hide in our room and try to find some peace. Then he would come in and want to make love, thinking it would make everything better. It got to the point where I would hear his footsteps approaching the door and I'd feel resentful that I couldn't have that time to myself that I thought I'd created by working so hard to get the kids in bed.

"Now I go to bed with piles of books on every subject from teaching kids manners, finance, gardening, home design, even a few steamy love novels. It's really the only time I have to myself each day, and I use it to learn new information or experience the fantasy world created in a novel. I've decided that if I ever do get married again, I want to have separate bedrooms so that we can make love if we want but also go back to our own beds and leave the light on all night if we choose."

Sometimes going back to school creates the needed intellectual stimulation, as Janet found out when she went back to school to study web page design. "When I was in high school," she says, "we didn't even have computers. During our court hearing the judge ordered that I go to career counseling since I'd been out of the workforce raising our three daughters for twenty years. My analysis came back saying that I needed to do something creative and challenging. I met with a career counselor, and we talked about job availability. I thought it was useless to get a degree in something I couldn't use. Through a process of elimination and after a few informational interviews with people in the professions I was considering, I decided on web design.

"Being back in school has recharged me. It gives me a place to put my mental energy that is positive and growth-oriented. I don't have time to sit around and moan about the divorce and all the problems it has caused me. Instead, I've chosen to get out there and start again. It's been fun and terrifying at the same time."

Feeling Good Spiritually

I was delighted by my interviews with single mothers on the broad, wide-ranging subject of spirituality. The many ways in which these women defined spirit and soul, and how to connect the two, were as unique and different as each woman's face. One common description of feeling good in your soul was the ability first to identify, then to listen to, and finally to follow some sort of internal voice. Some women called their internal voice God or Jesus. Others called it the universal consciousness. Still others labeled it intuition. It was always about connecting to an unseen, unprovable source of inspiration or direction.

I once read a fairy tale about a young girl who lived with a wicked stepmother and two stepsisters. The stepmother and sisters wanted the girl to die, so they told her the fire in their home had gone out. They ordered her to go out into the scary woods, to find an old witch, and to bring fire back to the home to relight the hearth. The girl did as she was told, and the stepmother and stepsisters rejoiced, thinking that the witch who lived in the forest would kill her and they'd never see her again. The girl had in her pocket a small doll that her real mother had given her. She asked the doll which direction to go, and at each turn the doll's small voice led her in the right direction. She found the witch, brought fire back home, and the wicked mother and sisters died when she returned.

The doll in this story represents a woman's intuition. We all have that small voice directing us if we stop to pay attention to what it calls us to do. We really do know what is best for our children. We know what direction we need to take in our careers. We know whether a love relationship is healthy. We just have to ask and wait for the answer. And sometimes the waiting takes a while. During my marriage the loss of soul in my life started when I stopped listening to my intuition. I knew the answers to my questions, but I didn't want to hear them. I had determined my direction and didn't want to stray from the path. That was the first step of Spirit separation for me—if I couldn't hear my own voice, how could I hear anyone else's? Once I started trusting that voice, my soul started revealing itself again.

"While I was going through the divorce process, a friend told me about her spiritual director," says Carol, a forty-eight-year-old editor with three children. "My friend said she read about it somewhere, then called a local church and asked if they knew anything about spiritual directors. They gave her a phone number to call. She went in for an interview to talk about where she was in her life. The interviewer listened, then gave her four names of spiritual directors she might want to call to see if any of them were a good fit.

"I ended up going through the same process and found a spiritual director. I was fairly religious during my life leading up to my divorce. I continued to go to church even though my husband wasn't really interested in devoting his Sunday mornings to anything but sports. The real reason I wanted a spiritual director was to ask her questions, to find out what to do when you feel like you've lost your faith. At first I thought I better show up and act like I still had a spiritual life or maybe I wouldn't be acceptable. But I decided to tell the truth. I sat down at the first meeting, and when she asked me where I was with God, I had to say, 'I don't know.' Then she asked where I wanted to be, and I said, 'There was a time when Jesus was alive in my life, but he is gone now.'

"We've worked together for a few years now, and I have developed a different relationship with Jesus than the one I remembered as a child. My director has helped me to see that this God relationship is a daily part of my life, that prayers can be ten seconds while I drive my car, that in offering kindness to my kids or other people I am teaching them about Jesus. I now believe that every person is made of many parts, and spirituality is one of them. I'm very pleased that I've decided to put time into discovering that part of myself."

"Last year I joined a shamanism group," says Ingrid, a forty-year-old receptionist with a ten-year-old son. "I didn't really know much about it, but the flyer I read sounded interesting and fun. I still go to my church, so it isn't like I expect shamanism to be a new religion for me, but I've always been drawn to Native American ways.

"In the group we've done creative projects. We made masks, then decorated them to symbolize the person we were working toward becoming. We made prayer sticks in silence as we contemplated what we were asking for, then we left our sticks out in the wilderness where we would never see them again. We've made pouches where we put pieces of plants, rocks, and other small things that are important to us. We bring our drums and make music together. Sometimes we chant or take a journey into our thoughts. I'm learning about my world in a different way, which is actually expanding my spiritual base. Instead of thinking that God is only in a church or can only be found through my traditional religious background, I've found that God is alive in many cultures and there are many ways to express the same divine spirit."

Throughout my life I had grouped spirituality with religion, feeling confined to a certain set of church ideas and rules. When I realized that I could find spiritual expression in beating a drum, painting a picture, cooking a meal, playing a game, or singing a song, I finally understood the divine presence in all things. What distinguished an ordinary experience from a spiritual one was how present I was in the moment. Playing a game of checkers had often bored me in the past. But when I started looking at my son's face as he tried to figure out his next move and let myself relax in that moment instead of thinking about everything else I wanted to accomplish that night, I felt the presence of Spirit within me.

I stopped praying years ago when I decided that God wasn't listening. My prayers were about what I needed and wanted. They were words. I've learned many other ways to pray since then. Sometimes being silent for five minutes and allowing the sound, movement, and action around me to sink into my body becomes my prayer. I simply say, "I'm listening, God." Other times I can be gardening and feel such gratitude for life that I unconsciously start saying, "Thank you for the dirt, for my hands, for the wind, for everything I can name." When I feel unable to focus, I play a Gregorian chant CD, and after a few songs I feel transported to another space.

Through these experiences I learned something I must have missed in my religious upbringing—the purpose of going to church is to be in a place where your mind is open to the divine. God is not contained in any building; God is in everything, so She can be found everywhere. Spirit is alive in everyone whether they have experienced religion in their life or not. It doesn't matter what religion people belong to or belief system they espouse, as long as they can find a way to experience the divine in their lives.

We are not just mothers who are destined to spend all of our waking moments feeding children, caring for a house, and playing taxi driver. We are not just career women who have financial obligations to fulfill. We are complete human beings who need to have places and times in our lives that make us laugh, that make us feel good, and that help us to grow. We orchestrate such places and times for our children, yet we set our own desires aside at the drop of a hat.

I was moaning recently to my mother about all the kids' appointments written on the huge calendar taped to our refrigerator.

She repeated what she has said for years: "It doesn't matter how much you do for them; they will still ask for more. It is your job to set the limits." It must be easier to be a grandma because you don't have to hear the disappointment or argue your case after a hard day at work! But I know that she is right. It's really true in everything: people will take as much as you're willing to give.

That means you have to take time for yourself. If you want to feel good physically, then decide what that means for you. Maybe you need to talk with family members and friends about the possibility of one weekend of free babysitting each year. You may want to make room in the family budget for a dance class, or maybe you just need to adjust the family schedule so that you can get to bed an hour earlier.

You can feel good emotionally by developing new friendships, starting a new romance, or joining a support group. Perhaps work is an emotional drain because you hate what you are doing so it's time to look at a career change.

Mental stimulation is difficult when you are surrounded by children and have no time to read or engage in formal learning. But maybe mental stimulation is as close as reading a magazine article each week on a topic you know nothing about, or visiting a chat room online.

Search your heart in silence, and you may find a piece of your spirit that you thought you had lost. In every area of life it takes a certain amount of introspection to determine what makes you feel good, what is interesting, what is fun. Once you know, make a pact with yourself to do something about it.

TWELVE

New Romance

When I divorced, I knew I wouldn't be alone forever. I had been devastated by love but was still willing to try again. Not every woman I spoke with, however, felt the same way. Joanne, whose husband left her after twenty years of marriage, was terrified to date again. She couldn't imagine making love with a man (or wanting to). Her confidence was destroyed as she watched her husband escape his life as the father of four children to travel the world with a twenty-five-year-old. Rebecca's husband physically abused her. She swears it will take years before she will be able to trust a man. On the other hand, some women had felt so alone before their divorce that they couldn't wait to establish an intimate relationship afterward.

However you feel about dating, be true to what you feel. It takes time to heal. It's also important to be aware of your reasons for choosing to be alone. If you find that your need to heal is becoming an excuse to eat or drink constantly, disengage from human interaction, or let yourself fall apart physically, you might consider getting professional help or giving yourself a time limit to mourn your loss. Tell a friend about your plan to move forward in your life in however many weeks or months, so you can get the support you need to get on with your life when the time comes. When your time limit to mourn is up, challenge yourself to go on one date or to improve yourself in some way.

There are many emotional traumas involved when you lose your partner even if you're the one who left. Every woman I know has been affected differently, but each has this in common: you need time to pull yourself together and feel the best you can before feeling secure enough to face the dating world. So how do you do it? How do you pull yourself together when your life feels raw?

You do it one step at a time, making sure not to overcommit yourself. "I wake up half an hour earlier each morning," says Sandy, a thirty-four-year-old manager, "so I can write in my journal before the kids wake. It's a safe place to put my hopes and dreams. Nobody will ever read it, so I write all sorts of things. I've written steamy love scenes that I want to create when I find a man I want to share my bed with. I've made a list of all the qualities I'm looking for in a new relationship. Sometimes I even write positive things about myself in areas where I feel like I need encouragement. My husband was pretty negative about my breasts after I had the kids, so I write over and over, 'My breasts are perfect just the way they are!'

"Thoughts come out in my writing that I didn't even know I had. There was a man at the grocery store that I was attracted to, and he seemed to be attracted to me, but I didn't have the courage to speak to him. I wrote about those feelings and decided to be braver the next time a similar situation occurs."

"I asked a friend to come over and rummage through my closet with me," says Janet, "in the hopes of putting a new wardrobe together. We spent the afternoon trying on clothes and making a list of outfits that went well together. At the same time she made a list of the clothes I needed to purchase in order to add a new look to my old outfits. This closet clean-out was something I had been thinking about for a long time but couldn't find the motivation to do. Having a scheduled date with a friend made it happen. A week later we did the same with her closet."

"I hike each morning," says Julia, a forty-one-year-old retail worker, "feeling heavy as I carry my burdens to the top of the hill. At the top I have a personal ceremony leaving my troubles behind." Some women cut their hair and change their style completely. Others go on diets or start exercise routines. Reading can be very helpful. One mother started jogging with her daughter—they use that time to talk about how they're each feeling about the change in their lives. I do yoga a few times a week and use that time to think up ideas to write about the next day. I also put together a five-minute makeup routine. I threw away all the makeup I never use and put the essentials for my five-minute routine in a handy basket. Even if I'm just driving the kids to school I put on my five-minute face. It makes me feel better about myself.

Often feeling good about yourself involves a change in attitude. We can't change ourselves back to the young woman we were before we had children, we can't change the fact that we have children who need us, we can't add hours to our day, and we can't change the damage done in our lives by the divorce. What we do have control over is how we feel about ourselves.

Part of the good news about starting over with a new person is that you get to decide who you will be in the new relationship. I don't mean that you act like someone you aren't; it just seems that most of us have grown more aware since our previous relationship, and you have better tools to bring to a new romance. Most men you meet won't know anything about you. Think of yourself as a character in a book that you're writing, and remember: this is a *new story,* and it can be anything you want it to be.

Meeting Someone

No matter how long you've been married, it's been a while since you've been in touch with the dating scene. You're a mom with kids—not exactly the "singles club" type—so how is it possible to meet an attractive, available, interesting man while driving the carpool to school? I admit it is more difficult to start a new romance when you have children to care for, a home to keep up, and most likely a new career. It *does* take a little effort, you *do* have to leave the house, and you *do* have to feel ready for a relationship of some sort—even if it's just dinner out once a month. It's also perfectly normal not to feel ready to have even a short conversation with a man. Don't push yourself. When you're ready, you'll know it.

"I joined a single parents group at our local church and have met many interesting people," says Janis. "Nobody has struck a romantic fancy, but I sure appreciate having a social outing to attend on weekends. We arrange events throughout the week, like a movie, dinner out, or meeting at a bar to listen to music. Whoever wants to attend just shows up, and we enjoy our time as a group. I have gone on a few dates with men in the group, and I find it's easier going out romantically with someone I already have gotten to know casually."

You could ask some of your friends to set you up with people they know. Just make sure you're clear with them about the type of person you're interested in. Sometimes even a friend will think you'll go out with anyone just to get out! "I've been on one blind date," says Sue, a forty-seven-year-old engineer, "with the brother of a neighbor. The way she talked about him, I expected this outgoing, athletic person who dripped with charm. He didn't say ten words over dinner, looked like he hadn't done a sit-up since his college days, and had almost no interest in socializing. When I asked my friend how she thought we would make a good pair, she said she just wanted me to get out of the house!"

A personal ad might be a good place to start if you have little time in your day for social interaction. At least you get a chance to write down the type of person you're looking for, so you are less likely to waste time with an uninteresting man you have nothing in common with when you could be relaxing in the bath at home. When you decide to look at the personal ads for the first time, promise yourself that you won't get discouraged when reading the men's ads. They usually start with: "Wanted, 25-year-old, beautiful woman with perfect body." No one like that exists, so sooner or later they get more realistic!

Romance is out there, and I found it where I least expected it. One day in February 1996 my then nine-year-old daughter Brooke brought home a flyer announcing auditions for *The Music Man,* the town musical. To my relief, all the children who auditioned were given a part. The idea of one nine-year-old being good enough but not another always seemed a bit brutal to me. The schedule arrived in the mail, and I was shocked to see the number of practices from March through July. Not only would I have to make the costumes, but I was expected to watch all the children in the cast during four practices and sell refreshments at show time. How would I ever find time to add this new event to a life I was already overwhelmed with?

I sat staring into space contemplating this newly made mistake when I saw a man to whom I was immediately drawn. I watched him for a while. He was playfully talking to a few of the kids; then he walked over to the piano and started playing. I'm not a person who usually feels this sort of immediate attraction, yet I found myself wishing this man were single.

Over the next few months there were many *Music Man* practices. I had been so preoccupied with preparing for our family's move into Rose's studio that I hadn't volunteered to help with any of the musical practices until the day after I was to move in, July 2. I arrived at the practice with videos in hand. The kids were all in two rooms playing games, drawing, or watching a video. It felt good to be there. Brooke had been talking for months about all the people in the show, so I was happy to finally get to meet them.

While I stood outside looking through the glass windows watching a dance number that Brooke was practicing, the man I had spotted months before walked up and introduced himself. There was some sort of commotion as one of the forty children I was in charge of, but had momentarily forgotten, lay crying on the tanbark twenty feet from me. I hurried to resume my position as babysitter, this time determined to pay closer attention to the children. He came to talk to me again. An internal voice reminded me that he might be married, but his presence was warm and we talked easily. I liked him. A few minutes into the conversation he put me out of my misery when he looked directly at me and said, "I'm getting divorced too."

I felt my stomach drop. I kept waiting for him to turn and look someplace else, but his eyes never left me, and the directness of his gaze forced me to look at the ground. It's been years since I've had to flirt. I found myself wondering what to do, how to act, what to say. My immediate reaction was to come right out with, "I like you, Al. Do you want to go out sometime?" Then I thought that would sound strange since we had just met and knew nothing but that delicious feeling of chemistry. It was instant, my body wanting to feel him holding me. It's funny how fast complete honesty vanishes when faced with the fear of rejection. I believe in honesty more than anything else, and most of the time I say exactly how I feel, but this time all I could offer was polite conversation about the play. All the time thinking about what it would feel like to kiss him, to feel him touch my hair, rub my hand across his face.

Then he did touch me, on my arm, as he walked away. I felt it everywhere. In those few short moments my need for new romance came alive, and I certainly didn't expect it.

Starting a Relationship

A few months after our first date Al called one day from work to ask me out to dinner. I looked out the window at my four children bouncing on our trampoline, covered with mud from jumping into the nearby dirt pile. I responded, "Why would I want to go out to a peaceful dinner when I could stay home, bathe the children, then spend the rest of the evening doing homework?" He said, "I'll pick you up in an hour."

It's not often that I take what I call "grownup breaks." Maybe that's because I get this guilty feeling when I think of the babysitter being in charge of correcting Wesley's essay, picking up Rhett from soccer practice, or going over Brooke's lines for the new play she's in. Worse than expecting the babysitter to be responsible for getting all this done is the chance that the sitter won't do anything—that the kids will be eating their cereal in the morning before school as I frantically help them fill in their math problems and correct spelling mistakes.

I said I'd go out to dinner, so my next job was to find a sitter. Lisa, the seventeen-year-old, and Eric, the fifteen-year-old, both had too much homework, so I had to call Lauren, the thirteen-year-old who can walk over to the house, thus saving me the time of going to pick her up. Since she could barely manage the children, however, I could count on no homework getting done. I yelled out the door, "All Ellison children inside to do homework!" I threw some dry pasta in a pan as the kids smiled at me, knowing that they were again going to get their favorite dinner, though I hate giving it to them because it has so little nutritional value: pasta with butter and Parmesan cheese. I did put raw carrots on the table with ranch dip so I wouldn't feel as guilty. They all got their books out, and I assigned my eleven-year-old to help the five-year-old. She moaned, "But, Mom, I have that historical fiction piece to write, and you promised to tell me how to write it." "Okay," I responded hastily. "Let's start. What period of history do you want to write about?" She responded, "I understand it—I just want you to start it." From my position at the stove, stirring the noodles and peeling the carrots, I replied, "I already went to school. Your homework is for you to do." That set a tone that nobody liked, since it meant I wouldn't be doing anyone else's homework either. I told them to help each other—I would be jumping in the shower while the pasta boiled. I got in the shower, and thirty seconds into shampooing my hair the shower curtain opened. Troy stood there crying, trying to spit out who said something mean to him. I told him to wait until I was out of the shower. A few minutes later I heard all of them screaming, "Troy, don't hit Rhett." I realized he took care of his own problem as I rested under the stream of hot water, getting more tense about my decision to go out as each moment passed.

There was so much homework to be done, the kids seemed agitated, and dinner still needed to be served. Even if I did succeed in getting everything done in time to leave, I knew I would return that evening to a house that looked like the kids had played tag in the dark. I would then be up until midnight cleaning dishes that were left on the table, putting books back in backpacks, and straightening the place for the early morning rush. That settled it—the whole thing was just too much trouble. I stepped out of the shower, dried off, and called Al. "How does Chinese food sound, with a nice movie in front of my television?"

I think it was his understanding, which came from his own parenting experience, and his flexibility that helped me feel comfortable with the reality of my life—I was a mother with responsibilities and a woman with her own needs. Al saw how harried my life was, how much I had to fit into each day, and he came to dinner most nights ready to roll his sleeves up. He was the first to reach the sink and swore that doing dishes was a form of meditation for him. He'd play the piano as I put the kids to bed and volunteered regularly to massage my tired shoulders. Who could say no to a visit from an angel?

Sex

The scariest part of a new romance for many of us is sex. It may have been years since you've been naked with a man. You can't even remember what passionate kissing felt like, much less how to do it. Relax. Sex is supposed to be fun, a playful way for adults to interact. It isn't a place where time should be wasted evaluating your weaknesses—like the set of stretch marks across your stomach or your sagging breasts. (If you feel anxious or you're worrying that the man you're with is judging you, you're with the wrong man!) If you can come to this intimate part of your relationship accepting your body and feeling good about yourself as a sexual human being, then your partner will see you the same way. If you constantly talk about your weight, or how insecure you feel about your stomach or the added cellulite you have on each thigh, your partner will notice those things.

Having a positive, sexy attitude is a great challenge. Sometimes I wonder how women in our society can admire anything at all about their bodies. Every advertisement, commercial, television show, and magazine cover depicts perfection. Don't buy into the media image. The body you have is the only one you have to make love with, so now is the time to start liking it! The first kiss may feel awkward, and there's nothing wrong with a few giggles or with telling your date that it's the first time you've kissed a man since your divorce. Men like honesty as much as we do; it may even make it easier for both of you.

Making love the first time might be embarrassing or feel uncomfortable, but it could also be the most liberating moment of your year. "My first experience was terrifying because my date had every light in the room turned on," says Angie, a forty-five-year-old homemaker. "When I asked if we could turn a few lights off, he said that I was too beautiful to miss seeing. His attitude had a profound effect on my mood!"

Remember, you are writing the story of your new life, line by line, choice by choice, and day by day, so use your imagination. You don't need to lug your old sexual experiences into a new relationship if you don't want to. The man you're with doesn't need to know that you were a virgin until you were twenty-five and so shy that it took six months before you slept with your fiancé. He doesn't need to know that you spent your college years in a sex commune. You've had children, so you've obviously had sex. Some things were great in past sexual relationships, and some things weren't so great. Start the relationship acting like the person you want to be both in and out of bed. If you never want to cook, tell the guy you don't know how and skip the domestic act. If he sticks around, you are in luck. You've been through marriage, kids, and divorce, and life is too short to change what you are just to attract a man.

Some mothers find it hard to find a place for sensuality in their postdivorce life. "After my husband left me for another woman whom he said liked sex more, I thought for a long time about my own sexuality," says Teri, the mother of three young children. "I decided I needed to change my attitude about sex and about my body. The next day I waited until the kids had gone to school, then I took off my clothes and looked in the mirror. I began saying to my reflection, 'You are very sexy.' I said it over and over. I thought that maybe with a little brainwashing I could erase the messages I had been giving myself daily for years—'You need to get in shape. You need to eat better. You need to lose weight.'

"Then I sat down and planned a special evening with the man I had been dating but hadn't found the courage to sleep with. I would simply take on the attitude of a sexy movie star on the set of a film. I would wear a bathrobe with nothing under it, then take it off nonchalantly as if I were getting ready to rehearse a scene. Instead of wishing for a body I didn't have, I spent the day engrossed in my plan, creating in myself the attitude that my body was sexy and desirable.

"Everything was arranged. My parents would pick the kids up

after school and take them to a hockey game. Later they'd have popcorn, movies, and a sleepover—not to return until noon the next day. It took me hours (and a glass of wine) to get myself psyched up to actually go through with my plan, but I did it. After we'd eaten dinner, with all the lights on I disrobed as casually as if I were folding laundry. When I saw his wide-eyed lustful stare, I almost panicked. I fought the strongest impulse to throw my robe back on and run out. Instead, I took a deep breath and decided to relax into the excited, loving reaction I was getting. What fun we had as we passionately kissed, laughed, and moaned! It was better than a scene from a movie, and it certainly lasted longer! I was proud of myself—I had taken the first step toward my new attitude of self-acceptance. This wasn't about impressing my date; it was about feeling good about myself, for myself."

"Sometimes I think sex is more fun if you don't care what the man thinks about you," says Susan. "I think my husband and I had sex maybe six times in the last year of our marriage so I was starving for a little physical action by the time we separated. Our love life had been pretty boring, no real effort on either of our parts to make it fun or interesting. Because I wasn't having sex I guess I read more magazine articles about how to turn your man on, what men like in bed, all those *Cosmo* covers that jump out at you when you're in the grocery store line. I decided that if I were ever to have another sexual relationship it was going to be completely different.

"I'm not an exhibitionist or anything, but when I fell in love a few months after the divorce, I decided to be creative and adventurous even though I was scared. One night I left a trashy novel on the bed with a note that read, 'Read page 89. I'll be waiting for you at 9:30 to reenact it!' A few days after that I asked if I could have a back massage after I put my kids in bed. I think he was expecting to give me a quick massage, on top of my clothes, as he watched the news. When he walked into the room and saw me lying naked, face down on top of the bed, with a bottle of oil on the night table and candles lit, I heard him say, 'Boy, it's my lucky week!' One morning not long after that when we were away for the weekend, I woke up early so I could surprise him in the shower. We soaped each other up and down, sliding skin to skin while we laughed and played like children. I was becoming addicted to the fun that I could create with my imaginative, care-free, sexy attitude."

Buried deep within every human being is the need to be loved and the need to feel connected to someone else both physically and emotionally. Kids are great, and as a mother there is no way to feel unconnected to them, but they can't fill our needs as women. Sexuality takes energy, but it also gives energy back. When going through a divorce, it is often impossible to imagine making space for a relationship that has the potential to cause more heartbreak. But romance can also be an integral part of the healing process. "Something happened to my energy when I started dating," says Kate. I haven't fallen in love with anyone yet, but dating gives me something to look forward to. So much of my day is full of concerns and responsibility. Whether I'm at work or at home, it seems that someone always needs me to do something. When I'm on a date, I'm just Kate, I'm not Mom, so I completely relax and enjoy myself. I feel this when I go out with girlfriends too, but I have so little time in my life for social-izing, and in the end I do want to get married again."

I have always had a voice inside my head that constantly dic-tates to me what a mother is supposed to be. Falling in love with Al has changed what I hear. The voice now says, "Relish your-self, experience life, be who you want—you're all you have!"

Build Realistic Expectations

There seem to be two kinds of women—those who have very high expectations for the next relationship, and those who have no ex-pectations at all because they were so disappointed by the expecta-tions they brought to their marriage the first time that they're afraid to expect anything. "The first three men I went out with fell far short of my expectations," says Shawna, a thirty-two-year-old nurse. "I had met them through an online dating agency, and the description they gave certainly didn't fit the men I saw seated be-fore me. It took many dates and conversations with men for me to realize that I was expecting too much right off the bat. I'd been in an intimate relationship with my husband for ten years. We knew so much about each other, had many shared experiences, and part of me had forgotten what it felt like to be in the beginning of a relationship just getting to know each other.

"I was also looking for someone to fall in love with, to take away my grief over the marriage. My goal was to throw myself into a new relationship as a way to get on with my life. I started dating a month after we split. By the time I dated the eighth man I relaxed and changed my goals a bit—having a good time replaced my need to fall in love. Things went much better once I lowered my expectations to the level of the human men that were actually in front of me instead of the ideal I was holding in my head."

"I felt almost emotionless after the divorce," says Bonnie, "like my feelings had been drained. I was a dull version of a once vibrant person. My self-esteem was pretty low, and actually I didn't spend any time thinking about a relationship of any kind. When a co-worker asked me to go on a date, I agreed just to have a night out. It felt good to draw a man's attention again. I didn't feel any real attraction, but then again, I wasn't feeling much of anything anyway.

"We ended up dating almost a year. By the time we broke up I was a different person. I'd worked through some of the emotional garbage from the divorce; I was healing and working toward becoming whole again. When I look back, I see that I would not have dated this man before the divorce. We had nothing in common, and he wasn't my type. I had no expectations of the relationship. It just felt good to have someone's arms around me. Even though the relationship didn't set off fireworks in my heart, the companionship helped me through the first year."

It is important to realize that expectations are a good thing. If we expect nothing, we get nothing. How do you discover what your expectations are? I've been working for a few months on a new, more functional set of expectations. I have a list of things I expect from a relationship that I've decided are absolutely necessary for me to be happy. To have time for each other in daily life, to be able to share ideas and thoughts, to feel valued and respected, to feel free to be honest, and to spend time developing a friendship. Then there is a list of things that I expect but could live without—punctuality, common hobbies or interests, and ability to talk about parenting issues.

The pain of the last four years has inspired me to think long and hard about the relationship I want this time. I have taken the time to look at the problems in my past relationship and have made a deal with myself to never repeat them. I'm thirty-nine years old now. This time I'm looking for a life partner who is exactly like me. I told my mother this, and she said, "Don't you think that's a little self-centered?" to which I replied, "Maybe, but I live with myself every day and don't have any problems." I have a long list of all the qualities I need and want from my next partner. I seem to add something to the list every day as I continue to heal and grow sure of myself. I know now that I'm not looking for a man to make my life exciting or different but instead to share life in a loving, peaceful, passionate, and engaging way.

Your new relationship will be with someone who is not the father of your children. How do you expect him to interact with them? I still remember a conversation I had with Al as we walked around San Francisco one day before he had spent any time with my kids. We were talking about whether we would say something in a corrective tone to each other's children. I hadn't thought about it until then, but I decided that I would rather he didn't say anything at all that was disciplinary. I felt it would be better if I handled everything with my own children, so he could be free to be a friend. I didn't want my children to feel any pressure from him.

Another expectation might be that you have a certain amount of time alone together as a couple. Or you may expect him not to work on weekends. Maybe you expect to be surprised with flowers once in a while.

No matter what kind of relationship you came from, it's important to take the time to examine who you are now. Know what your expectations are and communicate them to the new man in your life. This is the first step toward a rewarding new romance. If your new man doesn't know what you expect from him or from the relationship, chances are you'll get hurt and he won't know why. Having realistic expectations of what the relationship can and cannot be is important if you want to be content. Unrealistic expectations cause daily battles as you try to make your partner into someone he's not.

Introducing the Kids!

So, you've been romantically involved for a while, and you feel ready to introduce your children. There are many opinions about when (and if) children should be brought into a new relationship. I've always thought it better not to introduce the children until you're serious about the person you're dating. Many books have been written about children and divorce, and most of them agree that it's not a good idea for kids to see their mother dating a different man each month. That doesn't mean you can't date a different man each month—just that you may not want to bring him home or talk much about him.

I find it difficult to keep my boundaries defined when my children see and comment on everything I do. My two daughters want to know everything about my personal life. It seems that the older the children are the more perceptive, knowledgeable, and questioning they become about your dating life. When Wesley asked if Al had kissed me, I told her that was my personal business. A few days later I asked Wesley about a party she attended, and she said, "You tell me about your date with Al, and I'll tell you about the party." It took me a few minutes to explain to her that she was free to tell me whatever she wanted, and that I also had the right to reveal only what I wanted without her feeling hurt when I didn't tell her something. Keep it light, and let your kids know that they'll be the first to hear the news if you become serious with someone.

A sense of humor is most important, especially when your children first meet your new man. The first time we took all six of our children out to dinner together was a disaster—or should I say, my kids were a disaster. His kids, Adam and Eric, sat listening to everything we said, staring with disbelief at my kids, who were acting like escaped convicts. Wesley and Rhett were kicking each other under the table and screaming with each kick, Brooke was sitting on the dirty floor spinning quarters, and Troy was making spitballs and throwing them at us. (Adam and Eric later joined Troy in the spitball throwing, so I felt a little better.) Al kept looking at me and saying, "They're just kids." Actually those were the only words he had time to utter. I didn't even respond because I was too busy correcting my little convicts!

Later we went for a walk to get some soccer shoes, and Troy decided to lie face down in the middle of the sidewalk and scream because the other children weren't waiting for him. Rhett hit Wesley in the face with a bag he was carrying, causing a large red mark to appear on Wesley's face, and Brooke was parading up and down the sidewalk with a feather boa around her neck, pretending to be a movie star. That night I remembered a statement my ex had recently made: "You won't have any trouble getting married again. There are a lot of men who would love to have children!" When Al and his kids left that night, I cried for two hours.

Another time I invited Al and his kids over for game night. We were playing tabu in teams—Wesley and I were winning by about twenty points. Al looked at Wesley and said, "You remind me of myself—I used to be just as competitive!" She looked him right in the eye with no sign of a smile on her face and said, "I never want to be anything like you." So much for bonding. A few weeks later Al was playing the piano with Rhett and having a fun time. Rhett walked away to write a note. I thought to myself, *How sweet—Rhett is going to give Al a thank-you note for being so kind*. When Rhett gave him the note, Al opened it and read, "You suck."

This is the response I'm getting, and all of my children like Al! Remember: in the beginning your children would rather have you all to themselves, they would prefer you were still married to their father, and they will probably make things as difficult as possible. The motto of a single mother's dating life—"It just takes time!" Give your children some time to stop hurting and wishing for their old lives (forgetting sometimes what it felt like to have Mom and Dad in the same house!), and they will eventually want to see you happy in a new relationship.

It may even make them feel less responsible for you. The new relationship you model can be an example of a loving, communicative relationship. Depending on what your marriage was like, your new relationship could make a big difference in your children's lives and in the kind of marriage they choose to have when they grow up.

Building a Relationship

Falling in love was the easy part. Creating a new relationship without old patterns was the hard part. Both Al and I threw our hearts into the fire from the very beginning. We had no thought of protecting ourselves from possible heartbreak, as we professed our love like teenagers after only three weeks' time. We've been together for three years, still very much in love. I'm not writing this to set up another "happily ever after" fairy tale but rather to illustrate how pain plus growth can equal an entirely new view of love. I walked into this relationship as an emotionally whole person, knowing my direction, able to ask for what I want. I no longer wish to become one with anyone. I no longer feel the need to put myself aside in the name of love so that my partner can flourish. I knew all of this when I started my relationship with Al. Every card was placed face up on the table. We each showed up with our imperfections and with our fear of being hurt again beyond repair.

I found out that this man was drawn to my strength. He was happy that I had a career and children I loved fully. He didn't need me to complete him—he was already complete. There have been times over the last few years when I have wished for that prince I envisioned in my childhood to ride toward me, to love, cherish, and *support* me financially for the rest of my life. I usually feel like that when I'm really tired of working! What I've learned from being on my own is that there is no perfect prince. I can't expect anyone to save me, and I don't *want* anyone to have to save me. I have created my own life, as an already complete woman, and I've chosen to share that life with Al.

I don't have any really dramatic stories about us. He does what he says he will, he is consistent in his love for all of us, he is passionate about his work and my work, and we share our darkest moments and our highest joys. He says yes to just about everything I ask. The relationship has brought me more balance and insight than I could ever hope for.

Of course, I can't leave out the intensity and healing power of passion—sex for the sake of sex, sex for the sake of love, sex as an expression of what already is, kissing in the kitchen and touching whenever we pass each other to attend to our parenting duties. We aren't married yet. We live together, which is unconventional. In my heart I wish for our children's sake that we were married. I still don't want to set a bad example or live in what some might consider sin. But we aren't ready just yet. We're almost ready, but we don't want to put our kids through the saga of another divorce. We know that marriage is not just a ceremony that joins the two of us but one that includes six children who will also be joined as a family. Every relationship has its choices. There are always complications with love. What is thrilling for me is who I allow myself to be in this relationship, how openly I communicate my thoughts and feelings, and how emotionally safe I feel.

I've been involved with my single mothers group for a few years now. A friend jokingly asked me recently why they haven't thrown me out, since I'm living with Al. I told her that I plan to attend single mothers meetings even if I choose to get married. She laughed, but I was serious. I brought this up at the next meeting and asked the group if they thought it was time for me to say farewell. We then had a great conversation about how I continue to feel like a single mother even though I have a man in my life. All the issues have remained the same for me. I still have an ex-husband with whom I struggle, I still need to talk about visitation issues, and I am still the one responsible both financially and emotionally for my kids.

No matter how much help I receive from Al, no matter how often he does homework with Wesley or plays games with the boys before bed, he has his own set of financial and parental worries. I feel how much he loves me, but it is still hard for me to ask him to drive one of my kids to a practice, to be responsible for my kids when I'm out of town, or to help out with anything I consider my job. He has two of his own children who have their own sporting events, school functions, and chauffeuring needs.

When I thought of what it would be like for him to live with four more children and be expected to take on the responsibilities that belong to their father, I guess I was too afraid he'd run screaming from the house! So I've chosen to remain independent, to ask him only when I really need help, to not risk losing him because I expect too much. Many of the women in my group were surprised by my choices. They thought, as I had, that a new relationship would change how they felt, that it would be possible to start again, leaving the divorce and all the tiresome issues behind them. We ended the discussion in agreement: even though I was technically no longer single, I still shared many of the same feelings with the women in our group.

Creating Family

I've learned that the process of dating, falling in love, and thinking about marriage has the benefit of enhancing my life—I have more energy, I have someone to share my life with, I have an adult close by who loves me and values my contribution to our home. Even though Al's presence in my life has been positive in these ways, however, that isn't always how the kids see the situation. They often remind Al whenever he makes a disciplinary comment that he is not their father. When they hear me talking to Al about parenting issues, they tell me that it isn't any of his business. Al has the patience and interest to spend hours a week hearing about my kids and the challenges I'm facing. Yet the kids can't seem to understand, or maybe they don't want to acknowledge his fathering contributions. No, he will never be their father, but he can be an important role model, friend, and male influence in their lives. He doesn't look like, dress like, act like, or communicate like their father, and he doesn't want to be compared to their father. He is simply here day after day consistently backing me up and doing father-like things.

Blending families is the biggest challenge for me when considering remarriage. I remember the first few months of living together. We had moved into the cottage, which had only one real bedroom and one bathroom. Al's kids were in the living room on bunk beds; my kids were in a small den on two sets of bunk beds. Shower time in the morning was a challenge, and making six lunches while serving breakfast in an eight-by-ten-foot kitchen required patience and humor. The washing machine was attached to an outside wall, and we had no clothes dryer because our old house's electricity couldn't handle the voltage. Clothes had to be hung on the line. I was working out of the living room, and there were at least four construction workers on our property every day working to build the addition that would house our joint children.

For one year we lived together in what felt like a camping adventure. I had originally told Al that I didn't want to get married until we had spent a year living together to see how everyone got along. The amazing thing was that every one of our children rose to the occasion. They complained rarely, worked together to make a difficult situation livable, and were at times incredibly grateful about the new rooms we were building. We went as a group to the carpet store where everyone picked out their own carpet color. I worked with each child to pick paint and then helped each one design his or her own room. Al and I breezed through the construction process with one common goal in mind—keeping the project to the estimated cost. We had no arguments.

You think I'm lying, but really the process was a miracle. There are still the little kinks in adjusting to the individual ways our families were used to doing things. My kids had been used to doing a lot of chores, and Al's boys hadn't. I remember Al telling me one day that the boys called me a drill sergeant. It's been difficult for both Al and me to give each other's children the physical affection we want to give them. I don't want his boys to feel like I'm stepping into their mother's territory, and Al is afraid that if he's too affectionate with my kids, Adam and Eric will be hurt.

We keep reminding each other that time and shared experiences are what build a family, and even though it isn't happening as fast as I would like, it is happening. When I look at our challenges, I don't see that they are much different from those of any other family trying to raise six children.

THIRTEEN

From Survival to Living Again

It took two years before I was allowed to sell our house in New Zealand and bring the proceeds back to the United States. At that point I moved out of the eight-hundred-square-foot studio apartment off our friend's garage and bought a one-bedroom cottage. A week after the addition was completed, the kids moved into their new bedrooms. I was sitting at my desk in the middle of the family room, and everything felt different. I could breathe. I looked out the window and actually saw the beauty of the hills, the trees, and even the mud in the front yard. The work crew was gone. I looked at my calendar and realized that I had four unscheduled hours. In that moment I moved from surviving my life to living it.

Through every step of the divorce ordeal, through construction chaos and everything in between, I had chanted to myself, "I will survive." As I sat there thrilled with what I'd accomplished, I said to myself, "I did survive." I was now surrounded by the new life I had worked every day to create. Now my job was to start living.

There may not be any visible difference between surviving a life and celebrating a life. I still had the same job, the same daily responsibilities, and the same expectations. I had reached a major goal (we added on five bedrooms), but there was still a lot to do. I still had paint to buy and tiles to pick out. There were curtains to make and articles to write to pay the construction bills. To an outside observer, I might have been simply sitting at my desk, taking my usual morning tea and cookie break before hurrying on to my next activity. But I didn't feel the same as I did the day before. I had spent three years going full speed every day, working to change my life, to put the pieces back together, to create a new home for my children. In that one breath, as I exhaled into the beauty around me, I realized it was time to let life in. I was tired of being a survivor. I was tired of feeling poor. I began to believe that whatever I already had was enough.

The single mothers I talked to felt the same pressure. We all do whatever we have to do in order to care for and protect our children. We work long hours to be able to afford living in safe neighborhoods, and we sacrifice buying things for ourselves when our kids need new soccer shoes. We take on two jobs if need be, and keep going no matter how we feel, for as long as we have to. At least once, in desperation, many of us have thought that it would be easier to die than to start another day. Over time we grew stronger; we got used to survival. We stopped asking ourselves, "When will things get easier?" We started to accept that our new lives were going to be more difficult.

Yet somewhere along this courageous, heroic journey, there are flashes of knowing that this path cannot be sustained. That moment of knowing came for me that morning in my living room. It was time to let go of divorce as a handicap, to leave my protective cocoon of being too troubled to really enjoy life. I wrote in colorful, free strokes these words across the papers on my desk: "It's time to use your wings."

Creative Power

Some women are lucky enough to be raised knowing how much power they have. My mother never called it power when I was growing up. She didn't outline it or teach me how to use it. But I knew she believed I was capable of doing anything I wanted to do. One day during the summer of my sophomore year in college I told my mom I was going to make a chess set out of clay. I had never worked with clay before. I don't even remember why I wanted to make it. She showed up with a bag of clay a few days later, no questions asked, and I proceeded to spend the rest of the summer making ten-inch-tall chessmen.

When Wesley turned thirteen, I wanted to have a "coming of age" ceremony for her, so I picked a date, invited women friends, wrote a script, and created what I would have appreciated learning when I was thirteen. When I wanted a garden around my house, I started digging. When I decided to make a career as a freelance writer, I called magazine editors in New York and asked if they could meet with me. I learned to use my power to create what I wanted in my life, first by acknowledging that the power existed within me, then by watching how other women used their power. Our daughters learn by watching us.

"I call on my creative resources every moment, from the way I do dishes to the way I dress, to the way I decorate my home, to the way I approach challenges on a daily basis," says Frances. "People use this word in terms of the art world, but actually we are all creative beings. We use creativity in every waking moment in the way we make our choices, in the way we choose to live our lives."

"I have to admit that it took me a few years after the divorce before I felt like I had any creative energy at all," says Jenny, the artist. "During my pregnancy I was the most creative, painting every day. When we returned to the United States, I had a hard time redirecting my life. If I did feel the urge to paint, the result was disastrous: my color mixing was off, and I couldn't feel any attachment to the subject I was painting. It was kind of like my life had a quality of flatness to it.

"My sister was visiting one weekend, and she took me aside to talk. She told me that I had to start living my life again and that the only way to do that was to hold on to my strongest talent and put my energy back into it. I remember resenting her for that piece of advice; she had a good job, a great husband, and two children who were already in school. A few months later I had an insight that changed things. I realized that painting was just an activity, something my body did. The ability to paint came from my imagination. Then I understood that it wasn't about expecting myself to be a great painter again; it was about using my imagination to create the life I wanted. I think that is what my sister was saying that day. All the while I was expecting a product. Instead, I found a way of thinking. I was so excited and by then ready to begin painting my life."

At the core of the female spirit is the ability to create. After I told that to a friend, she laughed and said that she had no creative ability. I picked up her baby and said, "You created a human being." If you were raised believing that life just happens to you, that you aren't good enough, that you have no creative power, now would be a good time to examine what you believe about yourself and why you believe it.

I know a woman who has more talent as a singer than anyone I've heard on the radio. She tells me stories about her childhood to help me understand why she is so afraid to create the life she wants. No matter what she did, her mother made fun of how she did it. She would play a song on the piano, and her mother would say, "You think that's a song." When she wanted to sing, her mother would say her voice wasn't good enough. Later in her life, when she was molested by a family friend, the mother told her that she was making it up to get attention. When she told her mother it happened again, her mother said she must have done something to cause it.

Our beliefs are sown one at a time, starting at the youngest age. Psychologists say that we can't just wipe the slate clean and start again. But why can't we just set that slate aside for a while and decide, as adult women, that we are going to write another, far different story on a new slate? You have the power to decide what you now want to believe about yourself. You can find women who use their power to create the life they want. You can watch them and relearn. I know that every woman has a different set of tools at her disposal to help herself move from survival mode to accepting her new life and fully living it. The core of creative ability is within every woman—the challenge is to reach it and learn to trust it.

Being Out There in the World

Just as a caterpillar weaves a cocoon around itself before becoming a butterfly, I wove a protective coating to keep me safe and distant from society. The layers were as thin as string wrapped around and around, sealing me inside. The strings were my thoughts ("I don't really want to go to that dinner party alone, so I'll just stay at home with the kids."). They were my doubts ("I'm not a good enough writer to submit a piece to a magazine. I need to take a writing class first."). The strings were my fears ("There is no way that any man will want to marry me—a woman with four kids!").

During the months I spent within this cocoon I had time for a sort of internal inspection. I played with all the thoughts that surrounded me, that kept me living to survive. For the first time in seventeen years I was alone. Over time I had gotten comfortable being all wrapped up. It felt nice to be alone with myself figuring out who I was. Years later, when I chose to emerge from that cocoon, I was transformed, just like a butterfly. Unfortunately I hadn't become more beautiful physically, but I had gone into my cocoon feeling as if I were crawling on the floor, unable to cover much ground, and when I broke the strings of my "survival" thoughts, I came out flapping my wings.

In April 1999, four years after I left New Zealand, I realized that I hadn't taken a weeklong vacation since the divorce. Al and I went away for weekends whenever we could arrange it, but he usually used his vacation time to take his boys on a vacation. We hadn't quite worked out the concept of family vacations, and my kids spent most of their vacations with their father. When my kids were gone, I rarely allowed myself leisure time. Instead, I chose to work, catching up on overdue assignments. I made up all sorts of excuses, some of them extremely valid, like not having extra money to spend on myself, not really needing a vacation, and not wanting to ask anyone to watch my kids for a week.

Then one day my mom suggested that I join her for a week in Hawaii. She works in the travel industry and planned to be in Hawaii on her next job. I thought back to the time when I was married and had left home on a day's notice to meet her in Italy. My mom had arrived on location in Rome and found that she had a room of her own. Knowing that I loved art and was currently taking an art history class, she had begged me to fly to Rome as soon as I could arrange it. I easily managed to find child care, since I had unlimited financial resources at that time, and I was on my way the next day. When I arrived in Italy my mom was working, so I barely saw her, but I had time to explore on my own: the Vatican, the Colosseum, and later the art museums of Florence.

I thought a while about her offer to meet in Hawaii. It felt so indulgent. Did I dare to ask Al to take care of my kids while I was off vacationing? My life had a whole different set of responsibilities from those I had eight years before when I flew off to Rome with not a care in the world. I ended up in Hawaii a few weeks later, looking out at the ocean, hearing Polynesian singing in the background. I remembered my fears from the years before—that I'd never have a chance to visit a nice resort again, to go on vacation, or to have time or energy to nurture myself. I talked to the kids on the phone, and everything sounded so peaceful. Al and my father were managing the kids with ease and enthusiasm. Neither made me feel guilty. Instead, they said that I should take a week off at least three times a year. I hung up the phone and thought about this man who loved me enough to take care of my life and my four kids so that I could have time to enjoy myself. I'd never experienced that kind of sacrifice before, and Al was not even my husband! I remembered my old belief that I'd never find a man who wanted to share his life with a woman who had four children, and I laughed to myself.

Before the divorce, my self-confidence was based on how I looked, my success, my children—the attributes of my life that the world would have judged as positive images. It's hard to find the courage to be out in the world, exposed to other people who might judge or humiliate you when you feel weak and unsure of who you are, especially if your self-confidence has been based on qualities you no longer feel you have. Today I have a different kind of self-confidence that comes from knowing that I have survived something very difficult, more difficult than I would have imagined. I have an inner knowledge and strength that are more powerful attributes for me than all I possessed before. My friends laugh when I tell them that I think the divorce was good preparation for my fortieth birthday this year. Divorce was sort of like losing my youth—the marriage was like a beautiful unmarked face that became covered with wrinkles! I'm ready now for the real wrinkles, for my body to change, because I understand that change, although terrifying at times, can also be a catalyst for great opportunity and for rebirth.

There is one self-confidence trick I learned when I was still in my cocoon stage that I have to share. I was offered a media job with a large company to be their spokesperson. The job required going on TV and radio and talking about the company's product. I had done media tours when I was married, and even then television scared me. In fact, after my first experience I never wanted to do it again. But when the job offer came in, I needed the money, so I took it.

My client's company never knew how terrified I was because I convinced myself that the only way I could make it through the ordeal was to act like someone else. I imagined that I really was the capable, insightful author they had hired, even though I felt completely incompetent inside. When the tape of the media tour arrived a few weeks later, I had to watch it twenty times. It was eerie—I couldn't believe the person I was watching was me. I had done very well. This was an incredible lesson for me. I was forced to put myself out there in the world. I acted in a way I didn't feel at all inside, and I fooled everyone. From this point forward I understood how to use my own thoughts to project the image I wanted to project, rather than limiting myself to the reality dictated by my fears.

Opening Up

Gardening is an activity that regularly brings me peace. When my hands are in the dirt, I feel like a child. Everytime seeds that I've planted grow into beautiful plants I'm surprised. Planting things around our home is part of re-creating my life. I love to look at bulb catalogs and imagine hundreds of daffodils blooming each spring. I draw up designs and dream of what the five-foot-tall trees I planted this year might look like in ten years. I've designed my yard to have many different rooms, each with a mood of its own. Roses are probably my favorite flowers, so I have a small rose garden surrounded by bricks and gravel pathways right outside our dining room, so I can look at them whenever I sit down to eat. When we moved in, the yard was just a scrubby, weedy place with only a few bushes and an old English walnut tree. I've allowed my garden to be an outlet for my creative energy for two years now—it is my way of playing. The growth of my garden is a pretty accurate reflection of my rate of healing. To create something so beautiful from something as small as a seed inspires me!

My garden also reminds me that my life is a process of growth. Things die every winter in order to grow even more beautiful again in spring. I notice that vegetation planted in healthy soil grows the best. So it seems with human beings—those given the most care usually grow the best. Last winter a small lemon tree completely surprised me. It had frozen; all its leaves fell off, and not one leaf sprouted for a year. Just before I was ready to dig it up, a green shoot appeared. I still thought of digging it up because I knew it wouldn't be a very pretty tree with part of it already dead. But I decided to leave it in the ground until I had time to choose a plant to replace it. As I look out my window today, every seemingly dead branch on that tree is covered with healthy leaves.

I have felt like that tree, lying dormant for several seasons, not responding as my "gardeners" had hoped, only to sprout a green leaf or two just before everyone gave up hope. We all need time to sprout new shoots after divorce. I watch the flowers in my garden open to the sun; the rain beats down on them, and even the most delicate ones can be standing just days after being smashed into the dirt by my children's frenzied game of tag. I close my eyes and imagine myself a flower in my yard as I try to open up to the world, to let the sun warm my face, to let the water drip around me, to feel alive where I've been planted, and to bounce back whenever I'm trampled.

Opening up means trying out new behaviors. Paige, the mother of two grown children, says that she "was raised believing that the way to have friends was to tell them what they would want to hear. I remember my mom telling me that if I told one of my friends that I felt insecure, they would tell everyone and use it against me. So I went through life without validating my feelings or telling anyone the truth. What I realized as an adult was that the ability to open up, express your feelings, and admit to weakness is necessary if an intimate relationship is the goal. I didn't know this when I was married, so I didn't speak up for myself.

"As I look back on that time, I'm not sure that anybody really knew the person I was inside. I had a relationship a year after I was divorced with a man I didn't like very much, so it was easy to open up because I didn't care if he liked me. It was a huge experiment for me, especially in the area of sex. Now I know why young people today meet someone in a bar and sleep with them. It's much easier to make love freely with someone you don't care about. The good thing is that I've been able to draw from that carefree experience and incorporate that part of me into my current love relationship. Not once in my marriage was I able to tell my husband what I wanted sexually. I just went along with whatever he wanted.

"It isn't just in the area of sex where I've made great strides. The other day I went to a social function with about three hundred women. I only recognized one woman's face. Instead of pretending I was comfortable introducing myself to groups of complete strangers, I went up to the woman and said, "I feel so relieved to see a face I recognize. I don't know a soul here." She then introduced me to each friend of hers as they approached to talk, and I ended up sitting at her table for dinner. We are now friends, and contrary to my mother's advice, she did not use it against me!"

Part of the opening-up process is the ability to let others in, to be open to opinions, ideas, and new relationships that were scary to contemplate in the cocoon stage. What I've found amazing is how often women I barely know tell me their deepest pains. They must recognize a suffering in my life that they can relate to. In being honest with my struggles, in conveying an accurate picture of my life rather than pretending it is something else, I've drawn others out to share their stories.

The sharing of stories is what brings people closer together. My single mother support group allowed me to practice telling my story. They were there to listen to the past, to work through the present, and to hear my dreams about the future. Having a safe place to talk about parenting ideas, to celebrate a new relationship, and to allow intimacy and trust to grow with other women sparked my desire to participate fully in life.

Finding Your Center

In my survival mode every piece of information about a court order, a visitation, or any divorce-related item felt like an electric prod being touched to my skin. I would jump off center, be annoyed or preoccupied for days, and invent schemes for revenge or whatever else I needed to do to cope with the feelings of angst. After years of this kind of reaction I decided that in order to feel as if I were actually living my life I needed to learn how to stay centered.

I used to hate that word because to me it implied the impossible—that irritating things could happen around me, and though they might not be what I wanted, I could still respond to them from a place of strength and peace. I longed for the day when I could calmly reorganize a planned week off to deal with the unexpected presence of my kids after getting a call from their dad two days before they were supposed to go on vacation with him, calling the whole thing off. When a child support check didn't arrive for weeks, I wanted to be able to say, "Oh, well, it will be here soon." To me the word *centered* meant acting peaceful on the outside while inside the fires were still burning.

I was hearing two completely opposite views from people. The first was that if I held everything in and didn't express my feelings, I would get ill. The second was that if I lived with so much expressed daily agitation, no one would want to be around me and I'd never be happy. So I couldn't decide whether to hold it in or let it out. In survival mode I did a lot of both. It was kind of like being in a boat on the ocean during a storm. When the waves were rough, I was fighting for my life. When there was a calm, I would sit and complain about being in the boat!

I hear women discuss meditation and how they learned to center themselves. Centering seemed to take conscious effort and a resolve to change old patterns. I enrolled in a class to learn to meditate, but the silence and lack of movement made me anxious. When I met Al, the one thing that drew me to him immediately was the sense of peace I felt around him. I saw him get upset with his kids, but he expressed his anger in such a different way. When one of my kids began an argument with me, he would come up behind me, hold me against him, and whisper, "Let it go." Not that he encouraged kids to be disrespectful. He just didn't find it necessary to engage in negative energy while it was happening. Later, when the situation had cooled down, was the time to make your point.

When we disagree with each other, I'm the one who pushes for my way, who turns toward the wall in bed and acts like a baby. As I face the wall, he has often said, "You are more important to me than anything that we disagree about," reaching toward me with healing, love, and perspective on whatever issue I can't seem to let go of. So over time I started using the word *centered* to describe how I felt whenever Al was anywhere near me.

I was very sure, however, that I didn't want to depend on another person to get me to a state of mind that I needed to learn to arrive at myself. I began to look at the connection between breath and feeling centered and realized that I barely breathed at all. For a few weeks I tried deep breathing whenever I felt stress. When I hugged my kids each night before bed, I would hold them and breathe until I felt my body relax. The breathing awareness helped me slow down, to be more in touch with my body and the stress I was holding. Then I moved on to yoga and found that this was perfect for me. I could breathe deeply while having time to think and to move at the same time.

I asked Al once how he stayed so calm. His response triggered a change in my way of living each day. He said that awareness was both the most important and the most difficult part. Intuitively I knew that I had chosen to be unaware of my behavior. I had to cope with surviving the aftermath of divorce. I had no energy or desire to be aware of my own patterns. What he was talking about was developing the ability to pull himself, his thoughts, reactions, and interactions, into a centered place where he could respond calmly. I responded most of the time on impulse, with an immediacy that often had me saying I was sorry more often than I liked. It's taken me many months to get into the habit of watching myself, of actually asking how I feel about something or taking time to respond. I am learning more about who I am and beginning to believe that I can change the way I react to life.

Setting personal boundaries is a step toward feeling inner peace, as Vickie found out when she made it clear that she didn't want her husband to show up at her house unannounced. "It was partially my fault because I let him do laundry at our house even after he had moved out," she says. "We weren't divorced, and I wasn't sure that we wouldn't get back together at that point. He used to stand at the front door and kick it for me to let him in with a basket of laundry in his hands. He could have put the basket down and opened it with his key, or he could have done the laundry at his apartment. If it took me too long to answer, he would yell, 'You should open the door. You are still my wife, and you should kiss the ground I walk on.' I would be laughing on the other side of the door, thinking that this was insanity.

"The peaceful period started when I decided to stop the insanity by changing all the locks. Without him around it is much easier for me to react to the girls in a peaceful, centered way. It was difficult when our relationship was so stressful not to carry that stress into all the other areas of our lives. Now he is gone, and the stress is locked out with him."

"The key for me is simplicity," says Hannah. "I try to find my center in the simple activities I do everyday—to me that means paying attention in the moment. That can be as simple as cutting a piece of bread, watering flowers, gardening, sitting down and reading a story with the children, or writing in my journal. When I write, it helps me to get my feelings out of my head so that I'm not carrying them around. It also helps me to process anger and frustration as well as sadness and grief.

"I think that when I left the relationship, my feelings were very mixed up—like a big bag full of all sorts of things and I didn't know what was what. Writing helped me to separate all those things out. It doesn't have to be complicated or cost money, but for me it is about being present. Sometimes I tell myself that I don't have time to enjoy a bath, or talk with a friend, but when I'm really present in the moment I find myself slowing down and making time."

Compassion

Along with allowing myself to feel vulnerable again has come a sort of reconnection with the humanness of all people. There was a time when I would hear about a family's problems—a child who was addicted to drugs, for instance, or a teenage pregnancy—and I'd voice my opinion, "Where were the parents?" I would see a mother slap her child in the grocery store and want to call social services to report the abuse. My feelings have shifted. Now, instead of judging that mother, I feel like volunteering to watch her child so that she can finish her grocery shopping without incident. I've grown softer. My first feeling is one of relating to the parent's pain. I know what it feels like to be so tired, so defeated and overwhelmed that I've wanted to tie my kids up (with soft pieces of fabric!) so I could have just one hour of peace. This sense of feeling connected to everyone in my world has helped me to feel more alive. All of us have issues. Nobody's life is as perfect as it might seem. Troy's teacher just gave me a card to hang on the refrigerator that says, "Everyone is weird."

Volunteering had been a big part of my married life. Yet I admit that after the divorce I was often unable to reach out and do anything for anyone outside of my family. I guess we each go through times in our lives when we are able to give, and times when we need to receive from others. One afternoon I was thinking about the verse in the Bible that says to love your neighbor as yourself, and I had to laugh, thinking about my poor neighbors. I was having a hard time loving myself and thought that perhaps Jesus should have said, "Love your neighbors because in that love you will find yourself."

I often tell my children the story of how, when I was a child, my mother dragged all of my siblings and me to Christmas parties for disabled children. We would be the entertainment, singing or dancing or playing games of some sort. Those parties terrified me. There is a certain Christmas sugar cookie with sprinkles on it that reminds me of those parties, and I still feel sick to my stomach whenever I see that cookie. Nothing bad ever happened to me—the problem was that seeing all those handicapped or mentally disabled children made me so sad. I tried my best to persuade my mother not to take us, but she would say that they were children just like us who wanted to sing and laugh and have fun at Christmas. As I got older her explanation changed to: "Sometimes helping someone who has a difficult life can put your own life into perspective." My father would then add: "You can't spend your whole life taking without giving anything back."

Compassion was modeled to me; it was expected from me. It took a while for me to have the energy to care for others, but when I did, I understood what my mother was saying all those years ago about perspective. Compared to the problems surrounding me in the world, my life is pretty awesome.

"My volunteer work helps bring the focus off myself and on to others," says Frances. "In the beginning it was hard to move from 'poor me' to helping others. It took hard work, dragging myself out of bed, forcing myself to walk out the door no matter how I felt. I had been a hospice volunteer before the divorce. I knew that this kind of caring for others would move my energy into a giving space and from that I would receive energy back.

"So many people ask how I could go back to hospice work when my life was falling apart and death is so painful and hard to be with. To me the dying process is like any other, including the birth process. When you go through birth, you are dying to enter the earth plane, and when you die, you die to rejoin Spirit. I've always seen myself as a midwife for those who are making a transition back home to Spirit. It is very sad for those left behind, and I find that a majority of my work is comforting those left behind and helping them to let go. Helping other people let go of a loved one helps me to let go of parts of myself. Really, they are the ones who are helping me to heal."

There Is Always a Choice

Women would often tell me they couldn't believe my strength and then praise my coping methods. I would respond, "I have no choice." When I interviewed single mothers for this book, they said the same thing: "What choice do I have?" But we do have a choice. We can choose to fall apart, to give our kids to someone else to care for. We can choose to take drugs, to drink, to do many destructive things, but most of us don't. We choose to go on living, to rebuild our lives for our children's sake, and even when we don't think we can make it, we still wake up, put one foot in front of the other, and face another day.

Where do we each get that kind of power? Maybe intuitively we know that there is a choice and that the choices we make determine the life we will live. Maybe our power is similar to that of the wolf, tiger, or bear mothers who grow fierce if their young are threatened. Bonnie, the mother of four children under nine, says that it was her stepfather who clearly pointed out this choice to her. "I'd lost close to fifty pounds after giving birth to my twins. I just wasn't coping at all. He told me that I had to pull myself together or my ex-husband would get the kids. I kept telling myself that if I couldn't hold on, he would get them. I would think of the kind of life my ex-husband had, how he would roam the neighborhood when he was nine years old and get into all sorts of trouble. I knew that without me that is how my kids would turn out."

Moving from survival to living is a choice. It isn't an easy choice. In fact, it is often easier to stay down in survival mode because there is no risk of falling again. When life becomes something worth living, then there is something worth losing. It takes courage to use creative power, to get out in the world and open up to those around you. But think of the alternative—a lifetime of survival.

FOURTEEN

Time to Dream

When you reach a place in your life where you can dream again, you've completed the circle. You've taken the dive into the underworld, survived the pain, worked through the grief, and found the courage to crawl back to the surface. You followed the circle from the top, around the side to the bottom, and now, with a dream in your heart, you stand near the top again.

Sometimes I visualize the whole divorce experience contained as a complete story within a bubble. I then place my divorce bubble alongside other bubbles that contain different stories, other life experiences I've had—adolescence, leaving home, having children, graduating from college, getting married, and others. In the beginning I remember that each of those bubbles seemed huge. They surrounded me—I was inside of them. Over time, with all of them, including the divorce, the bubble is inside of me and I surround it.

My divorce bubble hasn't disappeared or floated away as I used to pray it would. Instead, it has added to my presence in this world. My divorce bubble is an inner scar I carry with me everywhere. Recently my friend Mary and I were driving our four girls to the musical *Rent* when one of the girls started to complain about all the scars on her legs from playing sports.

Mary began to tell the girls that female warriors were proud of their scars because they were seen as marks of courage. The scars helped tell the story of their lives. The girls responded in unison, "You are both so weird!"

Remember the Past

Remember the dreams of your childhood? I wanted a horse for as long as I could remember. I went to 4-H for years, learning all about horses in the hope that one day I could convince my parents to buy me one. When I was thirteen, my parents finally decided to move to the country so that my sisters and I could have horses. There is a delicious sense of excitement and energy in the beginning of an idea. Our 150-year-old stone house was miles from any of our friends, surrounded by sixty acres of fields, forest, and swamp. The place had been a monastery at one time, and one of the barns was new, with just the skeleton of walls on the top floor. I had the idea that one day I'd move my bedroom out to the top floor of that barn.

At that time I couldn't imagine a happier time in my life than the day the first horse arrived. I rode my horse every day, even in the winter, sometimes at 6:00 A.M. before school started. When friends slept over, we would sneak out of the house and ride the horses bareback through the woods as fast as we could in the middle of the night. In summer we'd take our horses to the creek and hold on to their manes, and as the horses swam across we'd dangle along. When the snow in Wisconsin, where I spent most of my childhood, was too deep to walk in, we'd pile the hay bales on a toboggan and ride to the barn in the dark of morning. I smoked my first cigarette sitting on that long golden grass that was folded over, like a picnic blanket that had just been picked up, with my horse tied to a tree behind me.

If you look closely, you may find that parts of your childhood dreams are still alive in your adult life. "When I was a little kid, I wanted to be an actress," says Vicki. "I wanted to be a doctor. I think I wanted to be everything. I used to put together little shows. Performing was really my thing. I wanted to go to New York and perform on Broadway. I'm lucky because I'm still involved in performance in some way in all the little jobs I've ac-cumulated. It's funny—I never dreamed of being married when I was in college. I didn't know I even liked kids until I got a job as an assistant where I taught little kids to act."

Later in life I dreamed of going to college. I remember filling out the applications and wondering what it would be like to live away from home. I could have chosen to attend the University of Minnesota with many of my friends, but I was ready to imagine a bigger life. The thought of being on my own scared me, but the dream of what might be was stronger than my fear. When the time came to leave home, my sister and I piled our belongings into the family station wagon, cried as we waved good-bye, and with our automobile club maps in hand began our cross-country journey from Minnesota to California. This was my first experi-ence in removing myself from the life I had known and dropping into a new reality. I did not know a soul in Los Angeles, but I didn't care. I was still filled with the reckless abandon of youth.

Early in life I didn't feel vulnerable. I never imagined the pos-sibility of running into a tree in the dark, falling to the ground, and being paralyzed as we rode our horses madly through the night. I thought that driving across the country would be an easy trip and that I would arrive at college and love every minute of it. I didn't waste one minute of my life doubting that it would turn out fabulously. We all have early memories of feeling inde-structible. The challenge is to call on those memories now, to re-member the energy we felt. Remember what it was like to dream and to believe that all things are possible. Then ask yourself whether it is possible to shed the burden of your adult life and use your memories to steal some of that energy back.

Create the Present

Immediately following the divorce, I seemed to have space only for little dreams. My only goal was to keep my children in the community where they had been raised. I found a way to do that. Then I dreamed of owning my own house again, of having a place to put my creative energy. It was a cottage, but I did it. Then I dreamed of making space in this home for my family to heal, to sink their roots into the place and to feel secure in their future for a while. I'm in the process of doing that. But I still keep dreaming. I want to write a novel, to get married again, to landscape my yard, and to become financially independent. I've learned that I have the right to want things. My dreams keep me going.

Dreams also take a lot of work; they don't just materialize on their own. Yes, I was able to remodel the cottage we bought and add bedrooms for all of our children, but I left out important details. During the last few months of construction Al and I spent every free minute doing most of the finish work ourselves. We went together to a tiling class where we learned how to cut and lay tile. We went to a flooring class to learn how to install wood floors. I painted all of the inside walls and trim. Al used his weekends to install a drip system for the yard so that I could plant a garden.

Once I have a dream in my mind, I seem to be filled with an amazing amount of energy to work in that direction. I remember when Al asked with a smile, "Can I see a list of what you expect to complete on the house before you consider it done enough to spend weekends doing other things, like taking a break?" I admit that my dreams can become a little obsessive. I did have a list, but there was no way it could be completed in the near future, so I created a smaller list that wouldn't scare Al as much. I still have so many things I want to do before my home is the way I want it. Maybe I'll never finish. But I've also accepted the fact that other people may not share my dreams to the same degree or may not be willing to spend their lives helping to make my dreams a reality.

I dream of being married again. As I write this, Al and I have discussed honeymoon locations and the general idea of a wedding, but he hasn't asked yet, and we haven't chosen a date. The dream itself is a very large picture, more like an idea. Being married has nothing to do with a wedding ceremony for me at this point. In order to go in the direction of my dream, all I need is the heartfelt desire to spend a lifetime loving the same person. Saying I want to be married again is not about love—I think it's possible to love many people in a lifetime—it's about choice and healing.

As a couple, Al and I have made the choice to take responsibility for who we are in this relationship. We have already made the choice of spending a lifetime together, whether there is a wedding or not. Loving each other has been as easy as breathing, but also as difficult as choosing—for us love is a conscious choice to be together every day. We both understand that love is not enough and that trust, once broken, cannot easily be fixed. Both of us had quite a bit of healing to accomplish on our own and within our relationship. We understand now that love is much more fragile than we had hoped when we were married to other people, that we have to be careful with each other, to be aware of the areas in our past that caused the most pain. Our hearts can never really commit fully to someone else before we've healed our own deep hurts. There will be leftover beliefs, expectations, and patterns of behavior that carry into the new relationship if the healing process is ignored or left incomplete.

The first time I got married, I spent my energy thinking about the event. What would my dress look like? Who would be in the wedding? Where would the reception be? What kind of cake would we have? I don't remember spending any time imagining what our life together would be like. This time I don't care where we get married; I haven't even thought of what I want to wear or who will be invited. We both want the ceremony to be more of a welcoming for our children, from both of us, into the new family unit that the marriage will create. Instead of planning an event, we are spending hours planning a lifetime that we want to share with each other. And we find that while we're both comfortable with dreams of our life as husband and wife, we spend more time discussing how our blended family will work to our mutual satisfaction. Those discussions go more slowly.

I also have a dream that all single mothers can find the strength and support they need to grieve the loss of their marriage, to rebuild their lives, and to reach a point where it is possible for them to dream again. This book has been part of that dream. It has been painful work at times. I've sat at my computer in tears, dredging up old feelings so that I could translate them into words to which a reader might relate. Sometimes in moving toward a dream there is a backward motion into oneself, an examination of beliefs and goals. I've often described writing this book as hanging on to the edge of a cliff by my fingertips, being terrified to fall. I'm sure the fall is about the fear of being known, of telling the truth, of handing others the right to judge me. In finishing this book and allowing it to be published, I have felt a sense of falling into the divine, of letting go of my cliff and falling backward.

I told a friend of these feelings, and she said, "You don't have to fall. You can write your story in other people's words to protect yourself." My response surprised me. I told her that I was asking every single mother who reads this book to let go of her cliff and fall back into the divine, to fall back into life. If I couldn't do it myself, then my words were useless. She didn't get it, but I instantly recognized my own truth, even though I had not spoken it before. I knew I had to keep moving forward with my writing, regardless of the consequences.

Dreaming is the first step in creating the life you really want. You can dream small or dream big, but dreaming of nothing will produce nothing. Once you've determined what you want, it's possible to set goals that will help you achieve your dream. At the times when reaching your goals seems impossible, listen to the stories of other single mothers who are out there in the world trying to make their dreams a reality.

I heard many stories from women like Hannah, who emerged from difficult times having discovered that she lost sight of her gifts somewhere along the course of her life. "After my divorce, I decided that I would use my gifts and talents in my career," she says. "Every person has gifts and talents. I challenged myself to really look and see what my gifts were. When I found out what I really loved and started doing it, my life fell into place.

"It's not always about being the head of some corporation or making a lot of money. There are many challenges in life, and one of the misunderstandings of a spiritual viewpoint is that everything should be easy. But it isn't easy. I have a sign in my office that says, 'Expect Joy.' Part of having the life I dream of includes the practice of gratitude for simple things. In our society we are always seeing what we don't have. There is a sort of addiction to seeing what isn't working instead of looking at what is working."

Stephanie, the woman who just completed law school, says that her dream is to come back to Stephanie and be the best Stephanie she can be. "For a long time I was a sort of shadow of myself," she said. "Now I am starting to ask myself, 'What do I want?' I guess rewarding and stimulating work is part of the picture, but I also want to have fun. The other day I went with a friend to the opera. It was a big effort. The tickets weren't cheap, and I had to find someone to watch the kids. I want to be a more balanced person, able to put my needs into the family equation. I want to exercise, to take care of myself, and to have a social life. I hope to find a man to share my life, but I have to admit there is a good chance that it won't happen. It hasn't been easy to find someone like myself, my age, who can accept the limitations in what I have to offer at this point, including my three kids and my new career as an attorney. So it's even more important that I have dreams that I can accomplish on my own, whether or not I find a new relationship."

"All my life I've wanted to live in the country," says Martha. "I want to have more time off work—maybe even own a working farm where I can help kids who are going through a hard time in their lives. My dream for the immediate future is to get Karen into a good high school, to create a healthy home and social environment, and to see her through her college years. Maybe then, if I've invested well, I'll be able to move to the country. My goals and dreams have changed and gotten more reasonable. They are more reality-based. I'm taking life slower and am more realistic, and I don't beat myself up for not being exactly where I wanted to be at this point in my life. I really want to have my own home again."

"I'm not quite as far along in the healing process," says Bonnie. "My dream is to have back the dreams I had before my husband left—to have a happy family. That has been my only dream since I was a girl. I want another chance in a new relationship to make it work this time. I'd love to go back to school, and I passionately want to become an attorney."

Believe in the Future

Someone asked me once what my heart's desire was. After a few minutes of thought, I said, "I can't answer that. I don't know."

Over the next few days I thought a lot and tried to answer that question for myself. I struggled with the challenge of identifying and then naming the one thing I might want most in my life. I remember going into San Francisco for dinner with Al when I was in a distant mood, contemplating this thought. A postal truck drove by, and I asked, "Do you think driving a postal truck is that man's heart's desire?" Al stared at me blankly. "Maybe," he replied, "if he really likes stamps!"

I hadn't lost my mind. I was just thinking that maybe the belief that we can have whatever we desire leads to feeling dissatisfied with the life we have. Then I thought about prayer and our expectation that prayers will be answered. I began to resent the question itself and thought, *Is it possible to attain your heart's desire, or do we all modify our desire as we go along in life?*

I realized something important about my way of thinking that day: I had been stuck in my own ideas, in a limited concept of what it meant to dream. It had been years since I had let myself imagine a future that sprang from my heart's desire. Not a future determined by how much money I needed to earn each month, by worry over my kids' college educations and the car's tune-up schedule, but a future with pieces not experienced yet. A future that might include walking on a beach in Greece, meeting friends for dinner, then retiring to a villa I've rented for the summer. Designing a garden that covers two acres in the country somewhere. Being interviewed for my best-selling novel after it's picked up by Oprah's Book Club. Learning to play the harp. Enrolling in a cooking school in France. Biking across the Italian countryside. Establishing a group home for single mothers. Walking through the Metropolitan Museum of Art in New York again (Al and I went there last summer), holding Al's eighty-year-old hand.

This fantasy thinking helps me to broaden the possibilities of my life, a life that in just ten years will be focused more on my own personal desires and not as much on my responsibility for my four children.

As Amy points out, it may not be possible to change your life immediately because of your financial obligations. "Right now I work in a big company, and I manage a lot of people. I travel quite a bit, and I think my life is stress-filled because of my job. When I think of the future, I see myself owning some sort of shop. I love craft activities, like painting old furniture. I recently bought a house that I am remodeling, and I get so much enjoyment out of that creative process.

"The divorce took some of my spirit, but I also see that my job is draining me in some ways. I am incredibly challenged by my job, but I also feel like there is a whole side of my life that is grossly neglected because my job is so demanding. When I visualize a future, when I think of my dreams, I see myself working for myself, maybe in a shop that I own, with lots of time off to be with my daughter. I also dream of having more kids, of being married again, of creating a new family unit."

"I've been working in advertising for twenty years," says Joanne. "If I could dream anything, I'd get a degree in natural medicine, homeopathy, aromatherapy, massage therapy, or some kind of physical therapy. I know it's a completely different path than the one I'm on. I'd have to go back to school for years, but I could see myself being very happy in a healing profession."

Pick a dream, any dream—you can modify it later. It really doesn't matter what the dream is. What is important is that the energy used to dream the future moves one's mind out of the now. For me the dreams I have balance the pain and challenges of my daily routine. They stand in the wings of my mind, hovering on the outskirts as a reminder of possibility when my reality feels mundane.

I've covered the walls of my office with at least a hundred pictures I've cut from calendars. I glued them to the wall in a sort of collage. They remind me of how important it is to use some part of each day to imagine. In one of my favorite pictures, which always brings me out of a pensive mood, a woman in a bathing suit is standing on a beach ball. She holds her arm high in the air, balancing her entire house on one finger, like a basketball player spinning a ball. In every window of the house is some sort of commotion: someone painting, a baby being thrown in the air, children dancing, a man being nursed, a bird singing in a cage, food being served, children hanging out of the window. And yet this woman stares peacefully ahead, perfectly centered on her beach ball, effortlessly holding up that house. What I love about the picture is how the artist, Jane Evershed, has so creatively communicated a woman's ability to hold a family's life in her hand. Behind her is the ocean, with a distant island suggesting paradise.

I remind myself that I've held and managed so much already. When I look at that picture, I find myself replacing the house with a box full of the dreams I have for the future. When it's time, I will be able to take the energy I'm now pouring into my children and pour it into myself. I believe that if I allow myself to dream, if I can see myself moving toward my dream ideas, I will have more energy to dance with the possibilities that lie ahead, enchantingly, in my future.

FIFTEEN

Passion Discovered

Many friends have asked me, "Why would you ever get married again? You already have your children." The simple truth is that I've always believed in love, commitment, and a shared life. I have found passion in my relationship, passion in my writing, and a new passion for life in general. For me blending a new family and starting the cycle again doesn't mean repeating anything. Everything about me has changed. I appreciate things like washing machines, flowers in the spring, making love, and the sound of my children's laughter in a way I never could before. I work daily to create the life I want simply by avoiding old patterns that didn't work for me the first time. I now believe that life is something I can create each day, instead of an event that just happens to me.

Passion is what life is all about. It is what moves us. There are all kinds of passion: passion in a love relationship, passion for gardening, passion for a career, passion for children, passion for yourself. When you're living in a problem marriage, you have no energy left for passion. Then the divorce process comes along, and there is only passion to get it over with. When you can actually feel within your body the excitement of possibilities, an opening up to new ways of being, then you've reached a place where you can celebrate the journey that has led you to wholeness and renewed passion for life.

Passion Begins with Feeling

I sat and watched the American team win the women's World Cup soccer finals. When Brandi Chastain fell to her knees and swung her shirt in the air with a look on her face of pure joy, I thought how lucky she was to experience that moment of triumph in her life. Later I read stories about that team; they had played years together through losing seasons before they won it all. The word *passion* came up often in the articles—passion for the game, passion for the team, passion for the sport.

Most of us won't get the opportunity to swing our shirts before thousands of fans or to be the best in the world at something. But there still can be moments when we fall on our knees with pure joy on our faces and feel the satisfaction of living a passion-filled life. "Single moms have a reputation for being worn out and in need. Not me!" says Vickie. "I stopped the abuse going on in my household. My children and I have better lives because I chose to be a single mom. So I see being a single mom as a positive thing instead of a negative. I love being a single mom. I have peace in my home and no longer have to be a parent to my two children and my husband. He was like having a bad teenage son. I love having my kids, my work, and my house!"

Can you hear the passion in those words? You don't have to be an artist, a performer, a sports star, or a success in the world's eye to feel passionate about your life. Passion is a part of all intense feeling. You just have to like who you are, be secure in your choices, and have energy to pursue the things that bring excitement and happiness into your heart.

I admit that it isn't possible to live in a state of passionate bliss all the time. Sometimes I go for days unable to feel anything. I don't feel depressed, I don't feel sad, I don't even feel mad when one of the kids does something wrong—I feel lifeless. I don't want to be touched or talked to, consoled or advised—I just want to be left alone. I'm overwhelmed with everything. These dead spells happen regularly to me. There is nothing chemically wrong, I don't have PMS, there is no tragic event on the horizon. I just can't find the energy I need to move in any direction.

I've learned that this is a normal process for me, that I need a sort of dead period before the energy starts to move again. I need to hear the silence, to face the empty page, to feel nothing for a few days at a time. During the dullness, and because of the dead calm, passion has space to move within me. I don't like to experience these low places in my life. I'd rather ride a high, moving constantly on to new projects, creating in all areas of my life without stopping to feel. So for a few days every six weeks, against my will, my body or emotions or both shut down, and I feel nothing.

The space my mind goes to is very dark. I play the scenes of my life over and over in my head and feel sorry for myself. I start to believe that I will have to make dinner every day for the rest of my life. Then I think about my lists of things to do. I hear a child arriving home from school and know that the homework is about to begin. My time to work is over, and I didn't accomplish what I wanted to. In that moment life is just too much for me to handle.

I was in this space one night in the beginning of the school year. My daughter Wesley had just started high school, and her back-to-school night was the same evening as Troy's third-grade orientation. I knew Troy's elementary school and all the teachers already, so I decided to attend Wesley's event. I arrived home after picking Wesley up from water polo practice with take-out Chinese food in hand, ready to serve dinner, change my clothes, and walk out the door for the high school meeting. It had started to drizzle outside, the sun was beginning to set, and the house was dark. The kids were sitting with the babysitter around the kitchen table instead of hanging out in their usual location, outside on the trampoline. They delivered the news that the electricity had been off for an hour. The babysitter left as I placed the chopsticks around the table and listened to the day's events.

I remember looking out the window and saying under my breath, "These lights better be on in fifteen minutes when I have to leave." My kids are brave, but not brave enough to stay alone in a dark house without me. I served dinner, got dressed, and kept moving forward as if the lights were going to be on when I needed to leave. I didn't have the energy to stay home and deal with the whole thing. I knew it would be much easier to sit motionless listening to Wesley's teachers than to navigate reading by candlelight for the rest of the evening.

Miraculously, the lights went on exactly two minutes before I was supposed to leave. As I drove to the open house, the sky lit up with a few flashes of lightning. The lightning continued throughout the class meetings, and by the time the open house was over there were loud bangs of thunder. I drove home knowing that my California kids had heard thunder only a few times in their lives so would probably be wide awake and scared to death. As soon as the garage door opened I could hear through the open windows shouts of "Mom's home!" and the sound of feet running. Their questions overlapped: "Can lightning kill us?" "Do houses catch on fire if they're hit?" "How are we supposed to sleep if it's so loud?"

What I wanted most was to sit on the porch and feel the thunderstorm. Nothing about it scared me. I couldn't take my eyes off the jagged marks that hung across the night sky. We pulled up chairs and sat together to watch the biggest and loudest thunderstorm of my life. I had been feeling lifeless for weeks leading up to that storm, but as I sat there completely at rest, in awe of the power and movement of the earth around me, something shifted. I was being jolted back to life!

I expect to generate passionate energy every day, and when I can't, I feel I've failed. And yet I do believe that it is in the times I sit motionless, unable to feel excited about anything, that my mind and body begin to unwind. I still need a more realistic understanding of the limitations of my body. My mind creates endlessly in a sort of passionate frenzy, but I wear my body out trying to manifest my creations. The thunderstorm was a great source of inspiration for me. It was a reminder of how powerful life can be. The sky was dancing with light, exploding like a conductor directing her symphony, or an artist slapping on the last brush stroke, or a mother watching her child take her first step. I could have missed it, I could have done the dishes or paid bills or taken a shower, but instead I sat down on the porch and recognized the importance of receiving energy and passion simply by noticing and experiencing life.

"I think I can finally say that love of life and my newfound freedom are my passions," says Martha. "But it hasn't been easy for me to learn to love my life or appreciate my freedom. During all the time that I didn't work, when I made the choice to be home for Karen so that we could both heal, I learned a great deal about slowing down and taking one day at a time. Sometimes I felt I was taking one minute at a time, and when that happens, all of a sudden the fact that there is food on the table for dinner becomes something to be really grateful for.

"Life is more alive with possibility for me now than it ever has been in years past. I have gone once a week to a support group for women who have experienced domestic violence. This group has been instrumental for me in specifically dealing with issues surrounding the abuse. After I attended the group for a few months it became very clear that there is a cycle to the healing process. When new women joined, I would see myself in their faces. Now I'm hoping to see myself in the faces of the veteran members of the group who have found new passion in their lives and have had the courage to rebuild their dreams.

"The love I have for my children and my desire to make life better for Karen and me became my anchor. Even when everything else was falling apart, I was still passionate about my role as protector mother. In a way that saved me, because it was a reminder that I still possessed energy toward life and growth somewhere in my heart. So even when I felt that I couldn't face one more day, that primal love kept me going."

Passion Requires Presence

I took Wesley, Brooke, and a few of their friends to the Lilith Fair, a concert of female performers organized by one of my favorite artists, Sarah McLachlan. The stage was beautifully decorated with images of goddesses painted on huge flowing silk curtains. When Sarah came onto the stage and started singing, she was completely present in that moment. I was pulled into the space instantly because her passion was so transparent. Her words, the motion of her hands, and her voice became one in a perfect movement. When we drove home, I told the girls that the con-

cert might be the closest they would come to experiencing goddess worship in our culture! The feminine energy was powerful
and confident—a reminder to the women in attendance not to
forget who they were. It was a personal reminder to me of how
inspiring it is to see someone passionately involved in life.

People often ask me how I get so much writing done in the
little time I have. They wonder if it's hard to get in the mood, or
if I need a special setting or inspiring thought to get me started.
My answers often surprise them. I write wherever I am no matter
how I feel. Sometimes I get a piece right in the first draft, sometimes I rewrite it many times. I do my best to write the article a
magazine asked for or to write the book my editor imagined. But
I don't hang on to my writing until I feel it's perfect. I let it
go—I send it out and go on to whatever new ideas are forming
in my head.

That's how I stay passionate about writing. I allow it to be a
living, daily thing that is part of who I am. When I enter my office and sit down at the computer, I feel completely absorbed in
the moment—the words are effortless, like breathing. Hours can
pass before I pause to look at a clock. I love what I do so much
that I'd fight to do it even if I were never paid.

For me passion is knowledge that I'm in the right place doing
the right thing. I bring fewer expectations to the things I'm passionate about. That doesn't mean I'm not hurt by a bad review
of my work, but I keep writing regardless. Finding something to
do that feels like breathing—effortless and affirming—is incredibly important in the healing process. There has to be something
in your life that makes you say, "I really like this."

Sometimes a passion develops out of an experience of pain.
"When I decided to become a childbirth educator, I was moti-
vated by my own pain," says Jodi. "I was angry with myself for
allowing a man who had walked out of our lives while I was
pregnant to waltz back into the delivery room to participate in
the most intimate event of my life. I became passionate about
spreading the message to other mothers that it is possible to give
birth without a partner or to give birth with a partner of your
choosing. Now I write articles to focus more attention on the
topic of choosing a birth partner. I feel excited with what I am

contributing as a birth educator. I'm taking a negative experience I had and trying to create new possibilities that might make the experience different for other women. In a way I feel like I'm pioneering what might become a new birth method, one that puts the woman's feelings first."

The Strongest Link in the Chain

There is a saying that, like a chain, you are as weak as the weakest link. But I believe I am also as strong as my strongest link. Often I have found myself measuring my life according to the weakest aspects of my personality. By focusing on areas where I needed improvement, I once believed, I'd be bettering myself. But I'm not so sure anymore if that is the best way to go about improving my life. Why not decide what my strongest link is and focus on that?

Recently I was asked to bring seven objects that represented my strengths to a class I was taking. When I was presenting the objects to the class, I became obviously passionate over one of them. I couldn't say enough. It was a blank piece of paper. The paper represented my life because everything to me is like a blank piece of paper. My garden is just dirt until I design something, a wall is blank until I put a color on it, and even a day is blank until something is scheduled. My creative ability is my strongest link. I use it in everything. Some leftover vegetables look like soup to me, rusted tools could be painted and hung as decoration on an outside wall, an idea floating in my head turns into words, into a story. I am passionate about the possibilities in my life for being creative.

"My strongest characteristic is perseverance and a positive take on life," says Vicki. "So what if I lost a husband? So what if I didn't get the traditional family thing? There are other great things in life, and so much fun out there to be experienced. I love being close to forty. I know who I am and what I want. Now I know the stuff that I didn't know when I was twenty, and I'm not intimidated by anyone. When my life is difficult—and it is financially at times—I just keep going. In a way I'm like the Little Engine That Could. I keep chanting, 'I think I can, I think I can,' and the amazing thing is that when I keep chugging along, I actually do accomplish what I set out to do.

"I've always been positive about life; I'm a passionate person in general. I think I learned early in life that when I was sad, depressed, or mad at someone, I didn't have much fun, so I learned to get on with things and let the negative feelings go."

"One thing I like about myself is my desire to learn new things," says Joanne. "Once I pick an area of interest, I can almost appear obsessive. I go to bookstores and buy books, I talk endlessly about the new information I've acquired, and I feel excited with the energy learning creates in my daily life. When things go badly at work, or at home with the kids, sometimes all I have to do is change the focus of my thoughts toward whatever subject I'm studying. My best friend calls this distraction. She says my life falls apart and I ignore it. I guess it can be a way to avoid whatever negative emotion is coming up, but is that so bad? I believe that the important thing is to heal from the daily pains of life. If I can accomplish this with a few new books or a class, well, I feel I've succeeded."

Life as a Playground

When other adults visit our house to drop off their kids for an overnight or an after-school play date and see half the neighborhood jumping on the trampoline, they often comment that my life would drive them crazy. I guess I came to the conclusion long ago that I could sit back and watch the circus being performed around me, being perpetually annoyed with the noise, the performers, and the constant motion, or I could jump into the ring myself. As a participant, I know that life is the noise, that the music, conversation, and even the arguing become life-giving energy. I'm walking the tight rope, I'm riding the elephant around the ring, I'm the clown, and I'm the midget. Life is the challenge of staying on the horse's back while I do an arabesque in a bathing suit that's too tight; it's the fear of falling to the ground if I miss the handoff on the trapeze. But when I place myself totally in that chaotic moment, it magically gives energy back to me.

Play makes us laugh and helps us to reach out to others, as Pam found out when she joined a coed softball league. "It has seriously been twenty years since I've been on a sports team," she says. "I was a little afraid to join because I thought that the participants would be mostly couples. The first practice I learned how to throw and catch the ball, I didn't hit anything that was pitched to me, and I pulled a hamstring trying to look fast as I ran to first base. Not quite the successful beginning I had hoped for, but I laughed, I sat on the grass without a blanket, I had a beer instead of a glass of wine, and I enjoyed adult conversation for the first time in months.

"As the season progressed I actually improved. Some of the men on the team gave the women batting and throwing lessons, not with the condescending attitude I remember when I was growing up, but with a belief that we could each hit a home run if we wanted to. This experience brought me many new friends, it got me out of my rut of staying at home and feeling sorry for myself, and it gave me a chance to find the childlike part of myself that I thought I had lost."

The word *playful* is rarely used to describe an adult's life. There seem to be more important goals, like financial security, healthy children, and successful careers. In this adult world of responsibility we slowly lose our passion for living because the magic is gone—we've seen it all, felt it all, and known it all. Yet it is in the everyday moments that life happens.

This is where my children rescue me. Even though they have taken the same difficult journey that I've been on, they have come through it still able to make magic. They know how to let bad experiences go, jumping on their bikes for a spin around the block with friends just moments after an argument. They are full of forgiveness and love, walking that difficult line between two feuding parents with amazing grace. They tell me when I'm too stressed and remind me not to take things so seriously. They laugh often, jump on each other, knocking furniture all over the place, race to get the front seat in the car, and volunteer to decorate anything. Their enthusiasm for life is my model. I watch them. Maybe if I race to the car, I'll begin my day laughing too!

This is the last chapter of the book, but it is far from the end. Your new life begins here. All of our lives begin when we are able to look at the little section of our past titled "Divorce" and realize that it is just one chapter in a huge book that is our story. There are many more pages to write—success, joy, sorrow, grief, wealth, poverty, and love may all wait for us in the future. What we learn from this chapter of our lives goes with us into the next. We are wiser, more prepared, and less naive, with a deeper knowledge of our self-sufficiency as well as our weaknesses.

I am a stronger woman because of the divorce. I have developed a sense of compassion and relatedness to other women that I never had before. We have survived as a family and grown into more interesting people. I have fallen to the depths of human darkness and lived to see the light. I am happy—happier than I ever remember being within the marriage. Yes, the journey was long and hard, and there were times when I thought I wouldn't make it, but here I am, and when I look at my reflection in the mirror, I am proud of who I see.

To all the women who have made the choice to be a single mother, to all who have had the choice made for them, to each woman who has examined who she is and who she wants to be, who has salvaged her life for the sake of her children—you have given something precious and rare to your children and the people around you: a living example of what the word *courage* means.

Epilogue

"I'm a bitch, I'm a lover, I'm a child,
I'm a mother, I'm a sinner, I'm a saint,
I do not feel ashamed."

There are many people in my life. Each of these people has his or her own opinion about me and the choices I have made. This is what people had to say about me. It was a challenge for me to have the courage to believe my own truth in the middle of it all.

"I called her in response to an ad in the paper. She was looking for a tutor who had worked with disabled children before. As soon as she said hello, she was telling me about this elaborate plan, a way of teaching her son that she had learned or read or something. She wanted someone who could work with him every day. Would I be willing to learn, she wanted to know. I was willing.

"We started working together every day. The behavior modification process she taught me was slow in the beginning, but then, after a few weeks, the progress was amazing. Before long there were observers from our special education department coming to take notes so they could also learn this program. The nursery school teacher called them because the improvement in the boy was so obvious.

"This mother was determined to heal her son. She had a clear vision and a sense of direction I'd never experienced before.

When she didn't know what else to do, she'd call every professional available to get answers. When she couldn't find the answers she needed, she took her son to the United States where she thought she could find the answers. I haven't seen them since."

"I can't believe what she's doing to those children," Alice said as she chatted with Brenda on the phone. "To make them live in that tiny place, all five of them, with one bathroom. I can't imagine how they must feel going from that huge beautiful house to a room off a garage."

"I'm sure it's hard for the kids, but she probably has her reasons for choosing this," Brenda said.

"I would never humiliate myself or my kids like that. She could have moved close by and rented something with some dignity. Her daughter told me that she hated living there. That's why she's always at our house." Alice was shaking her head.

"They are great kids, though. Maybe all the trouble has made them tougher or something," Brenda said, "and besides, I don't know where I'd go if the same thing happened to me."

"She's a whore," her husband said to himself as he crumbled up the note he found under the bed. "She's been with someone else. This is a love letter, this guy loves her—that cheating bitch. I swear I'm going to send this letter to everyone she knows, to my family, to all our friends, so they all know that this is her fault."

"Mom, are you home? You won't believe what Ben asked me at school when he found out we're moving into the Elliots' garage. He said that you and Rose were probably lesbians. This is all so embarrassing! How would you like to be me having to answer all these stupid questions and trying to make it look like it's going to be fun to move into a garage? This is all your fault! If we'd stayed in New Zealand, everything would be all right, and we'd still get to see Dad!"

"I can't believe how she manipulates people, using that poor single mother routine to get people to do things for her. I wish my husband had not given her such a good deal on his construction costs."

To my dearest friend,
  I have to write this to you because I love you. Somehow I feel you've disappeared. That outgoing, loving spirit I met in Poland, the woman who was able to bring such energy to everyone, she's gone. Where is she? Your eyes look empty except when you hold that beautiful godson of mine, and then I see something. I don't know what is wrong or why you won't tell me. That day in Gdansk (18 years ago, can you believe it?) when we met in the train station. You knew me only two days when you took my hand and said that we were going to be great friends, that I would come and stay with you in the United States. You remember the church camps in Poland, how you convinced the priest that I could be your translator even though I spoke little English. You stayed up all night with me trying to teach me what you were going to say the next day. Day after day we pulled it off. I thought you were just like me, with a sleeping bag, a backpack, and a few pieces of clothing to your name, until you picked me up at the airport in Minneapolis driving a van that was as big as a bus! I want my old friend back. How can I help you?

                                                            —L

"Whenever we talk, I hang up the phone thinking what an amazing person she is. To be able to juggle her life, all those kids, and still be creative. I think about my own life and how I can barely manage myself. She's always been strong, but this time she sounded so vulnerable, like she couldn't find anything but her kids to live for."

"Well, how do you expect him to take on responsibility when you make him feel like everything he does is inadequate?" the seminar leader said in response to her question. "In a family it is the woman who controls the relationship. If things aren't working out, there are things you can do to make them better. Don't expect a man to be your best friend. That is why it's so important to have women in your life who can support your telling your truth."

The woman asked, "What if you're able to say the truth but the man you love can't hear it?"

He responded, "Then you aren't saying it in such a way that he understands. Practice with your women friends to make sure you aren't rambling on. You know, men can only understand things when they are simple and concise." She made a commitment to try these new methods.

It was hard to remain focused on my journey toward wholeness with these words floating in my heart. As a woman I have worn many societal masks—mother, wife, and daughter. I tried to be perfect and fulfill others' expectations in each of my treasured roles. Near the end of my marriage I began to peek out from behind my mask to see what I really looked like. It took my tears to wash the masks away. Today I have only one unmasked, bare face, and I'm not afraid to tell my truth—my part of the story.

We all have a story.

Acknowledgments

My deepest thanks and admiration go to the women who were willing to share their stories with me. You gave of yourselves without recognition, with the expressed hope that other single mothers would be supported by your words. Your lives have redefined the word *courage* for me.

Enormous thanks go to Liz Perle, my editor and friend—who knew exactly the kind of book she wanted me to write! Your organizational genius and direction kept me going. To my agent, Al Zuckerman, and to Writer's House for believing in me to begin with. My heartfelt thanks to Karen Bouris Newton for presenting my proposal to Harper—you have been my personal marketing specialist, my editor, my cheerleader, my coach, and my friend through many books and projects.

One day I received a phone call that forever rearranged my life! I want to express my gratitude to the *Oprah Winfrey Show* and the producers at Harpo Productions for creating from my book a workshop format. When I wrote this book, it was my personal story. I had no thought that the things I did to become whole myself could be offered to others and perhaps have the same effect. From you I received direction. Thanks also to my extended family—Kim, Amber, my parents, aunts, uncles, cousins, and friends—who showed up for the show and showered me with their support.

I would not have survived the difficult years following my divorce without the support of my family: Dave and Nancy Maley, Susan and Dale Ferdinandi, Karen and Steve Gold, David Maley, Brian and Terese Maley, Brennan and Martha Maley. Thank you for standing behind me, for helping me to raise my children, for sharing your sense of humor, and for surrounding me with love when I needed it most.

My sincere thanks to my single mother support group for their support, advice, friendship, and direction. You were all instrumental in giving me personal feedback that helped me move forward with my life.

I consider myself incredibly fortunate to have lifelong friends who have walked beside me through good times and bad: Liliana Kochanek, Gabby Crescini, Julia and David York, Carolyn Berg, Bunny Bauernfeind, Faith Coolidge, Mary MacGrath, and Bryan Hidalgo. Thank you for being true friends.

One of my greatest blessings is the community in which my family and I live. My thanks to the coaches who took my children under their wings, who drove them to meets and practices and helped them to believe in their abilities. To the best schools, teachers, and administrators a single mother could ask for—you offered a safe and loving place for my children to learn about themselves and the world. To my neighbors and friends who shared after-school activities, drove carpools, and volunteered to host sleepovers.

To the other parents on soccer, volleyball, swimming, basketball, and track teams for volunteering to drive my kids and for taking them on team overnight trips when I couldn't be in two places at once—your kindness gave me hope.

My last and greatest gratitude goes to the people who fill my home and my heart. To my partner, Al, for reading every word, for listening, for editing, and for helping me to organize my thoughts and my story. You have brought the greatest balance and passion to my soul. To Adam and Eric for being adventurous enough to join in the journey of blending our families with open minds and hearts. To my daughter Wesley for being true to who she is, for inspiring me with her dedication to everything she does, for talking to me about her life even though she is a teenager, and for being someone I can always count on. To my daughter Brooke for her sense of humor and warmth, for taking life and enjoying everything about it, for reminding me what fun looks like, for being at home on any stage, and for her compassionate understanding. To my son Rhett for baking shortbread cookies and sharing them with me, for loving art as much as I do, for laughing at me every time we play basketball together, and for being a leader in so many ways. To my son Troy for showing me how much fun a trampoline can be, for laughing in a way that always makes me smile, for nose kisses, and for all the special drawings and paper airplanes displayed on my desk that remind me that I am loved.